WITHDRAWN

D0814278

Remember Sago

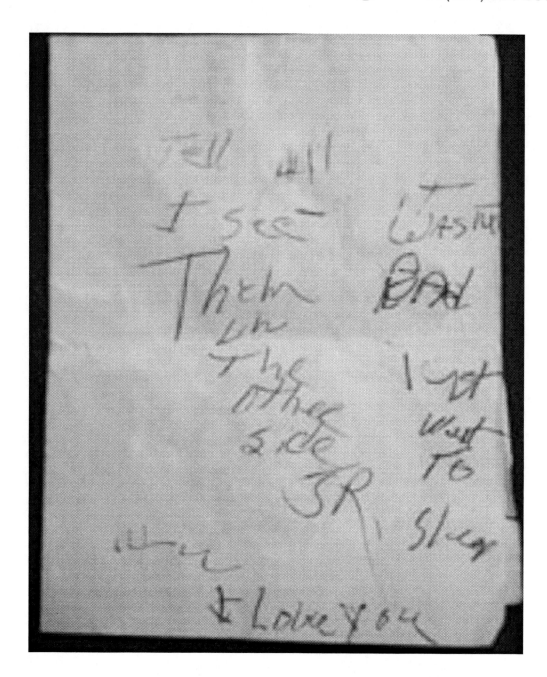

"TELL ALL I SEE THEM ON THE OTHER SIDE. IT WASN'T BAD I JUST WENT TO SLEEP. JR. I LOVE YOU"

This note was found with the body of Sago Mine Foreman Martin Toler Jr.

Note: Courtesy of Tom and Karen Toler

Readers express sympathy to Sago miners' families

Sammie Wade, Florida

It is hard to know what to say. I will think. I prayed for them, as did millions of other people, and I feel a personal grief that they are lost. The mines really are the beating heart of West Virginia. Without mines most of us would never have come to West Virginia. Even if we never worked in the mines, we are connected, blood and sinew, to them. The people who do the dangerous work of the Sago miners do it for all of us. I guess the only thing we can do for the miners is to remember their families.

Builder Levy, New York City

Coal miners are among America's unsung heroes!

What began in 1968 as a ten-day trip became fourteen years of visiting and photographing in coal mines, miners' homes, and communities in the hills and hollers of West Virginia, eastern Kentucky, southwestern Virginia, and western Pennsylvania. I was attracted by a rich cultural heritage that included the rejection of British colonial rule, support of abolitionism, and the collective struggle of coal miners since the late nineteenth century to make life better for themselves, their families, and the American working people. With the help and encouragement, in 2002, of a commission from the Appalachian College Association, followed by an Alicia Patterson Foundation Fellowship in 2004, I have begun to revisit the Appalachian coalfields. I have been looking at mountaintop removal mining, slurry impoundments, and other coal industry practices and developments to see how they are affecting the communities in the surrounding valleys and hollows. My primary focus continues to center on the lives of the people and their enduring humanity, but now more than ever on their mountains, whose fate affects them so intrinsically.

Larry Gibson, Kayford Property, Cabin Creek, West Virginia

I am from a family of miners. The price the miners pay is too high. If they don't die from black lung, they die from cave ins or explosions. The price is too high to sacrifice our family and friends in the quest for energy when there are alternative methods.

Nelson Tinnel, Muddlety Valley Road, Summersville, West Virginia

"The Working Man" The Backbone of The Country. 1/9/06

Brian S. Clendenin, Craigsville, West Virginia

We are human by nature and coal miners by trade,
We are proud of our heritage
We are brothers.
We are West Virginians.

Miner Operator, Brian S. Clendenin
Craigsville, West Virginia

Helena Edwards, Coalville, Leicestershire, England

It is no consolation, but I just wanted you to know I shed tears this morning for the poor families whose hopes were raised and then tragically destroyed this morning. Mining communities across the world are thinking of you and sorrowing with you.

I live in Leicestershire England, Coalville in the north west of the county was centre of our local mining communities but the pits all closed in the eighties, with huge consequences for the people. Slowly things improved, investment and jobs arrived. Now the area is site of a new National Forest project. Natural beauty arisen from destruction.

The legacy of those who labored and lost their lives in mines will never be forgotten, it lives on in the spirit of their communities. with deepest sympathy, Helena Edwards

Josephine Zando and Mary White, War, McDowell County, West Virginia

My sincere sympathy goes out to all the families of the Sago miners.

Jane M. Martin, BA, CRT

Author of *Breathe Better, Live in Wellness*

A Message to Miners and their Families,

The Sago Mine Disaster will, no doubt, take its place as a major event in the history of Appalachia. As time goes by the memory of events, even those of this magnitude, unfortunately, tend to fade. But, you can be certain that the heartbreak and loss felt at the Sago Mine will never be forgotten.

With a heart for the Appalachian people, especially coal miners, author Betty Dotson-Lewis has lovingly taken oral histories and preserved them by putting these accounts down on paper – in an everlasting form. As writers, our task is to keep stories alive, not allowing the world to overlook things vitally important, so hopefully, tragedies such as this will never happen again.

The toil and loss suffered at the Sago Mine will never be forgotten as long as there is the written word. Share your lives in order to inform and inspire the world. Tell your stories. Never stop telling them… and we will never forget.

Sago Mine Disaster

Featured Story
Appalachian Coalfield Stories

Coal en route (near Williamson, West Virginia 1971)
Photograph by Builder Levy

B. L. Dotson-Lewis
Summersville, West Virginia

Infinity Publishing has made it possible for me to record these stories verbatim, uncut, in original format, and dialect.

ISBN 0-7414-3478-4

Published by:

INFI∞ITY
PUBLISHING.COM

1094 New Dehaven Street, Suite 100
West Conshohocken, PA 19428-2713
Info@buybooksontheweb.com
www.buybooksontheweb.com
Toll-free (877) BUY BOOK
Local Phone (610) 941-9999
Fax (610) 941-9959

Printed in the United States of America

Printed on Recycled Paper

Published January 2007

Summersville, Nicholas County, West Virginia
March 2006

About my books: Capturing the spirit of the Appalachian coalfields

Dear Readers,

We are in a critical stage of preserving our mountain history, culture, and traditions. Our elders are leaving us daily taking their stories with them. A large number of WWII Veterans have already taken their compelling war stories to their graves, gone forever. These stories should be recorded and passed down from generation to generation. For so many minority cultures, it is already too late. I fear we are losing ground here in Appalachia as well. It is also important we chronicle significant events as they happen today in this region such as the Sago Mine Disaster, the Aracoma, and Boone County, West Virginia, mining accidents. We have a greater possibility of recording an accurate account if we document the facts now. In a year or so, the facts will change as people tell their own version of the stories. We cannot depend on educational institutions, filmmakers, or even publishers to capture the stories of this culture. It is extremely difficult for outsiders to get a true picture of mountain life from a distance. It is even more difficult for outsiders to get mountain people to open up to strangers. I believe it is up to people like you and me to preserve our history – just ordinary, common people who live here - whose own ways are the ways of the mountain people and who care deeply about the storyteller as well as the story. I am convinced the best stories come from first-person interviews – giving someone a voice to record history as they see it. My commitment to the people here is to do something toward the preservation of this unique mountain culture. I want to give a voice to the mountain people, my people. I want to be someone they feel comfortable to talk with freely. I want to let them paint an intimate, colorful portrait of their lives through their own words.

Although technology and major highways have finally made their way through these isolated mountains, the people here still live a life apart from the modern ways of most of America and their ways of life are the stories I want to record.

These stories not only tell us about the different stages of building this country, but they tell us who the mountain people are, how and why they settled here. They tell us who we are. They tell us about our strong ancestors. Their stories tell how they survived backbreaking jobs, terrible tragedies and developed total self-sufficiency. They looked after their neighbors and kin people. These stories tell us how they entertained themselves. Out of need, they became artists, musicians, and quilters. These stories tell us how they were able to live off the land by becoming expert gardeners, hunters, and fishermen.

We can all learn something about self-reliance and community service when we learn about the spirit of the mountain people of Appalachia.

Take care,
B. L. Dotson-Lewis

About the author
B. L. Dotson-Lewis
Summersville, WV

During my senior year at Nicholas County High School, a small rural school located in the Appalachian coalfields of West Virginia, my high school counselor called me to her office one day to find out what I was planning on doing with the rest of my life after high school graduation. My reply was, "I plan on going to college." That was it. I planned on going to college. I didn't know where or how.

You see my parents and five brothers had moved from West Virginia to the west coast between my 9th and 10th grades in high school. My Father was lured to the western states of Oregon and Washington by talks of big timber and big game hunting, both of which he was heavily involved. Several uncles, aunts and cousins moved simultaneously to the same area and lived within sight of each other and both my grandmothers moved later. In essence, they moved a mini-Appalachian village to the west coast. Wherever they landed and because they moved as a clan, they were always home in Appalachia. The biggest part of the clan involved in the western movement, finally settled in the foothills of Mt. Saint Helens, Washington.

I went west on one trip with my family. I can't remember exactly how we traveled, but my brothers and I probably rode in the back of a pickup truck with a cab on it. I do remember sleeping in sleeping bags under the stars at night and my Mother cooking our meals on a Coleman Camp Stove and my Father telling stories around the campfire at night. But on the final trip west from the 42 acre farm located on a rural one lane road where coal miners and farmers lived in Nicholas County, I stayed behind in West Virginia with my sister. When I think back on it, I was 15 years old and pretty much on my own. That was a big responsibility for a 15 year old girl making her own decisions and earning a living, at that time my life centered around school, church and doing housework for people to earn money.

When I told my counselor I had no idea where I would be going to college, especially with no funds, she suggested Berea College in Kentucky. I said O.K. even though I did not know one thing about Berea College. I had taken the SAT and ACT tests earlier in my senior year or junior year in preparation of college entrance somewhere. My counselor was able to put in an application to Berea for me along with my college entrance test scores. If I remember correctly, I had to take additional tests to qualify for entrance into Berea College. She was able to administer those tests. I was accepted as a student at Berea College.

I did not have an opportunity to visit Berea before the school year started simply because I had no means of transportation or extra money to spend on travel and lodging. It was good enough that I was accepted at a college where you did not have to pay tuition and you had the opportunity to work for room/board and spending money. I was thrilled with this setup.

That summer after high school graduation I was able to go visit my parents on the west coast. I had not seen them since they left West Virginia. For most students high school graduation is a big night for the family. I remember the night of my graduation, my sister was the only member of my family able to attend, but I didn't expect my parents to travel that far to see me graduate from high school. The thought never crossed my mind. I was proud to receive several awards on that night. I knew my parents would be proud even if the subject never came up. It never did.

This trip west was by Greyhound bus, 17 years old and alone on a 4 day and 4 night bus trip across the United States. I made notes along the way of people I met and things I saw out the window as we sped across the states. I spent that summer with my parents and brothers. I worked as a waitress at one of the local diners. The lumberjacks were amused with my West Virginia twang. My parents, who migrated from the southwest town of Grundy, Buchanan County, Virginia to West Virginia held on to their original southwest Virginia dialect, which made them even more popular with the westerners.

This was also the summer one of my brothers, Sam, came home from the Army on leave. It was the Vietnam War era. My Father had spent a great deal of his time lobbying the President of the United States and the Governor of the State of Washington in regard to his boys and Vietnam. He presented his case: That he had five sons, three had served in the military or were currently serving, and he wanted assurance his two youngest sons, drafted, and would not be shipped to Vietnam. After countless letters and phone calls, he won his case. So, Sam, son #4, was coming home for leave and would be shipped overseas, but not to Vietnam. His bus would arrive around 3 a.m. in a town about 40 or 50 miles from our home. My Mother told me that we would need to be there at the Greyhound Bus Terminal to meet him. The only odd thing about this seemingly normal situation was that I would be driving. I had no driver's license, nor experience behind the wheel. My Mother did not drive. We had a large flatbed truck. Around midnight my Mother woke me up and told me it was time to go get Sam. We got into the truck with me under the steering wheel and my Mother on the passenger side. I got the truck started and in a gear that moved forward and we took off. The midnight surrounding the two us in that flatbed truck was blue-black and a heavy fog hung over the lake as we drove by Mossy Rock at the base of Mt. Saint Helens but the road was straight and wide with no traffic. We were very happy to see Sam.

August rolled around and it was time for me to go to Berea College in Kentucky to pursue a degree in higher education. My Father had never mentioned my good fortune in attaining entrance to college with free tuition. In fact, he never brought up the subject of my education during the entire summer. Neither did I. But the time came for me to leave my parents and return east. There was no plan in place to finance this trip. I had worked off and on during the summer but had helped my parents out with living expenses.

A few days before it was time for me to leave in order to arrive at Berea in time for freshmen orientation, three of my brothers got together and came up with a plan to get me a one way ticket from Seattle, Washington to Berea, Kentucky. At that time, wood shakes were in demand on the west coast. My brothers raised the money for my bus ticket by cutting down a couple of trees, sawing them into shakes and selling them on the spot. My father was still not very high on my leaving home and returning to the east. A college education was something for others to obtain, but he didn't have a good stand since both his sisters were graduates of Radford Teachers College in Virginia near Grundy, Buchanan County where he grew up. It would have suited him better had I just stayed at home with my family.

When the day came for me to leave, my Father was not around, he had gone to the woods. My brothers picked up my old olive green army footlocker, given to me by my oldest brother when he returned home from the Army. They loaded the footlocker up on the flatbed truck, stuck me inside between two of them and headed off to the Greyhound Bus Terminal in Seattle. They went inside with me, purchased my one way ticket, gave me spending money and told me to sit up front on the bus. I headed back East on the front seat of a Greyhound Bus with a few dollars in my purse, a few more dollars pinned in my underwear by my Mother and everything I owned packed in an army green footlocker tucked underneath in the storage unit.

I sat on the front seat and got acquainted with my traveling partner, a just released jailbird traveling from Seattle to Arizona to reunite with her children. She had just served four years and was missing her family. She was broke so I gave her one of my $20.00 bills my brothers had given me and told me to hold on to. We became pretty good friends by the time she got off. I got acquainted with a few more people along the way but did not get as close with the others as I had with the jailbird. I remember her vividly. She had reddish blond hair with dark streaks. It was shoulder length, wavy and needed combed. Her red dress buttoned down the front and several buttons were missing. She had long fingernails. One of her front teeth was missing and she carried her high heels in her hand and just walked around barefoot. She told me all about being in prison. I remember feeling so sorry for her and wanting to help her.

On the fourth day, late in the evening, the way I remember it, I arrived at Berea College. The bus station was in a popular drugstore/restaurant, The Carlton, where the college kids hung out. I waited for my footlocker to be unloaded. Some of the college students were there to meet the bus and help freshmen, like me, find my dorm room and get situated. I stayed at Berea College year round for over three years.

(B. L. Dotson-Lewis lives in the coalfields of West Virginia)

* I recently read in a news magazine, a scholarship to Berea College is now worth approximately $80,000.

The first book published in this series capturing the spirit of the Appalachian coalfields by B. L. Dotson-Lewis, is Appalachia: Spirit Triumphant (a cultural odyssey of Appalachia) in May of 2004.

Self Portrait of a Coal Miner

Self portrait, Paul Given, Richwood, West Virginia. Courtesy of Paul Given

CONTENTS

Pictures   1-32

Introduction – Life and Death of the Mountain People   33

Part 1 – Stories of Tragedy in the Appalachian Coalfields   35

Featured story – Sago Mine Disaster   37

    Events of January 2, 2006   37

    Last Mantrip Out of Sago Mine – Essay   38

    "Shock" of the Event Brings Home Memories   42

    Sago Mine Disaster   43

    Heartbreak Ahead   48

    Sole Survivor   48

    Profiles of Miners Who Died at Sago   50

    Second Left Crew   56

    Sago Blows   61

    Rescue Efforts Underway   62

    Is Anybody Out There?   63

Days that Followed   65

    State and National Officials' Response   65

    Ex-MSHA Official Appointed to Oversee Investigation   65

    MSHA Goes to Court for Union   66

    Timeline   67

    Memorial Service and Eulogies   90

    Homer Hickam's Tribute to Sago Miners   92

The Company   95

    Background – Mine has History of Bad Top and Violations   95

    Sago's Tangled Web from Wilbur Ross to Enron to Hills of W.Va.   96

    Sago Mine Company Profile   98

    Profile of International Coal Group Officials   98

    Notes Left by Miners   99

Former Sago Miner Speaks Out   100

    Nelson Tinnel, Former Sago Dispatch Officer, Speaks Out   100

Charleston Gazette Newspaper Article – April 28, 2006 by Ken Ward   106

    McCloy: Sago Miners Hit Gas Pocket 3 Weeks Before Blast   106

Randal McCloy Jr., Sole Survivor of Sago Mine Disaster   109

    Letter to the Families of the 12 Miners Who Died   109

    Owen Jones Interview Transcript from January 17, 2006   111

    Viper Miner Cannot Shake Memory of Sago - Narrative   149

    Aracoma Mine Accident – "Fire in the Hole" Narrative   150

    Boone County Miners Die – Narrative   156

    West Virginia Law Makers Pass Mine Safety Legislation   157

Updates   158

    West Virginia Health and Safety Director Resigns Post   158

    Sago Mine Scheduled to Re-open   158

    Sago Survivor, Randal McCloy, Jr., Making Progress   158

    W.Va. Governor Calls for "Mine Safety Stand Down"   158

    Public Hearings on Sago Rescheduled from March to May   158

Hawks Nest Tunnel Tragedy   159

Part 2 – Stories of Strength and Survival   183

    Eula Hall – Mud Creek Clinic   186

    Dr. Donald Rasmussen – Miners for Democracy   194

    Ralph Baber, WWII Soldier, Invasion of Luzon   198

Part 3 – King Coal Expands His Realm   219

    Appalachian Experiences Mountaintop Removal   220

Part 4 – Black Lung's Legacy   229

    King Coal and the Coal Miner's Soul   230

    Black Lung Bulletin, February 1970   232

    Cold Days, Dark Nights by Jim Branscome   234

    2004 National Black Lung Association Conference Highlights   237

    Letter to UMWA President – Black Lung Claim   240

    A Christmas Wish – Black Lung Victim   242

Part 5 – Coal Camp Memories   245

    Whatever Happened to Widen Coal Camp   246

Part 6 – Stories of Mountain Culture and Tradition   251

    Last Fiddler on the Mountain, Ralph Roberts   253

Stories by Mountain Man, Earl Dotson   261

    Copperhead   261

    Shootout in the Moonshine Capital of the World   263

    Coon Hunting with a Cripple   267

    No Sleep   269

Appalachia Crosses the Great Divide   271

Agony of Defeat   271

Bobcat Hunting   273

Lost Bull on Strawberry Mountain   276

My Father's Journey to His Last Hunting Ground   277

Part 7 – A Legacy for Young Mountaineers – Genealogy   279

Coal Miner's Family Tree   279

Part 8 – Acknowledgments   285

Photograph Credits   286

Glossary of Coal Mining Terms   287

Sago Mine Disaster

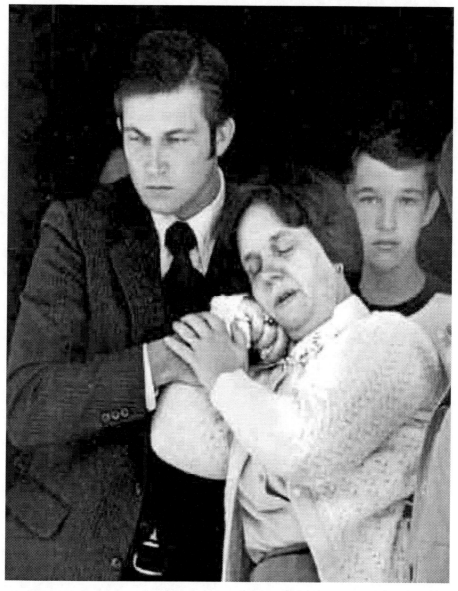

Mourners leave a 1980 funeral for one of the five miners killed in the explosion at Westmoreland's Ferrell No. 17 Mine in Uneeda, Boone County. Photograph: Courtesy of Charleston-Gazette

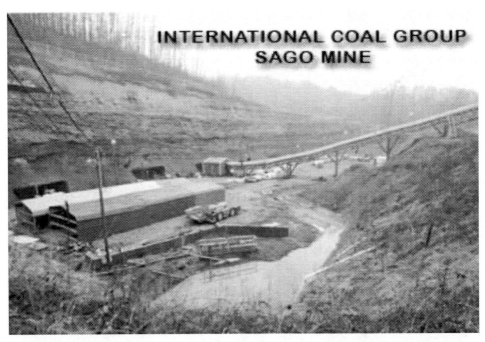

Sago Mine. Photograph: Courtesy of U.S. Department of Labor, Mine Safety and Health Administration

VIGIL. *A candlelight vigil for the dead miners held at the Sago Baptist Church was attended by many of their families, people from the area, and photographers.* **Photograph by Todd Maisel-New York Daily News**

Photograph: Courtesy of Todd Maisel-New York Daily News

State Police guarding the mine entrance. Photograph - Inter Mountain Newspaper

Judy Shackelford braces against the cold wind as she walks away from
Sago Mine, the place where her brother, Terry Helms, worked and died.
Illustration by B. L. Dotson-Lewis, January 2006

Crosses on the hill is a common scene along West Virginia highways. The coalfields of West Virginia
are filled with mountain people steeped with strong religious convictions. I took this photo in
Braxton County on my way to Sago. Photograph by B. L. Dotson-Lewis 2006

Entrance to Sago Mine - railroad crossing signals flank the sides of the narrow bridge leading to Sago mine. A large coal truck is on its way out of the mine entrance. Photograph by B. L. Dotson-Lewis

Drawing by B. L. Dotson-Lewis

A common scene throughout the area.

Photograph by B. L. Dotson-Lewis

Pastor Weese Day of Sago Baptist Church offers a prayer.
Photograph by Randy Snyder. Courtesy of The Herald Dispatch

Candlelight vigil at Sago Church. Photograph: Courtesy of Herald-Dispatch

REFLECTING. *CNN'S Anderson Cooper takes a quiet moment to reflect while watching television monitor while waiting for news of the miners.* **Photograph by Todd Maisel-New York Daily News**

Photograph: Courtesy of Todd Maisel-New York Daily News

Sago mine is located in Upshur County where both farming and mining take place.
Photograph by B. L. Dotson-Lewis

Nazelrod, fire chief in the small town of Adrian, arrived but was told to move his crew across the Buckhannon River for safety reasons. Photograph by B. L. Dotson-Lewis. Jan. 2006

Photograph by B. L. Dotson-Lewis

Vehicles are parked all along the one lane muddy road waiting
to get word on the trapped miners. Photograph by B. L. Dotson-Lewis

Drilling Above the Ground.
Photograph by Becky Wagner - Inter-Mountain Newspaper

Mine Rescue Robot – retrieved when it became mired in the mud.
The camera lens became foggy. Photograph: Courtesy of MSHA

Trapped miners family and friends gathered here at the
Sago Baptist Church. Photograph by B. L. Dotson-Lewis

Friends and family members sing "How Great Thou Art" outside Sago Baptist Church near the Sago mine late Tuesday, January 3, 2006, in Tallmansville, West Virginia. Thirteen miners were trapped inside of the mine following an explosion Monday morning. Photograph by Randy Snyder. Courtesy of The Herald-Dispatch

CELL PHONE NEWS. *Miner families celebrated after mistakenly hearing that the 12 trapped men were alive, as the false reports to them also spread to the journalists who were around them.*
Photograph by Todd Maisel-New York Daily News

Photograph: Courtesy of the Todd Maisel-New York Daily News

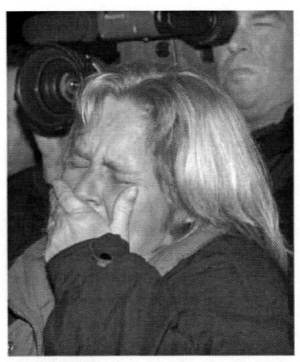

JOY TO SORROW. *The celebration turned to sorrow when the truth was learned, that the miners were not alive and the reports of their survival had been a mistake because of poor communications.*
Photograph by Todd Maisel-New York Daily News

Photograph: Courtesy of Todd Maisel-New York Daily-News

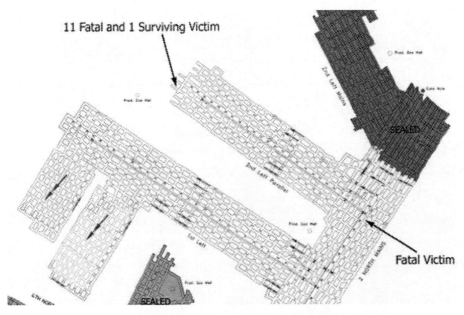

11 Fatal and 1 Surviving Victim

Fatal Victim

This Fatalgram shows where Sago miners' bodies were found.
Photograph: Courtesy of Department of Labor Mine Safety
and Health Administration

A Service of Honor, Hope, and Healing

Buckhannon

West Virginia

Sago Mine

20 06

WESLEY CHAPEL
JANUARY 15TH, 2006

Courtesy of Angelic Designs – angelicdesigns.com

A Service of Honor, Hope, and Healing

Gathering Music

Piano Selections .... Dr. Melody Meadows, Professor of Music
West Virginia Wesleyan College

"I'll Fly Away" .... Heather Miller, Laura Davis, T.J. Short, Natasha Osburn

"Let Your Gentleness Be Known" .... Community Choir
Stephen Benson, Director

Posting of the Colors .... Local Scout Troop Representatives

"My Home Among the Hills" .... West Virginia Wesleyan Concert Chorale
Dr. Larry Parsons, Director

Organ Prelude .... Dr. Melody Meadows, organ
Dr. Susan Radcliff, trumpet

Candles of Honor .... Randal McCloy Jr.
Thomas P. "Tom" Anderson
Alva Martin "Marty" Bennett
James A. "Jim" Bennett
Jerry L. Groves
George Junior Hamner
Terry Helms
Jesse L. Jones
David Lewis
Martin Toler, Jr.
Fred "Bear" Ware Jr.
Jackie Weaver
Marshall C. Winans

Welcome .... Angela Gay Kinkead
Dean of the Chapel, West Virginia Wesleyan College

Greeting .... Joe Manchin, III
Governor of the State of West Virginia

Courtesy of Angela Gay Kincaid, West Virginia Wesleyan College

*Call to Worship

Leader: The angel of the LORD encampeth round about them that fear him, and delivereth them.

People: The eyes of the Lord are upon the righteous, and his ears are open unto their cry.

Leader: Many are the affliction of the righteous, but the Lord delivereth him from them all.

People: The Lord redeemeth the soul of his servants; And none of them that trust in him shall be desolate.

*Hymn - "How Great Thou Art" .... Hymn #77 (stanzas 1 and 4)
Jerry Murrell, Pastor
The Way of Holiness Church

*Opening Prayer .... Wease Day, Pastor
Sago Baptist Church

Psalter Reading - Psalm 91 .... "Ti" Anderson
Son of Tom Anderson

Remarks .... Homer Hickam, Jr.
Author, Rocket Scientist, Native of Coalwood, WV

Anthem - "Precious Lord" .... West Virginia Wesleyan College Concert Chorale

Meditation - "They Lit Up Our Homes" .... Ed McDaniels, Pastor
Christian Fellowship Church

Tribute - "Homesick" .... Matthew Keefer

Remarks .... Mike Rose (Son-in-law of Jerry Groves)
Cheyenne Police (Great niece of Terry Helms)

*Hymn - "Amazing Grace" .... Hymn #378 (stanzas 1,2,5 and 6)

Psalter Reading - Psalm 23 .... Frank Spears, Pastor
Living Word Church of God

Anthem - "Let Not Your Heart Be Troubled" .... Community Choir
Stephen Benson, Director

Scripture Reading - Romans 8:28-35, 37-39 .... Dennis Estes, Pastor
Buckhannon Union Mission Church

Courtesy of Angela Gay Kincaid, West Virginia Wesleyan College

17

Gospel Reading - John 1:1-15 .... Mark Flynn, Pastor
First United Methodist Church

Meditation - "There is No Darkness With God" .... Mark Flynn, Pastor

Special Music - "When I Get to Where I'm Going" .... Dan and Rebecca Nesbitt

Benediction .... Randy Hughes, Pastor
Weston Church of God

Postlude .... West Virginia Highlanders Bagpipe Band

How Great Thou Art

1. O Lord my God! when I in awesome wonder consider all the worlds thy hands have made,
   I see the stars, I hear the rolling thunder, thy power throughout the universe displayed.
   Then sings my soul, my Savior God to thee; how great thou art, how great thou art!
   Then sings my soul, my Savior God to thee; how great thou art, how great thou art!

4. When Christ shall come with shout of acclamation and take me home, what joy shall fill my heart.
   Then I shall bow in humble adoration, and there proclaim, my God, how great thou art!
   Then sings my soul, my Savior God to thee; how great thou art, how great thou art!
   Then sings my soul, my Savior God to thee; how great thou art, how great thou art!

Amazing Grace

1. Amazing grace! How sweet the sound that saved a wretch like me!
   I once was lost, but now am found; was blind, but now I see.

2. 'Twas grace that taught my heart to fear, and grace my fears relieved;
   how precious did that grace appear the hour I first believed.

5. Yea, when this flesh and heart shall fail, and mortal life shall cease,
   I shall possess, within the veil, a life of joy and peace.

6. When we've been there ten thousand years, bright shining as the sun,
   we've no less days to sing God's praise than when we'd first begun.

The Rohrbough Memorial Organ played in today's service is a gift
from the late G. I. Rohrbough, in memory of his mother, Etta Maude Lynch Rohrbough.

Cover design provided by Angelic Designs - angelicdesigns.com

Courtesy of Angela Gay Kincaid

ICG Officials, Ben Hatfield at press conference.
Photograph by Becky Wagoner - Inter-Mountain Newspaper

W.Va. Governor Joe Manchin, Photograph:
Courtesy of Keith Pride-West Virginia Pictures
Fairmont, West Virginia

Nelson Tinnel's Underground Mining Class

Left to right: William Dodrill, Eric Swartz, Fred Boggs, Joe O'Dell, Chris Bailes,
Gary Justice, Joe Strickland, Instructor (Nelson Tinnel), Billy Williams,
Nathaniel Rader, Kevin Stover, Joe Marts

80 hour underground mining class. I sat in to become better educated about the world of
underground mining. Photograph by B. L. Dotson-Lewis, 2/8/06

Remember Sago

Pallbearers carry the casket of Jesse L. Jones from the Tomblyn Funeral Chapel in Buckhannon on Sunday. Jones was one of the 12 victims in the Sago Mine accident in nearby Tallmansville. Photograph by Kenny Kemp – Charleston Gazette

Miners hats on crosses. Photograph: Charleston Gazette

Aracoma Mine Accident

Photograph: Courtesy of the Logan Banner

West Virginia Governor Manchin talks to a miner at Melville.
Photograph by Randy Snyder. Courtesy of The Herald-Dispatch

Hawks Nest Tunnel Tragedy

"Get on Board, Chillen', Chillen, Chillen'. Get on Board Chillen', Chillen', Chillen', Chillen'.
Get on Board Chillen', Chillen'. There's room for many-a-more"

Looking inside Hawks Nest Tunnel. Photograph:
Courtesy of Gauley Bridge Historical Society

Notes: Hawks Nest Tunnel
6/7/05 - woman living in Gauley Bridge
area told me that a man she knew
had a summer job when he was a teen
digging graves in Summersville to bury
tunnel workers - it was her Daddy.

Looking inside Hawks Nest Tunnel. Photograph:
Courtesy of Gauley Bridge Historical Society

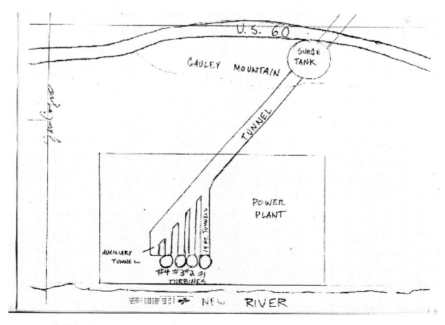

Drawing of Hawks Nest Tunnel courtesy of Gauley Bridge Historical Society

Strength and Survival

Oglesby Bedroom, Stotesbury, W.Va. 1982. Photograph by Builder Levy

Johnny Crabtree and Jim Ed Whitt preaching, Sprigg, Mingo County, West Virginia, 1970.
Photograph by Builder Levy

Picket line for the United Mine Workers of America, Brookside,
Harlan County, Kentucky, 1973. Photograph by Builder Levy

Appalshop in Whitesburg, Kentucky. Photograph by B. L. Dotson-Lewis, July 2005

Eula Hall – Appalshop
Photograph by B. L. Dotson-Lewis

Invasion of Luzon

Photograph: Courtesy of Ralph and Mary Baber
Gen. Leonard Wing, congratulates Pfc. Ralph Baber, Silver Star recipient, WWII

Message on back of postcard

SWP-SigC-45-30578   31 July 1945

Pfc Ralph M. Baber, son of Mrs. Minnie
V. Baber of Craigsville, W. Va., is
congratulated by Maj. Gen. Leonard F.
Wing, (CG of 43rd Inf Div), after receiving the Silver Star during ceremon-
ies at (Camp LaCroix, Luzon). The award
was given for gallantry against the enemy
during the (Luzon Liberation Campaign).

Photog: Art Gould

PASSED BY CENSOR
3

Photograph: Courtesy of Ralph and Mary Baber

We had little fold-up cots. (Ralph Baber on cot)
Photograph: Courtesy of Ralph and Mary Baber

Mountaintop Removal

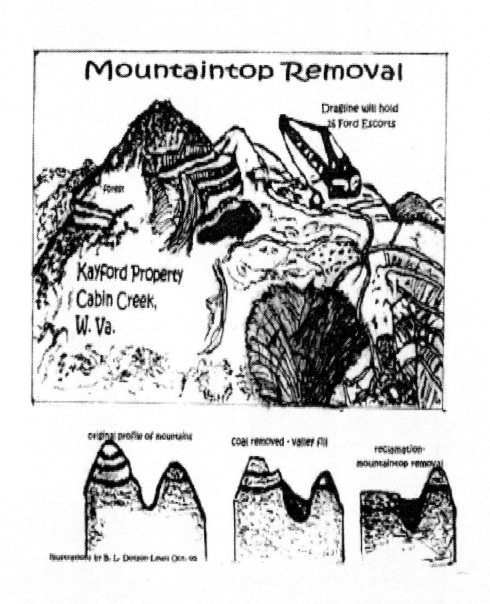

Drawing by B. L. Dotson-Lewis

Introduction

Life and Death of The Mountain People

This special collection of stories has been a roller-coaster ride for me, up and down, not knowing from one story to the next whether it was going to be tragedy or triumph, most of the time a mixture of both. Who would not be torn apart by the tragic events of this region, such as the Sago Mine disaster, Aracoma Mine accident and the deaths of the two miners in Boone County, West Virginia? We were never given time to recover from one, when another occurred. Sixteen miners died in one month. All the deaths were tragic events. The first stories in this book were my last stories recorded, and it is a good thing for I was left totally exhausted and feeling low. I do not know if I could have gone on. I am still trying to pull myself up. I can only imagine how the families must be grieving.

On the other hand, it was with jubilation I sat underneath a shade tree at Camp Washington Carver with hundreds of old-time musicians. Ralph Roberts, one of the last old time fiddlers rosined up his bow and sawed out tune after tune for me. We ate tomato soup and grilled cheese sandwiches his wife, Charlie, made in their little camper. I was the guest who got the bowl and Charlie ate her soup out of a red thermos lid. We sat underneath shade trees in lawn chairs, Ralph talked about his life, his relatives, the musical Hammons family, and Ralph talked about his love for music. After Ralph's stories, we walked over to the lodge, watched, and listened to Celtic music as the dancers pranced around the floor, joining hands and making circles and watching as men twirled their ladies around and round.

My connection with Ralph and Mary Baber has turned into a solid friendship. Ralph, a decorated WWII soldier, lives quietly and unassumingly with Mary, his wife, in a small mountain community. His story is a timepiece of the war with Japan. Ralph, so precise with details, did everything possible to make all the other soldiers in his story the heroes.

It was an unexpected meeting with Eula Hall in Whitesburg, Kentucky. Her story needs to be told over and over again. She represents all the goodness of these mountains.

The Hawks Nest Tunnel tragedy came to me through my own naiveté. Taken advantage of by someone from a large legal firm in Texas, so I was told and I believed. Told I was to do the research and I would receive payment well above my efforts. I had no idea I was on a wild goose chase with as many as 500 civil suits filed against the company, and I was to find one name in all those rolled up, tied pieces of onion skin paper over 70 years old. I was already knee-deep in the story of Hawks Nest Tunnel tragedy when this book got underway.

Miners for Democracy, Appalachian Experiences Mountaintop Removal, Cold Days Dark Nights, and my involvement with the black lung movement are all bits and pieces of the coal miners' struggles from environmental to health issues - from the cradle to the grave. Even though laws were passed to eradicate black lung in 1969, the chronic lung disease is still with us, and the only finality for the disease is when the Good Lord comes to take the miner to his heavenly home, then, the hacking cough ceases.

Stories by Mountain Man, Earl Dotson, is my own father's stories filled with humor and family connection symbolic of some of Appalachia's most treasured traditions. His death was two years prior to the Sago miners' deaths, but both left notes to their families to ease the pain and loneliness, a tradition honored by mountain men.

Coal Miner's Family Tree is a child's introduction to genealogy. A simple light-hearted tale about a young boy who learns his roots are in the coal mining mountains of Appalachia. Darkness and light, laughter and tears, hardships and joy, a unique region filled with mountain people who are capable of bearing the worst of all times, rising above the deepest sorrow and finding joy in something as simple as a fiddle tune.

I am hopeful this book reflects my people in the truth of life in these mountains and the sacredness of death. As I have said before, my books were not planned. I did not sit down at a desk in an office and map out a legend. These stories came randomly, some out of the blue, some by chance, or unforeseen circumstance. My stories have fallen together in this book in much the same way they came to me, in no particular order, but in the same way the people live their lives and the same way they face death, sometimes in tragedy, sometimes in triumph, but always with hope, faith and the knowledge that out of darkness comes light.

Part 1 – Stories of Tragedy in the Appalachian Coalfields

Featured story – Sago Mine Disaster
      Viper Miner Cannot Shake Memory of Sago
      Aracoma Mine Accident
      Boone County Miners Die
      Hawks Nest Tunnel Tragedy

Coal Camp near Grundy, Buchanan County, Virginia 1970. Photograph by Builder Levy

Incorrect reports of a "miracle" rescue spread like wildfire throughout the United States before it was learned it was false. People all over the country awoke the next morning to incorrect headlines. The confusing and incorrect reports were blamed on miscommunication.

Photograph: Courtesy of the Charleston Gazette

Featured Story – Sago Mine Disaster

Miners enter the mine on a "mantrip" the vehicle that transports miners into, out, and inside the mine, and, by extension, the term refers to the trip itself as well.
(Eastern Coal Company; Stone, Kentucky, 1970)
Photograph by Builder Levy

The events of January 2, 2006

Author's note: This essay written as a result of my feelings of shock and sorrow following the tragic explosion occurring at the Sago #1 Coal Mine in Upshur County, West Virginia on January 2, 2006 where 13 miners were trapped for more than 40 hours. I visited the site on the day after the explosion. It was a long ordeal for us who make our homes in the West Virginia coalfields, waiting and watching rescue efforts. The public watched as family members of the trapped miners became the focal point of the national media. As heartbreaking events took place, cameras zeroed in on this small, coal mining community recording in real time each teardrop that fell. Tallmansville, location of Sago No. 1 Coal Mine, became the main attraction of this nation and beyond during the rescue efforts and ultimate failure except for one survivor. Writing this essay was the only means I had of getting a handle on my own feelings.

Last Mantrip out of Sago Mine

By B. L. Dotson-Lewis
Summersville, W. Va.
January 4, 2006

I'm still reeling and stunned along with the rest of this nation by the events that took place this week at Sago No. 1 Mine in Upshur County, West Virginia.

On Tuesday, January 3, one day after the explosion in that mine, I traveled 84 miles to Tallmansville and Sago Mine because our coal-mining communities are closely connected. Members of my community are employed at that mine: Arnett Nicholas, Darrell Lucas, and Teddy Johnson, to name three.

Arnett's mother told me it was due to a shift change during the Christmas holidays that these men were not working on the morning shift of January 2, 2006, when the explosion occurred. Arnett is off from work with a foot busted on the job in October.

Kim Toler of Canvas lost her uncle, Martin "Junior" Toler, of Sutton in this explosion. At least two individuals who came into my office today had relatives there. One was Jerry Groves, who died in the explosion. So, our mining communities are connected not only in heart and spirit but in reality as well. But it doesn't matter whether employees of Sago No. 1 Mine live here or in other coal-mining communities – they are all blood brothers. They share the dangers of their profession.

When I walked into the Sago Baptist Church yesterday afternoon, a strange feeling was in the air, a feeling hovering over the people much like what I have read and heard about in old times when wakes for the dead were held at people's homes.

The church was filled to capacity and beyond with all ages, young children, teenagers, young and middle-aged adults and elderly people. All were family or friends of the 13 miners trapped 260 feet underground. I didn't know at the time that it was death hovering over those family members waiting in that little church.

The pews were filled with people and long, narrow, brown tables used for church dinners and bazaars were set up in the back of the main sanctuary. One young, freckle-faced girl with curly, red hair who wore glasses with light-blue tinted frames, gave me a half smile as she laid her head on her folded arms. She was waiting. Four people escorted an elderly woman dressed in a pink church dress and coat down the aisle of the church, out the double doors and down the steps. Someone on each side held her arm, someone walked in front, and someone walked behind her. She was distraught, having a rough time. There was whispering, once in a while you would hear a soft laugh, they were talking about the miners, remembering better times with the men and waiting for their return.

People were milling in and out. A sign on the double doors read, "Keep Doors Closed". Volunteers were carrying in blankets and food, making preparations for a long night of watching, waiting, and praying for the rescue of their loved ones. West Virginia State Police and Red Cross were acting as security to maintain privacy and keep the media out.

The small, white church is located across the road from the mine entrance. The church has a community/family room attached on the right, and a small porch has been built on the upper end of the front of the church. The church bell, used to ring for special joyous occasions or to announce church taking up, hangs on top in the steeple.

On the porch, three or four separate groups were huddled together; a few people were standing, leaning against the wall or bent over with both elbows on the railing surrounding the porch. A young couple sat in a corner with their metal fold-up chairs pointed toward each other in a way to keep others out. She was pretty with curly, thick black hair, twisted and pinned up on the nap of her neck. He wore a light gray ball cap. They both had hollowed, sad eyes.

In the yard, vehicles of various volunteer organizations took up most of the parking space, which was limited. A short distance back from one of the vans stood a group of people huddled together in the cold January drizzle under an umbrella. Rain poured down on everyone. The governor's security force was out talking with people and trying to make sure no unauthorized personnel gained entrance to the church.

Sago No. 1 Mine is located three miles behind the high school up a narrow road. It had rained all night and all day, creating a muddy quagmire for rescue workers and family members traveling in and out of the site and the church on the dirt road. Many of the vehicles were parked deep in the mud. Heavy equipment trucks, emergency vehicles, and media were traveling at a steady pace up and down the road. I passed the church and drove on up and parked on the one lane muddy, dirt road. I walked down the hill through the mud and rain to reach the church.

The tragedy began between 6 and 6:30 a.m. on the day after New Year's Day. The mine had sat idle during the holiday weekend. During 2005, West Virginia posted a glowing year in mining with only three fatalities. Then, on the first working day of 2006, an explosion caused the death of 12 miners and left behind a lone survivor—Randal McCloy, 26 years old, who lies in Ruby Memorial Hospital in critical condition suffering from a collapsed lung and severe dehydration. He is in a coma, and when he wakes up, he will live with the bittersweet knowledge that he is the only survivor. His wife, Anna, told that Randal kissed her each time before leaving for the mine and said to her, "God Bless You". They are the parents of two children, a son 4 years old, and a daughter.

Eleven hours passed before workers could begin rescue efforts, according to reports, due to the high level of dangerous gases venting from the mine. Most of the rescue work had to be done by hand, moving slowly and cautiously. A robot brought in with hopes it could travel into areas too dangerous for men, became mired in the mud, and was brought out. A camera was lowered through a drilled hole for possible communication with the miners but again mud became a factor and the camera was retracted. Carbon monoxide and methane gases remained at a dangerous level throughout most of the rescue efforts.

Sago No. 1 Mine is non-union. Its owner, International Coal Group, is headed up by New York billionaire Wilbur L. Ross, Jr. The company was formed in May 2004. In March 2005, ICG bought Anker West Virginia Mining Co., which was in bankruptcy. The Addington brothers of Ashland, Kentucky, formerly owned it. The initial purpose of the formation of ICG was to purchase the remaining assets of the Addington Empire for $768 million, according to newspaper reports.

We, as residents of these coalfields, are familiar with the Addington brothers. They were the owners of Horizon Resources. When this coal company was allowed to declare bankruptcy in 2004, it had a devastating affect on our own Cannelton Hollow miners in Fayette County, leaving miners without jobs, health care or pensions they had earned.

Sago No. 1, a mine with approximately 145 employees, has a long history of violations -- 46 over the past three months, according to the U.S. Department of Labor. Occupational safety expert Ellen Smith reports 13 of those violations were serious safety violations including seepage of volatile gas.

Coal is an important resource, with over 50 percent of electricity produced from coal. Employment in the coal industry in West Virginia is often for the money, but the danger is always there. It has not been determined what caused the explosion at the mine which shook the windows in Clifford Rice's new clapboard house on Sago Road.

Family members gathered at the Sago Baptist Church when they heard the news. Several hours passed before a rescue team arrived. We learned rescue teams were not on standby, but had to be assembled from certified men throughout West Virginia.

Today, the dead miners were brought up the hill one by one in a somber procession – their last mantrip out of Sago Mine.

"Shock" of the event brings home memories

Tallmansville, West Virginia -The worst mine disaster in West Virginia since Farmington where 78 miners died, nearly 40 years ago. This news, on everyone's lips and in their eyes, was coming out of a small coal mining community in Upshur County, West Virginia, 84 miles to the north of me. Thirteen coal miners were trapped beneath one of our steep West Virginia mountains at the Sago No. 1 underground coal mine following an explosion. Location and fate of miners, unknown.

As the hours of this tragedy of the Sago mine disaster moved forward, my mind went back, back in time, back to my childhood, my life in coal mine country. I went back in time to our 42 acre farm on the hill. It was the only place suitable my dad said for a family with five growing boys. I remember our neighbors down over the hill, Johnnie and Ann Groves. They lived with their children in the little white house on the side of the road in the sharp curve. My parents thought a lot of Johnnie and Ann. Dad always said, "Johnnie was a good man." His occupation: Coal miner. He used to come up on the hill to visit with Dad. He would come to the door and ask, "Is the General home?" meaning Dad. They would sit around the fireplace, telling stories and laughing. My dad told lots of hunting and fishing stories. Johnnie told stories about working in the coal mines and the men who worked underground with him. He would talk about the jokes they played on each other. Dad always said, "Johnnie loves to work in the coal mine, and I believe he works with a good bunch of men."

Some days while we were playing down that way, we would see Johnnie getting out of a truck. He rode with another miner to work each day. He carried his lunch bucket and hard hat in his hands. His miner's hat had a light attached to the front. I can't remember if his lunch bucket was round and silver or black, shaped like a little house with a place for a thermos in the lid. But when he started toward the house his little kids would run out to meet him.

Johnnie was killed in the coal mine, electrocuted, they said. He was a young man with a young wife and family. I remember Mom and Dad going down to the house. Cars and trucks came. They lined the narrow road on the steep hill almost to our gate. Mom told us not to come down there. She said, "It is no place for kids."

But we went there anyway, not in the house, because the house was small and people were coming and going and carrying in food. The kids were like stair-steps, close in age and small. They were running around. I don't think they understood their daddy had been killed in the coal mine, but Ann understood. We could see through the windows, the curtains were pulled back and tied. Ann was crying and bent over like a limp, rag doll. She was small, pale with dark hair and high strung. The neighborhood women were holding her up and dabbing her forehead with a cloth.

Later, Johnnie's brother was killed in the coal mine.

James Moore, Elza's brother, got his arm torn off at the shoulder in the coal mine.

Rabbit Groves, coal miner, walked with a limp, but I don't know what caused that limp.

Those people lived up or down the road from our house. They were our neighbors and friends of my parents.

I live in coal mine country.

Sago mine disaster

I am deeply involved with coal miners; recording their history, culture, traditions, and all those who surround him such as mountain fiddlers, veterans, health care workers and others. I had nearly reached publication stage of my second book when the Sago Mine explosion occurred on January 2, 2006. I put a temporary hold on the Tom and Pat Gish oral history interview and turned my full attention to recording the story of Sago.

I began following the story of Sago from the beginning, developing my own timeline and writing down key events as they happened. I wrote down many of the interviews, comments from the experts and information from press conferences as they occurred. Forty-eight hours of nonstop national news coverage by television, together, with daily newspaper stories and editorials, gave me a mountain of information. Also, I could draw from my own background of growing up and living in the coalfields. I had a plan.

I planned to record this historical event as it unfolded. I planned to write segments of the account which would reveal the bravery of coal miners. I planned to write bits and pieces of this story which would reveal the trust these miners gain in each other. I would note ways in which they depend on each other, like family, like brothers, never feeling alone as long as one more miner is present. I planned to tell of the miners' technical skills, how they go deep into the mountains, digging and shoveling coal; operating machines as big as half a mountain. How they take the risk of breathing in dust, knowing down the road they too, will take up the hacking cough of their fathers and grandfathers, taking them all to an early grave. I planned to write about the jokes they play on each other, like hiding another man's lunch bucket or giving names to the rats which become underground acquaintances. I planned to talk about these miners who love to mine coal, men who hum and whistle those coal mining songs such as "16 Tons of No. 9 Coal" and "Big John" as they walk around in their secret mountain habitant covered in a coat of black dust. I planned to tell of their survival skills, masters of mountain living surviving on next to nothing when the mine is closed and jobs are gone. Miners are able to scrape by, living off the land by digging ramps, raising potatoes, corn and killing a deer for winter's meat. I planned to write down how they could pick up an old fiddle after working on their hands and knees all day long and saw out a lively tune. All those things I planned. I planned on writing details of these miners' lives, not details of their deaths. I had no plans for that.

I asked her, "What do you do when you send a husband and four sons off to work in the coal mine each day?" Delores Tinnel said, "I pray."

On January 2, first working day of the new year 2006, an explosion occurred at the Sago No. 1 underground coal mine. Sago is near Tallmansville and Buckhannon in Upshur County, West Virginia. Sago has a population of a few hundred, Buckhannon has a population of 5,700 and Tallmansville is somewhere in between.

Thirteen coal miners were trapped 260 feet down and two miles back in the mountain. Cable news and national news networks swiftly turned the entire nation's attention toward the small coal mining community where Sago Mine is located in West Virginia. You could not get away from news of Sago or coal mining. News networks reported on this story as events developed minute by minute. To fill in gaps between press conferences with coal owner, Wilbur Ross, Jr.; CEO and President, Ben Hatfield; V-President Gene Kitts; and coal experts, J. Davit McAteer or Bruce Dials, reporters conducted interviews with family members of the trapped miners. After talking with family members, they searched for friends of the trapped miners to get an opinion or

West Virginia

Drawing by B. L. Dotson-Lewis

a personal story. They found John Casto who spoke so eloquently about the situation in Sago. Community leaders and preachers were interviewed as well. It was full coverage. News reporters such as CNN's Anderson Cooper came into our living rooms, kitchens, and work places to explore all facets of coal mining in this state, broadcasting live from Sago.

Reporters announced, "Coal is King in the hills of West Virginia" but for those of us who were born, raised and live here, that is a familiar phrase. A phrase that has been around since coal was first discovered in 1742 by John Peter Salley in what is now Boone County. Those watching and listening found out West Virginia leads the nation in underground coal production and approximately 50% of all coal exported comes from West Virginia coalfields with 315 underground mines and 229 surface mines. The West Virginia Coal Association reports West Virginia produced 544 million tons of coal during 2005.

It didn't take long for reporters to realize the phrase "Coal is King" echoes loudly from coal operators and investors as the demand for coal grows with a price that doubled over the past two years. "Coal is King" echoes from the steep hillsides as the price of natural gas soars and electricity consumption in the U.S. is projected to increase 40% by 2025, according to the Energy Information Administration. "Coal is King" with the construction of more than 120 coal-fired power plants nationwide proposed. That phrase is resulting in rich investors, who have never set foot in West Virginia, commonly known as absentee land and mineral owners, buying up floundering coal operations, problems and all, such as New York billionaire, Wilbur Ross, Jr., who purchased the Sago No. 1 Mine, cited by U.S. Mine Safety and Health Administration with more than 200 violations of federal regulations during 2005.

Experts interviewed on news broadcasts agreed King Coal has not enjoyed such a reign since the 70s. Jobs are so plentiful, coal operators have launched aggressive recruiting strategies offering high salaries and sign-on bonuses. The Inter-Mountain newspaper of Elkins writes as many as 800 new coal mine jobs are projected for Marion

County, West Virginia, alone - the county where Sago mine is located. These times are a throw back to the early 1900s when coal operators employed coal agents to recruit right off the boats as they landed on Ellis Island. Non-English-speaking immigrants were promised jobs, housing, medical services and education in the Appalachian coalfields, "The American Dream." We are not far from that today. Two weeks before the Sago mine disaster, Charlie Bearse, an official with Sidney Coal Company, a subsidiary of Massey Energy in Coal Run, Kentucky, wrote a letter to the Kentucky Mining Board alleging coal miners' work ethics have declined, and they are on drugs in Eastern Kentucky. The company wants permission to bring in non-English-speaking Hispanics to mine their coal.

The Sago mine disaster opened the eyes of this nation to coal mining. National news reporters became fascinated with coal mining, how and why it is done. They would say, "Mining seems so dangerous why would anyone do it?" Reporters dressed in Ivy League casual wear would approach a miner dressed in a flannel shirt and jeans or his dirty mining clothes. The reporter would stick a microphone to the miner's mouth and say, "What is the lure of coal mining? Why do you choose coal mining as your occupation?" (As if workers here have numerous occupational choices.) They soon found out, the lure of coal may be nothing more than a good paying job or just a job. The average income in West Virginia is $35,000; for the coal miner, the average salary is $50,000 exclusive of overtime and benefits. A job in the coal mines means you can stay in West Virginia near your family and friends. You can hunt and fish with buddies you have known since childhood. You can live in a rural area, raise a vegetable garden or have a horse. Also, you stay close to your roots. For many, coal mining is a family tradition, following in the footsteps of fathers and grandfathers. Coal mining is said to be "In the blood."

Through persistent and extensive broadcasting of news about the Sago mine disaster, our nation discovered coal has been King in West Virginia for centuries, but the focus had shifted away from the coal miner to the coal mined due to mechanization and a decrease in the need for miners as the job market slacked off and surface and mountaintop removal methods of mining gain in popularity. This nation, for thirty odd years has turned its back on coal mining and the coal miner, until now as an aging group of miners face retirement – the remainder of their days filled with bad lungs and a bad back.

Coal mining has been evolving over the years, but at a slow, steady pace drawing little attention to itself. The majority of coal mines in West Virginia are non-union. The UMWA is hanging on by its fingernails with only 32-35% union shops. Technology is playing a big role in the mining industry but we learned through this tragedy at Sago that technology is confined to methods of extracting, processing and hauling coal. Technology is at least 20 years behind for the coal miner in the area of safety and rescue. Tracking devices developed at least 20 years ago in Australia have still not made it in the mines here in West Virginia, the nation's second largest coal producing state. Instead of the latest tech methods, such as text messaging devices, our miners are equipped with antiquated walkie-talkies which at times serve no better than two tin cans with a wire strung between them. During this tragedy, West Virginia's Senator Robert C. Byrd barked out on the Senate Floor, "We can talk to people on the moon but cannot locate or communicate with miners trapped two miles away."

On the surface everything appeared to be honky-dory, rosy and status quo in the mining industry with no big news splashes since the mine disaster in Alabama in September 2001, where 13 miners died at the Jim Walters No. 5 mine. But individuals familiar with the changes occurring in the coalfields in West Virginia told me a different story. They told me they were not surprised to learn of a disaster. They used the old phrase, "One was waiting to happen." They told me agencies in charge of overseeing health and safety issues had become laid back about our miners in regard to safety enforcement, and implementation of new technology which could benefit miners. They told me the current administration had tabled proposals toward the advancement of safety measures in mining when presented in 2002.

So, this coal boom brought the focus back to the coalfields and the coal operators, but a mine explosion at Sago No. 1 underground coal mine in Tallmansville, West Virginia on January 2, 2006, brought that focus back on the coal miner.

January 2, 2006, the day of the mine explosion became a day of reckoning for those living in the coalfields of West Virginia; coal operators, government officials, coal miners and their families. This explosion which jarred the living daylights out of West Virginia and this nation, put wheels in motion that had failed to turn in favor of mine safety for over 30 years. This explosion resulting in the death of 12 miners, leaving a sole survivor, critically injured, took this nation on a 48 hour spree of waiting, praying and watching the fate of those miners. The finality came in the form of three hours of false jubilation and then total and complete heartbreak over the terrible outcome, leaving behind an unforgettable memory of Sago and coal mining.

In times of trouble or triumph, people of these mountains go to the Lord, and on the occasion of the Sago disaster folks ran to the House of the Lord at Sago Baptist Church, situated across the road from the entrance to Sago Mine. The church doors opened within an hour of the blast and at least 200 family members and friends gathered there to kneel, pray and sing hymns while watching and waiting for their loved ones to emerge from the deep, dark mountain. Wease Day, Preacher at Sago Baptist, was at his church tending his flock within the hour. Wease is a tall man with a big, angular face and broad shoulders. His speech and mannerisms convey kindness and understanding. He had a big job

Sago Baptist Church.
Photograph: Courtesy of Herald-Dispatch

on his hands as Preacher of Sago Baptist Church. He could use all the help the Good Lord could give him during this time of crises. Sago Church is a replica of the small, white churches seen throughout the hills and hollows of West Virginia.   Preacher Wease Day described his church at the memorial service this way, "Sago Baptist Church is a big operation, no physical address, no phone and no website. If you want to contact someone at Sago Baptist Church, you have to go there."

Many thoughts and questions raced through my own mind such as: How did a miner feel working underground in a closed in space, tearing loose the coal amid water dripping, dampness and pieces of coal and rock falling about him randomly, was he afraid? How did he conquer those fears? Did they talk about being afraid or the dangers they faced daily? Nelson Tinnel, a miner with 42 years experience came into my office on the morning following the Sago explosion. We began talking about Sago and coal mining and I said to Nelson, "Do you discuss with each other the dangers in a coal mine? Are you afraid? Do you talk about that?" The miner with 42 years experience told me, "I always tell a miner when I see him, 'Be careful'.   If it is a group of miners, I say, 'You all be careful'. That is my way of telling miners I will be thinking of their safety during their shift of work. I believe it is harder on the miners' families than the miner himself."

State Police protection was soon requested at the Sago Baptist Church for the trapped miners' families because of a media blitz. The publicity was overwhelming to the folks who were already dazed with the news of their men trapped in that mine.   Reporters with microphones and videos machines relaying soundbites and photos via satellite trucks flooded the small hollow within a couple of hours of the explosion. However, without continuous coverage of this tragedy, West Virginia miners may still be facing a future of mining coal under conditions outdated 20 years ago in the area of safety.   On the downside, West Virginia's people were revealed in living color to the world; their false jubilation, tears of heartbreak and uncontrollable anger; all these private emotions went into everyone's living room. The people of Sago and all their emotions were broadcast live and in color during their most vulnerable moments.

People living outside this region were given a bird's eye view to every facet of coal mine community life; the outpouring of friends and neighbors to the families of the trapped miners. People were seen carrying baked pies, hams, jugs of coffee and blankets into Sago Church.   People in the church were filmed and photographed kneeling in prayer, singing and raising their hands to God asking for 12 miracles.

A coal miner's daughter told me, "I hurt. I felt as if it were my family trapped there in that mine. I did nothing for 42 hours except watch the events at Sago as they unfolded."

I felt the same way.

Heartbreak ahead

From the time of the explosion until confirmation of the dead, for us, 48 long hours passed. For 12 miners it became an eternity.

Sole survivor – Randal McCloy

Randal McCloy was alive, barely alive, clinging to life as the ambulance sped out of Sago mine entrance. The ambulance crossed the bridge and headed for St. Joseph's Hospital, 10 minutes away in Buckhannon. Randal didn't know it but he received a huge round of applause as he passed the crowd on the river bank and in front of Sago Church. It was miserably cold, rainy, spitting snow, just past midnight night, but the people didn't know it, 12 more miners, their miners, alive, maybe banged up, but alive, would soon be coming down the same road Randal McCloy just came down. That is what they believed. They didn't mind the rain or snow. They didn't even feel it.

Anna McCloy was in the group at the church. She didn't know it was her husband – the man she had been a couple with since junior high – the father of her two children, their son and their daughter. She didn't know he was the one in the ambulance. She didn't know he was the sole survivor.

No one knows for sure how or why Randal McCloy survived and the others didn't, but what we have learned is the federal government sets clear rules for mine rescue: Five members to a team accompanied by a MSHA regulator. When the trapped miners were found, if federal rescue procedures were followed, the team first counted the men, then checked each one for vital signs. The rescuers check pulse, signs of breathing, skin and pupils. It was during this regulatory procedure when the unit was looking for survivors that they heard the faint moans coming from a miner lying on his left side, turned away from them. It was Randal McCloy. The team began reviving him, bringing him back to life. First they stripped off his gear, applied an oxygen mask and neck collar. It took the unit an hour to get Randal stable enough to carry. Rescuers carried him one half mile on a stretcher, loaded him on a train car which transported him the two miles to the surface of the mine. He emerged from Sago mine at 1:00 a.m. The E.R. crew at St. Joseph Hospital in Buckhannon were ready to receive Randal. He was in bad shape. He was near death. It was reported he was in a coma, dehydrated and had an irregular heartbeat. They immediately inserted a breathing tube and began routine medical checks.

After doctors at St. Joseph stabilized him, he was transported by helicopter to Ruby Memorial Hospital in Morgantown. On Wednesday morning, doctors reported McCloy suffered from a collapsed lung and his kidneys were damaged. His airways were inflamed and congestd. He had breathed in lots of dust and dangerous gases. He lay near death all through Wednesday and Thursday. He was put on a ventilator and his lung inflated.

After he was stabilized, Randal was transferred from Ruby Memorial Hospital to Allegheny General Hospital, near Pittsburgh, Pennsylvania on January 5, 2006. This move to Allegheny General was for treatment in a hyperbaric oxygen chamber which forces pressurized oxygen into the body. This treatment is for patients suffering from severe carbon monoxide poisoning. Dr. Antonios Zikos, a pulmonary specialist, reported the treatment is a preventive measure to stave off long-term psychiatric deficits which may appear weeks or months later.

McCloy's condition was classified as critical despite slight improvements after arriving at Allegheny General. His attending physician described his medical condition resulting from the more than 40 hour entombment in the gaseous mine as numerous injuries resulting in multisystem organ failure and some brain damage.

During McCloy's stay at Allegheny Hospital, besides treatment inside the hyperbaric oxygen chamber, McCloy was kept in a drug-induced coma as part of his treatment. The attending doctors described the treatment as a way of allowing the body to heal itself without fighting the ventilator and IV tubes. He had a tracheotomy before he was transferred back to Ruby Memorial Hospital. Randal was equipped with breathing and feeding tubes before returning to West Virginia.

On Saturday night, January 7, 2006, under heavy sedation Randal was flown back to Ruby Memorial Hospital in Morgantown, West Virginia. By January 7, 2006 Dr. Richard Shannon reported Randal was awake underneath the medically induced coma. Dr. Shannon said that when the medication was eased up, Randal's eyes flicker and he bites down on his breathing tube.

The media provided continuous coverage on McCloy's progress as he slowly came out of his coma. We hovered around our television when the news reported Anna saying that now when she asks him if he wants more chicken fingers he can say, "Yes or no." His family stayed by his side playing his favorite heavy metal music, gospel, and country.

When Hank Williams, Jr. found out he was one of Randal's favorite musicians he visited Randal McCloy and his family at Ruby Memorial Hospital on Wednesday, January 11, 2006. Hank told the media Randal's accident reminded him of what had happened to him in the '70s when he fell 400 feet down a mountain in Montana. Doctors said he would not live. June Carter and Johnny Cash visited Hank while he was in the hospital. He said that meant a lot to him.

Doctors still do not know why Randal is alive after breathing in so much carbon monoxide there are no textbook answers as to why Randal is among the living and the others are dead.

Randal is dubbed, "The Miracle Miner."

As of January 16, 2006, news reported Randal McCloy, sole survivor, of the Sago disaster upgraded from critical condition to serious condition. Randal was ready to quit coal mining according to Anna McCloy, his wife. "It was too dangerous."

Profiles of Miners Who Died at Sago

The miners who went in Sago Mine on January 2, 2006, were an experienced group. Several of the miners had 25 years or more of mining experience.

1.   **Thomas Paul Anderson**, 39, of Rock Cave, West Virginia

   Job: Shuttle car operator

   Years of mining experience: 10

   Family and background: He married Lynda Hyre Anderson on April 5, 1991 who survives him. Tom had one young son, Tom (Ti), older sons, Randy and Mitchell, and four grandchildren. He was a religious man. He attended the Church of God in Lewis County.

   Special Interests: Tom was an avid hunter and fisher. He loved the outdoors.

   Note: During the Memorial Service on January 15, 2006, at the Wesleyan Chapel, a story was told about Tom's 10 year old son, Ti, who picked up a Bible at the Sago Baptist Church while waiting for his dad to come out of the mine so they could go home. He went around to anyone who would listen to him including Governor Joe Manchin reading his dad's favorite scripture verse. When it was found out he was dead, young Tom went to his mother and told her, "It is going to be O.K. Everything is going to be O.K. I know where my dad is going. He is going to heaven."

2.   **Alva Martin "Marty" Bennett**, 51, of Buckhannon, West Virginia

   Job: Continuous Miner Operator

   Years of mining experience: 29

   Family and background: Marty had been married to Judy Ann Lantz for more than 32 years. He came from a coal-mining family and he loved coal mining. Marty followed his father into the mines. Marty's only son, Russell, worked at the Sago Mine on the shift after his dad's. His brother-in-law, Roger Perry, was in the group who escaped the explosion.

   Special Interests: He owned and operated his own backhoe and bulldozer service. He enjoyed hunting and fishing.

3. **James A. Bennett**, 61, of Volga, West Virginia

   Job: Shuttle car operator

   Years of mining experience: 25

   Family and background: He married Lily M. Foster on October 31, 1962. He had a son, John, and a daughter, Cheryl Ann Merideth, and several grandchildren and great-grandchildren.   He planned to retire this year.

   Special Interests: He attended Buckhannon Union Mission Church. Jim was described by the Sago Mine Second Left crew as their spiritual leader. Each day, when Jim Bennett came home from his shift at the Sago Mine, he began to pray for the men who went underground on the shift after him.

4. **Jerry L. Groves**, 56, of Cleveland, West Virginia

   Job: Roof bolter operator

   Years of mining experience: 28

   Family and background: Jerry married Deborah A. Groves on March 7, 1977. Debbie said that she had been in love with Jerry since the fourth grade. They had one daughter, Shelly Rose, and three grandsons.

   Special Interests: "He loved the work," said Raymond Groves, his older brother. "He wouldn't have stayed if he didn't."

5.   **George Junior Hamner**, 54, of Glady Fork, West Virginia

Job: Shuttle car operator

Years of mining experience: 26

Family and background: George was married to Deborah with one daughter, Sara. He attended Glenville State College from 1969 to 1971. He grew up on the Sago Mine site. A mining company bought out the family farm.

Special Interests: George raised cattle on his farm.

6.   **Terry Hellms**, 50, of Newburg, West Virginia

Job: Fireboss

Years of mining experience: 29

Family and background: Terry had a son, Nick, and a daughter, Amber. His fiancée was Virginia Moore. His daughter said that her father worked hard to put her through college so she could get a good education. Terry did not want his son working in the mines. He encouraged him to pursue other employment opportunities. Nick is pursuing a career in golf. Terry's fiancée wore a beautiful heart around her neck, a Christmas present from Terry.

Special Interest: Terry enjoyed hunting and fishing. He was a life member of the North American Hunting Club.

7.   **Jesse L. Jones**, 44, of Pickens, West Virginia

Job: Roof-bolter operator

Years of mining experience: 16

Family and background: Jesse was the father of two daughters, Sarah and Katelyn. His brother, Owen, made it out safely from the explosion and another brother, Lynden, was out sick on January 2, 2006.

Special Interests: Jesse spent half his life underground in the mine. His grandpa on his daddy's side died in a coal mine explosion. Jesse loved, hunting, fishing, camping, pitching horseshoes and digging ramps (ramps are wild leeks – they have onion like roots and are found in the mountains of West Virginia – ramps have a smell as strong as garlic. Ramps are dug in the early spring).

8.   **David W. Lewis**, 28, of Thornton, West Virginia

Job: Roof-bolter operator

Years of mining experience: 1 year, 8 months

Family and background: He was married to Samantha Dawn Rankin. He had three daughters, Kayle, Shelby and Kelsie. David was working in the mine so his wife could go to school. She is working on a master's degree in health care administration. With this mining job, David was free in the evenings to care for his little girls while Samantha went to school.

Special Interests: David was an avid hunter and fisherman.

9.   **Martin Toler Jr.**, 50, of Flatwoods, West Virginia

Job: Section Foreman

Years of mining experience: 32

Family and background: Junior was married to his wife, Mary Lou, for 32 years. She survives him. He was the father of a son, Chris, and a daughter, Courtney. He had a special nephew, George Toler. Previously, he worked four years in the mine with his son, Chris. While huddled with 11 other fellow miners trying to find shelter from poisonous air, Martin Toler, Jr. took an insurance form and a pencil and scrawled out a farewell letter steeped with religious conviction to his family.

Special Interests: Martin Toler, Jr. was a church deacon. He taught Sunday school and adult Bible study; he had six grandchildren.

10.   **Fred G. "Bear" Ware**, Jr., 58, of 127 Sago Road, Buckhannon, West Virginia

Job: Continuous miner operator

Years of mining experience: 37

Family and background: Fred had a son, Darrell, and a daughter, Peggy Cohen. His fiancée was Loretta Ables. They had been engaged for six years. Fred suffered a broken ankle, punctured lung and broken several ribs in previous mining accident.

Special Interests: Fred Ware lived across the road from the Sago Baptist Church where he was a member. Preacher Wease Day described Ware as someone good-natured who liked to talk. He remembered him as the sort of man who didn't mind being awakened to help install gutters at the church. He was buried in a flannel shirt and camouflage cap.

11. **Jackie L. Weaver**, 51, of Mt. Liberty Road, Philippi, West Virginia

   Job: Section electrician

   Years of mining experience: 26

   Family and background: Jackie was married to Charlotte Poe Weaver and had a daughter, Rebecca, a son, Justin, and two grandsons. Jackie is survived by many coal mining brothers. He was a member of the Corley United Methodist Church. He always wrote "Jesus Saves" in the coal dust on his vehicles.

   Special Interests: Jackie Weaver was a avid sportsman who enjoyed hunting and fishing.

12. **Marshall Cade Winans**, 50, of Rt. 1, Talbott, West Virginia

   Job: Scoop operator

   Years of mining experience: 23

   Family and background: Marshall married Pamela Denise Pharis on July 18, 1974. Marshall is survived by his wife, Pamela, and three daughters, Mandy, Holly and Tiffany. He was a member of the Loyal Order of Moose, Lodge 598 of Buckhannon and a member of the United Mine Workers of America. He was a Methodist.

   Special Interests: Marshall was an avid hunter and fisherman and enjoyed NASCAR.

Second left crew

Terry Helms would be the first man on the job at Sago Mine on January 2, 2006. It was planned that way. Terry was fireboss and must perform a safety check before the regular crews arrived to begin their 10-hour day shift. He would check for firedamp, dangerous gases or other safety hazards that could result in injury, death or slowing down of production in this underground mine. On this day, his shift began at 3 a.m. because the mine had sat idle over the long holiday weekend. Following a holiday, the previous shift fireboss would do the inspection before the day crew arrived. Terry, a miner since the age of 18, would perform other duties throughout the work day, such as checking beltlines, walking throughout the mine with a shovel in his hands to remove debris and perform other tasks needed done.

Terry made his home at Newburg, West Virginia, making it more than an hour's drive to his job. He had gotten a job with Sago last fall. It was not uncommon for miners like Helms to commute an hour or more to a steady, good-paying job. Unlike large urban areas where commuting is bumper to bumper traffic inching its way along a city block, out in the country, commuting is driving on the highway or rural roads you know like the back of your hand. One of the common dangers in rural commuting is deer crossing the road in front of your vehicle in pre-dawn haze or fog.

Fifty year old Terry worked hard to raise his children and even though he had been injured by falling debris previously in a mining accident, he stuck with it because it was paying off. His son, Nick, 25, an aspiring pro-golfer, was living and working in Myrtle Beach, South Carolina. Terry had urged his son to pursue a career in a field other than coal mining because of the many dangers. Terry would welcome Amber, his 22 year old daughter, home when he returned from this shift of work. Amber had just graduated from college with a major in journalism. She was filled with excitement because she landed her first job with the local paper, Morgantown's Dominion-Post. Amber talked about her dad working so hard to put her through college. He wanted his children to have opportunities only an education could ensure.

Terry, engaged; a steady, good-paying job with Sago; two children, educated and succeeding, sum total; all was right with the world on Monday, January 2, 2006.

While Terry Helms dove an hour plus south to reach Sago, Martin Toler, Jr., drove 53.3 miles north from Flatwoods in Braxton County to Sago Mine. Martin was section foreman, a job requiring sound judgment, good rapport with the crew, ability to perform a delicate balancing act between coal operator and coal miner. Also, he must hold a certificate awarded after completion of the certification process.

Toler had a reputation as a note taker, making things-to-do lists on pieces of papers he routinely stuffed in his pockets along with a pencil or pen. He was prepared to scratch out a list anytime the notion hit him. Also, he needed paper and pencil to note items for discussion with the mine superintendent.

Martin, 51, like Terry Helms, was an experienced miner. Martin's brother, Tom Toler and family live in my community of Summersville which is 30 miles south of

56

Flatwoods. They are a family of miners. Martin would rise early on January 2, 2006 drive to Sago and lead his production crew into Sago No. 1 Mine.

Randal McCloy, Jr., roof-bolter, was only 26 years old. When Randal landed a job with Sago, he was able to return to West Virginia from Maryland. He had worked as a miner in Maryland. Randal did not profess a love for mining, but the money was good and he could keep his young family in West Virginia close to their relatives. They made their home in the tiny community of Simpson. He and his wife, Anna, had been together as a couple since junior high school. They had two adorable children; Randal 4, and Isabel 1.

Roof-bolting was an important job in the mines. The roof-bolter makes sure the roof or top over the mined-out area is well supported, providing a safe environment. The roof-bolter uses a roof-bolting machine to drill holes and position the bolts which are tightened or secured in place with a metal rectangle plate or glue. Several layers of strata can be bound together making it a strong support system or the bolts can be anchored to another structure to shore up a weakened roof area.

Miners are required to carry methane detectors or meters underground. Any miner operating a machine must check poisonous gas levels each time before crossing the threshold into another area with his machine. Randal's gas meter was going crazy weeks ago, according to Anna. That was what he had told her. Any type of friction can set off an explosion in an underground mine, but Randal had told Anna he didn't believe the drilling he was doing was creating a dangerous situation. That relieved some of her anxiety. Early on, Randal had gotten into a habit of hugging and kissing Anna, and his two children before leaving for work each day and saying, "God Bless You".

In photos shown by the media, Randal has on a ball cap. He has a big smile. He is holding one of his babies. In other photos he is dressed in his white wedding tuxedo. Randal is lean looking. His brother describes his fitness condition; "Randal is like a machine."

Randal lived only 25 miles north of Sago. It would not take him long to make it to Sago No. 1 mine, board the mantrip, and begin his earnings for calendar year 2006.

Jesse L. Jones, 44, was a member of this crew. Two of his brothers also worked for Sago. Owen acted as foreman of the First Left crew. Lynden was sick and unable to work on Monday, January 2, 2006. But the Jones family was a family of miners. Jesse's grandpa had died in a coal mine blast.

Jesse was a country boy. He enjoyed the simple things in life, hunting, fishing, digging ramps and listening to the clang of metal when he scored a ringer pitching horseshoe. Jesse came from Pickens in Randolph County to mine at Sago.

Fred Ware, Jr., 59, operated the continuous mining machine. This machine has a large, rotating, drum-shaped cutting head studder with carbide-tipped teeth that break up the seam of coal. Large gathering arms on the machine scoop the coal directly onto a built-in conveyor for loading into waiting shuttle cars and transported to the outside. Fred controlled this massive machine with the touch of a button. Fred lived across the creek from the entrance to the mine.

He was a religious man and served as a deacon at the Sago Baptist, but he was not the kind of man who felt it necessary to be in church every time the door opened to show his faith. He led by example. He helped the church out with annual donations. Fred lived in sight of the Sago Baptist Church in a little white house heated with a coal-burning furnace.

He was about to try marriage for the second time according to fiancée, Loretta Ables. They had planned a Valentine Day's wedding.

This miner, like so many others I have talked with, felt at home in the mines. They loved the smell and feel of the coolness and dampness of the black shiny face of Mother Earth.

Early Monday morning on January 2, 2006, Fred Ware finished his daily Bible reading, laid his Bible on his chair, picked up his keys, his lunch bucket and drove across the bridge to Sago No. 1 Mine.

Fred's son, Darrell, worked in construction work even though his dad encouraged him to follow in his footsteps. Peggy Cohen, Darrell's sister, said she thought Darrell was afraid to go to the mines. Peggy is a nurse.

Another crew member, George "Junior" Hamner, 54, had spent 26 years mining. George quit the mines when his weight got out of control, so he turned his energy to running his cattle farm in Glady Fork in Webster County where he grew up. Hamner decided to do something about his weight. He opted for surgery and dropped 200 pounds. This gave him the option of returning to the mines. He filled a position as an experienced shuttle car operator. The coal boom brought on by high oil and natural gas prices was opening up jobs in the coal field for miners like Hamner who were experienced but had left coal mining. Now, they could return. Hamner was known as a private person.

Jerry Groves, 56, roof-bolter, came from a long line of coal miners – his father, grandfather and a brother were all miners. Jerry drove to Sago from Cleveland in nearby Webster County.

Thornton in Taylor County gave the crew David Lewis, 28. David did not aspire to work underground. He had worked in timber and on construction but that kept him away for home and his family. He took the job as a roof-bolter at Sago regarding it as temporary employment. He had earned his license as a certified electrician which could land him a job above ground when a position came open. David was raised on a farm. The money paid at Sago gave him the means to support his wife, Samantha, who was pursuing a master's degree in Health Care Administration. He was free evenings and nights to care for their three young daughters while Samantha went to class.

"This was a good way to make a living until we could find something else," said Lewis, whose father, grandfather and stepfather also worked in the mines. "It's just a way of life. Unless you're a coal miner or you have a college degree, you don't make any money."

Martin Bennett had a passion for coal mining. He loved the business and the way in which it provided for his family. He viewed coal mining as no more dangerous than driving a car. So, Marty Bennett was one of the miners who looked forward to riding the mantrip to the face to see what he could accomplish during a shift of work. He was in sync with

Mother Nature. Marty followed in his father's footsteps. His son, Russell, worked on the following shift.

Rock Cave, Upshur County, West Virginia, was home to Sago miner, Tom Anderson, 39 years old with 10 years experience in mining. He operated a shuttle car. The shuttle car, under Tom's command picked up newly mined coal and hauled it to the conveyor belt or a pile to be transported to the outside. Tom, like many of his co-workers, would meet on that early morning of January 2, 2006 to make up the Second Left Section crew. Tom was a devout Christian.

Crew member Jim Bennett, 61, was a shuttle car operator like Anderson. Bennett loved coal mining. Twenty-five years into it had not dampened his spirit or enthusiasm. He had in common with fellow miners a religious conviction. He prayed daily for the men on the shifts following him. Bennett came from Volga in Barbour County to join his crew of Second Left.

Jackie Weaver stayed right where he was born in the little community on Mount Liberty Road in Philippi. Weaver came to Sago with 26 years mining experience. He was a certified electrician.

The Second Left crew had their own preacher, Marshall Winans, 50. This scoop operator at Sago had been a minister for 20 years. He was a seasoned miner with 23 years experience. Winans was a member of the UMWA (United Mine Workers of America). He was a big NASCAR fan. Marshall made his home at Talbott in Barbour County. There was always news about NASCAR when Winans caught up with fellow crew members after a long holiday weekend.

Members of the Second Left crew at Sago traveled from all directions, 12 crew members and fireboss, Terry Helms, but they shared many common interests. These men enjoyed the out-of-doors. Jack Weaver, was noted for hunting and fishing as well as his religious convictions. He demonstrated his devout faith by going around scrawling "Jesus Saves" on vehicles dusty with coal dust. Jim Bennett was another outdoorsman. He was also a devout Christian. He offered prayers up for miners daily and recorded on the end of his telephone voice mail the question, "Do you know the Lord as your Savior?"

Ron Grall, member of First Left crew talked about how well this crew got along. They had common interests, respect and cared for each other. He said when a mine superintendent gets a crew together like Second Left, they like to keep that crew together as long as possible.

Fireboss, Terry Helms, was finishing his checklist as the remaining 12 were arriving at the mine. The last leg of the trip to Sago Mine, the miners would drive three miles up Sago Road behind the high school before approaching a small bridge with grey metal railings on each side. Sago Baptist church sat down the road in the distance on the right. The miners would cross the bridge, park their trucks in the gravel area, pick up their lunches and head for the entrance of the mine in the pre-dawn darkness. It was getting close to 6:00 a.m. on Monday, January 2, 2006.

Terry Helms gave the "all clear sign" and Second Left crew of 12 boarded a mantrip. Helms joined them. The 13 miners rolled down the mainline tracks into the mine traveling about two miles to their destination, the face of the coal. Helms would split from the crew at the left turn.

First Left production crew was also returning to work. This crew ran into trouble resulting in a slight delay. The mantrip sent to transport this crew into the mine was new and all the men couldn't fit into the vehicle. They did not get started on time. They were about 10 minutes behind.

Sago mine is shaped like a backward capital "F" and operates on the "room and pillar" mining system which uses a continuous miner to cut out the coal in chunks. Large blocks "pillars" of coal are left standing to support the roof while more coal is being mined. Rooms are created. Sago is a drift underground mine. A highwall was constructed and a drift mouth opened to gain access to the mine. After entering the mouth, the mine slopes down gradually in line with the Kittaning coal seam they are mining. Miners are transported in and out of Sago mine by a vehicle called a mantrip which runs on tracks.

On the left of the entrance of the mine, older mined out areas are sealed off as shown on the drawing. These areas were mined out by Sigler's mining company. Crews are currently mining areas called First Left section and Second Left section which run parallel to each other. Rock falls from bad top forced the closing of one section deeper in the mountain, a few months earlier. It appears on the map the company backtracked closer to First Left section to open a new section referred to as Second Left section.

Thunderstorms and lightening hit the area during Sunday, January 1 and all through the night into Monday. Ron Grall, member of the First Left crew, commented on the odd weather for West Virginia in January, rain pouring down, when the mountains are usually covered in snow during this winter's month.

Sago blows

Conventional shifts- 8 hrs.

Day   7:00 a.m. - 3:00 p.m.
Evening   3:00 p.m. - 11:00 p.m.
Midnight/Hoot-Owl 11:00 p.m. - 7:00 a.m.

Modern Shifts - 10 hrs. - 12 hrs.

10 hours or 12 hours per day (2 shifts)
4 on, 3 off
Weekend Warriors Thursday - Sunday

Second Left crew had reached their destination, 260 feet down and two miles back, but First Left was not quite there when Clifford and Victoria Rice were shaken from sleep by a bolt of lightening cracking and popping out their window. In the next second, what Clifford described as an earthquake, jolted them out of bed, all three of them; Victoria, Clifford and their German Shepherd dog. The Rice family had finally gotten use to the big, loud coal trucks thundering by their house on early morning runs up and down Sago Creek, but they were shaken by this blast forceful enough to bust out two windows in their house. Their new, clapboard house was built a few hundred yards from the entrance to Sago mine. Later, they learned, house trailers in the neighborhood took a beating by the blast felt as far away as French Creek. This explosion had come out of Sago No. 1 mine.

Minutes or seconds before the explosion, First Left crew had arrived at their turn off from the main track back in the mine. Roger Perry got off the mantrip, walked over to throw the switch to turn the track. That never happened. It was 6:30 a.m. The mine mountain began rolling, rumbling, belching and spitting out hot smoke and deadly gas.

The First Left crew nearly two miles back and 260 feet underground felt the mighty blast. The explosion took them by surprise, they had no time to think. It literally threw them for a loop. One miner was thrown out of the mantrip. Metal bolts, lunch pails and hard hats went flying in all directions. Someone was shouting, "Go to the intake!" "Go to the intake!" Meaning head to the outside. Foreman Owen Jones, Jesse's brother, managed somehow to get his self-rescuer strapped on, giving him one hour of oxygen to do whatever it took to get his men and himself out. But what about Jesse? His brother, Jesse deeper in the mine. Where was he? What was his condition? Did he survive this blast? Owen fumbled around until he found the phone. He called the surface for help. He told the dispatcher, "Get someone down here. There's been an explosion!"

Ben Hatfield, CEO and President of Sago, reported twenty-eight miners were underground at the time of this explosion; First Left and Second Left production crews and support staff.

First Left crew began half stumbling, half walking in the dark, backtracking the best they could with coal dust blinding them; stumbling on foot, trying to get to fresh air. Their mantrip was sidetracked, covered in coal dust and mud. The heavy black, gaseous smoke roared from the back of the mine forward to the mouth and the outside, Owen's men knew they were up against two deadly enemies of coal miners: lack of time and lack of oxygen. The invisible, silent killer would come first. This killer came in the form of a halo of gaseous smoke, as deadly as a viper. The gas would weaken them and the tiny bits and pieces of coal dust and rock would blind them, burning and stinging their eyes. Making them hurt like the devil but at least it was visible. The invisible killer lulls its victims into a slumber, then attacks from all sides and angles, front, back and center simultaneously, covering them in an invisible veil and finally, finishing off its victim by taking their breath. Time was of the essence for First Left crew. One hour of oxygen from here to eternity.

So, an explosion had occurred in Sago No. 1 mine instantly turning a steady, good-paying job into a death trap. Sago Mine became New York billionaire, Wilbur Ross's Hell hole for 13 West Virginia miners.

As the smoke wound its way to the outside, anything and everything in its path was coated with black, greasy coal soot. The supply of oxygen became thin in the shaft; deadly carbon monoxide was its replacement, the byproduct of a fire in poorly ventilated shafts.

No word from Second Left crew.

Rescue efforts underway

According to ICG CEO and President, Ben Hatfield, during testimony before the United States Senate Committee on Appropriations Subcommittee on Labor, Health and Human Services, Education and Related Agencies which took place on Monday, January 23, 2006:

"At 6:31 AM, Sago mine management heard the audible alarm of the mine monitoring system indicating the presence of carbon monoxide underground and electrical power was disrupted."

Owen Jones called for help following the explosion. I asked Tinnel how could Owen Jones call the surface if communications were cut off as reported. He explained that one way he may have communicated with management on the outside was using two-way radios which are stationed on mantrips, making it possible to communicate with the surface as long as the battery holds out. Owen told dispatcher that thick smoke was coming from deep in the mine as well as a cloud of dust. Management told First Left to evacuate out of one of the escapeways. No one had been able to establish communication with Second Left crew. Owen would not leave. He started deeper in the mine. He wanted to find his brother. His crew tried to stop him. They knew if Owen made it in to Jesse, chances were slim he would make it out before his oxygen supply was depleted.

Ten minutes after the explosion at 6:41 a.m., Mine Superintendent Jeff Toler, whose uncle was one of the missing miners, and three other mine supervisors headed underground to investigate. About a mile and half in, the superintendent and three supervisors traveling in a mantrip met First Left crew attempting to find their way out on foot. First Left crew's mantrip had been stopped by debris. When found, the lights were still on.

Instead of coming out to the mouth of the mine and fresh air, Owen Jones joined the makeshift rescue unit of four, making it five. They had tools and ventilating materials with them. They forged ahead on foot after turning their mantrip over to the First Left crew for transportation to safety.

Owen's crew, dazed from the blast, covered in black soot and already feeling the effects of oxygen depleted air, got into the mantrip, backed away and headed to the outside and fresh air. When First Left crew made it to the outside, they waited. Owen's First Left crew watched and waited for Second Left to come out.   The mine superintendent, Jeff Toler's uncle, Martin Toler was behind the wall of smoke. Roger Perry, member of Owen's crew had a brother-in-law, Alva "Marty" Bennett, behind the wall of smoke. Roger had been hit with shards of metal in his eyes and could not go back inside to look for Marty.   Owen's older brother Jesse was behind the wall of smoke.

The mine was equipped with stationary phones, after that communication had been knocked out, the men began yelling, "Anybody inside?" "Anybody inside?" No one responded. Rescue attempts had to halt for fear that an explosion would ignite as they directed fresh air toward Second Left section. The management group exited at 9:45 a.m. It is reported Owen Jones walked out alone an hour later at 10:45 a.m. Second Left crew was only 500 yards away. 40 hours of Hell would pass before anyone would get close to the missing miners again.

Is anybody out there?

"We don't hear any attempts at drilling or rescue. The section is full of smoke and fumes, so we can't escape. Be strong, and I hope no one else has to show you this note. I love you both and always have. I'm in no pain, but don't know how long the air will last." George Hamner Jr. (Note found in George Hamner's lunch bucket)

Notes reveal the miners were still hopeful at least 10 hours following the explosion. Did they know we had not given up? Did they realize people on the other side had not forsaken them or forgotten them. Did they know rescue units were working non-stop to find them?   It must have been hard sitting there in a confined space behind a brattice curtain with death closing in.

Do preachers like Wease Day know what men think while they were waiting to be rescued or to die? Does it tell you in the Bible how to wait to die? Did they talk to each other, pray? Were they scared? Did they see the white, bright light like coal miner Elza Moore saw when he was half way to the other side after his heart attack and the Lord called him back. He described the experience as one of the most beautiful experiences of his life.   These are hard questions. Questions no one wants to ask but deep inside those thoughts have crossed our minds. Somehow, someway, we hope those 12 miners knew they did not die alone or in vain. This entire nation suffered with those miners. Surely they did not for a minute think rescue efforts were abandoned. It hurts to know efforts were not enough, not quick enough, not technically advanced enough to save their lives. It is a strange helpless feeling to know we are on one side of the Jordan River and just two miles away, they are crossing to the other side of Jordan.

Those outside the region wonder how Appalachians survive such tragedies. How do mountain people get so tough and strong? One answer is because of the hardships they endure but there are other reasons: mountain people/coal miners are raised as one with God and Nature. They have indisputable ties with both. Mountain people are blessedly trapped between old rivers and old mountains. A beautiful dilemma. Mountain people have common sense which comes from doing common things according to Nelson Tinnel. Mountain people have a large family/community support system.

West Virginians are caught in a love/hate relationship with the black gold. They know of the dangers. One of my relatives whose husband works as a miner told me the other day as we talked of Sago, "The dangers of coal mining becomes a part of your life. You know it is there. You accept it. You try not to dwell on it or even talk about it. That is just the way it is."

Coal miners are sometimes a prized commodity, sometimes they are of little use, but the coal miners know if they are to survive in the coal fields they must understand the x factor. The x factor is what I call the unspoken but well known factors miners must obey to stay employed. I have been told one of the x factors in coal mining may be when you are hired on, you are told no work on the weekends; however, if you want to keep your job you will work on weekends whenever asked. The x factor may be a "redhat" working unsupervised posing dangers for others. The x factor may be demand for complete loyalty to the coal company, 24/7 by the miner and his family. The coal miner knows the rules of the game. These games have been around longer than the Olympics.

Coal owners/operators are telling us the coalfields are not prepared for this coal boom. Miners are in short supply. One reason for the lack of qualified workers is our young people were forced to leave the area to find jobs before the coal boom got off the ground. The lack of experienced miners raised a concern when the explosion occurred at Sago. One of the first thoughts was the level of experience of the miners trapped. Were they a bunch of "redhats" who may lose their cool or not yet knowledgeable in the area of survival in the deep, dark mountains with no lights and little air?   It was a relief when it was revealed the miners trapped had from 3 – 30 years experience. They were well trained in survival techniques. We thought that was enough.

Days that followed

State and national officials' response

"Where is MSHA?" 'Where is MSHA?" In 1978 legislation created Miners Health and Safety Administration under the Department of Labor Bureau (MSHA). MSHA is a regulatory agency, protecting the miner – watching over the miner like a guardian angel. But something went wrong when Sago blew, MSHA was nowhere in sight. Through public inquiry it was learned MSHA kept at least two public officials at the Sago mine site during the disaster, but it was ICG officials who briefed the press. CEO and President Hatfield told reporters: "We determine when we make media releases."

Those familiar with MSHA operating procedures during past mine disasters and accidents were surprised by this turn around of public relations. They said it was not suppose to work that way. Whenever, a disaster occurs, MSHA officials issue an order that puts them in charge. The outcry of the public was, "Where is MSHA? Where is MSHA?" Officials at MSHA failed to respond to that.

When MSHA finally made an appearance the agency became defensive with data highlighting the decrease in fatal accidents with a 34% drop since 2000. However, data also shows over a period of 5 years through 2004, West Virginia, Virginia and Kentucky produced about one fourth of the nation's coal and those three mining states have accounted for over one half of the nation's fatalities. UMWA President Cecil Roberts, reflects a state of concern by UMWA stating as the demand for coal rises, so will our mining accidents and fatalities. Roberts sees more small non-union operations producing coal. These operations have less resources for safety programs and due to the drop in mining accidents and fatalities, a philosophy has emerged that mines are safer. We don't need all of the enforcement we advocate. Roberts noted MSHA has been showing signs of problems for the past four years.

In my discussion with coal miner, Nelson Tinnel, on the subject of mine safety, he tells me he is concerned about the same philosophy or new culture Cecil Roberts refers to in his statements. Tinnel says he is afraid this philosophy is spinning out of control. He said, "During the 70s and up to the 80s everywhere you looked you would see a sign, "Be careful today" or "Safety First". You don't see anything like that now. Our focus has turned away from safety to production."

Nelson comments on the new structure of mine shifts from the normal, three-eight hour shifts per day to miners working 10 or 12 hour shifts so there is no shut down time for the expensive machines. For the coal operator, it is important that production does not stop but Tinnel is not sure the human body can be programmed like the expensive machines. Tinnel, "But I think a person does better if he spends 8 hours working, 8 hours sleeping and 8 hours with family and doing things he enjoys. The extended shifts of work takes a toll on a miner's alertness."

EX-MSHA Official appointed by Governor to oversee investigation

"We will pursue every lead," Mr. Davitt McAteer said. "We will take every step necessary to find the problems and to fix those problems."

Governor Manchin appoints J. Davitt McAteer, a Fairmont, W.Va. native to oversee the investigation into the Sago mine disaster. McAteer is a WVU College of Law graduate, 1970.

McAteer has a long history of involvement in coal mine health and safety beginning in law school when he developed and directed a study of the West Virginia coal industry. He became active in the Ralph Nader movement during the 70s. McAteer served as OSHLC executive director until 1993 when he was named assistant secretary for the Mine Safety and Health Administration in the U.S. Department of Labor. He held that position until the Bush administration took office.

Sago now joins Farmington, Monongah, Sewell, Hominy Falls and other West Virginia Mine Disasters.

In addition to the MSHA investigation, the West Virginia Board of Coal Mine Health and Safety will conduct its own investigation. Hamilton, a member of the board, said its inquiry will start about halfway through the government's investigation and will offer an independent verification of the results. Hamilton said the appropriate agencies are getting ready for what they know will be a highly scrutinized investigation. For now, the bereaved families will have to wait for answers. He went on to say the investigation into what happened in that mine will not only serve the mourning families by giving answers but will help prevent a recurrence. Also, it could change training manuals used to instruct miners on what to do in situation like what faced the trapped miner.

According to Mr. Terry Farley, and based on MSHA investigation reports of other fatal mine accidents, the investigation likely will include:

➢ Interviews with the sole surviving miner, Randal McCloy, 26, who was still in critical condition yesterday at a West Virginia University hospital.
➢ Geologic surveys on lightning strikes and mine data on roof collapses, both of which are considered possible causes of the mine explosion.
➢ Examinations of the mine interior, including mine walls, equipment and coal dust buildups.
➢ Carbon monoxide monitors and the mine's ventilation system.
➢ The mine's history of citations and fines issued by federal and state inspectors for safety violations.
➢ Autopsy reports on the 12 miners—state officials reported yesterday they died of carbon monoxide poisoning—to determine if any other gases were in their blood.
➢ Determining whether rescue teams could have responded any faster to try to save lives.

MSHA goes to court for union

The investigation hit a snag when International Coal Group attempted to keep the UMWA officials off company property during the onsite investigation. Sago is a nonunion shop but at least two of the Sago miners have requested representation by UMWA officials. Federal mine officials went for a court order to allow UMWA on site. The judge ruled in UMWA favor. Later, ICG filed an appeal.

Timeline:

Monday, January 2, 2006

➢ <u>6:00 - 6:31 a.m</u>

Monday morning, January 2, 2006 Sago Mine production crews were returning to work after the mine had sat idle for 48 hours during the long New Years' holiday weekend. Christmas and New Year holidays were over, so, the miners could now get serious about producing coal; the latest hot commodity hidden deep in the Appalachian Mountains. According to Ben Hatfield and Gene Kitts, a safety inspection was performed by fireboss, Terry Helms, an hour before the production crews arrived and nothing unusual was found. Helms and the others are unaware of a deadly bomb waiting to be detonated behind the recently sealed off section.

The Second Left crew loaded onto the mantrip, Helms, then joined the 12 miners and entered the mine. Their destination was more than two miles back into the mountain and 260 feet down. The first mantrip rolled past the sealed off areas. They traveled past the First Left section turnoff before making their left turn. First Left crew traveled a shorter distance to get to their work station. First Left crew had not made it to their turn off when the explosion occurred.

Ben Hatfield said two production crews and mine support members – a total of 28 miners were underground at the time of the explosion. An explosion which occurred at 6:30 a.m. in the mine was so forceful it shook nearby houses and trailers. The First Left crew was able to escape the blast by the skin of their teeth. They entered 10 minutes behind the Second Left crew. Four miners attempted rescue of the Second Left crew who were trapped, but were turned back by smoke and a "wall of debris".

Ron Grall, a member of the First Left crew who escaped, said during a televised interview the explosion was so forceful the dirt and wind blinded him totally and affected his hearing.

Another miner who escaped told friends and family that the first crew went into the mine. The second crew was following when they heard an explosion, they were able to turn back and escape. Communication was knocked out by the blast.

Until the morning of January 2, 2006, Sago was a small coal mining community approximately 10 minutes out of Buckhannon. It was an ordinary rural community until the morning the first working day of the new year. Tall barns, arched along the roofline making room for storing hay, are seen along the narrow roads. Cows are in the pastures grazing the wintry, brown grass. The landscape is clean with round bales of hay, neat wood frame houses, winding creeks, wooden bridges and mountains, beautiful mountains in the background. Small white churches dot the landscape - picturesque rural America, that was Sago. That was Sago until 6:30 a.m. on Monday, January 2, 2006.

The small town of Tallmansville became a popular hangout for the media during their news broadcasts out of Sago as well as Buckhannon. Buckhannon, Tallmansville and Sago are three close knit communities strung together with rural living, coal mine culture and a ribbon of road lasting 7 or 8 miles.

> ## 6:41 a.m. – Monday

Owen Jones, First Left foreman begins exiting with his crew when he comes upon a mine phone at the second man door. He calls out to the surface and said, "We've had something happen in the mine, an explosion or something! Get the people in here!" ICG official, Nicholson says the mine superintendent headed underground shortly afterward to investigate and ordered the dispatcher to begin the notification process. The mine superintendent made it about 9,000 feet into the mine before encountering dangerous levels of carbon monoxide and turning around.

> ## 7:30 a.m.- Monday

Preacher Wease Day opens doors of Sago Baptist Church where 200 family members and friends of the trapped miners gathered.

> ## 7:40 - 7:45 a.m. - Monday

State and federal mine agencies were called. When state officials were contacted, Director Conaway said that the agency was not told an explosion had occurred.

From the time of the explosion, nearly an hour-and-a-half passes before the world gets its first inkling of what's happened inside the Sago Mine. Monday, January 2nd, 7:55 a.m. A call is made from the mine to the Upshur County 911 operator.

Transcript of call:

OPERATOR: Upshur Emergency Squad.
UNIDENTIFIED MALE: Yes, ma'am, we need an ambulance at the Sago Mine.
OPERATOR: OK. It's the one up on the Sago Road?
UNIDENTIFIED MALE: Yes, ma'am.
OPERATOR: OK. What's going on?
UNIDENTIFIED MALE: You know, something happened inside the mines here.

Less than 15 minutes later, the rescue unit is on the scene.

Transcript of call:

UNIDENTIFIED MALE: Be advised, we're being informed -- we are on the scene, we're being informed that there are several men trapped inside. We're going to need a lot of help.

LOUISE BLEIGH, UPSHUR COUNTY 911 SUPERVISOR comments: Certainly hearing that there were several men trapped inside came as quite a surprise, quite a shock. And then I think your adrenaline kicks in and you just start doing what you are trained to do.

Benny Nazelrod, fire chief in Adrian, West Virginia, told news reporters his station is less than five miles from the mine. His teams get there quickly. But by law, only specially trained mine rescue teams can go inside. You do feel helpless. You know there's only a certain amount you can do and your normal instinct when you're in any type of rescue is to go help.

After Nazelrod arrived on the Sago mine scene he found out the miners were trapped in as far as 10,000 feet, he knew they were in for a long ordeal. Firefighters from surrounding areas were on hand to assist but they were soon ordered to move to the opposite side of the Buckhannon River for fear of high levels of carbon monoxide.

➢ **8:04 a.m. - Monday**

More than 90 minutes after the explosion - a specialized rescue crew was called. In anticipation that mine rescue teams were going to enter the Mine soon, the first call to the Barbour County Mine Rescue Team was made at 8:04 AM.

➢ **8:10 a.m.- Monday**

According to MSHA logs, the first call from the mine to MSHA personnel at home came at approximately 8:10 a.m. The first two calls were made to individuals who were out of town. The third call to MSHA was received by Jim Satterfield, Field Office Supervisor, at 8:30 a.m. and he responded immediately.

➢ **8:30 a.m. - Monday**

During the two hours that had passed Ben Hatfield, ICG CEO and President, described the scene at the mine as sheer chaos and confusion.

Mine officials refused to release names of the trapped miners but the public and the media soon knew who they were because mines operate on a check in, check out system. A board is often used with tags and numbers identifying miners. One way mine officials keep track of who is underground is through identification tags hung on hooks on a board, when a miner goes underground he will remove the tag from one area on the board and place it on an area designated as underground or out. The procedure is reversed when he comes out. The same tag number is stamped on his hard hat and may be stamped on his mining belt. This is a simple tracking system. Officials knew immediately who had not made it out after the explosion at Sago.

➢ **8:32 a.m. - Monday**

At 8:32 a.m., MSHA Inspector Jim Satterfield orally implemented an emergency mine closure order (a "103k order") prohibiting further entry to the Mine. At about the same time, State mine inspectors began monitoring the air quality at the Mine portal. High concentrations of carbon monoxide were found, indicating significant risk of an active underground mine fire that could ignite an explosion, so state and federal mine regulators on site determined it was not safe for mine rescue teams to enter. This agonizing process of monitoring the carbon monoxide and methane levels in the Mine air and having to wait and wait for confirmation that it was safe to enter would continue throughout the day. (Ben Hatfield)

> ## 10:30 a.m. - Monday

Ray McKinney and other MSHA personnel arrived at the mine site. The supervisor was contacted at his home at approximately 8:30 a.m. He made initial telephone calls to obtain support and assistance from other MSHA personnel and then traveled to the Bridgeport office to pick up his mining apparel and a government vehicle. Travel time from his home to the MSHA office was approximately 10 minutes. Travel time from MSHA office to Sago mine was approximately 60 minutes.

> ## 10:40 a.m. - Monday

Barbour County Mine Rescue Team arrived on site at approximately 10:40 a.m., and waited for state and federal authorities to approve their entry into the Mine. Other mine rescue teams were also contacted, and continued to arrive at the Mine through the course of the day, with eventual deployment of 13 to 15 mine rescue teams at the site by late afternoon on January 2.

> ## 12:00 Noon - Monday

Two rescue teams arrive from Barbour County, West Virginia. These are the two teams the company made arrangements to have available in compliance with federal requirements: Each mine must establish two mine rescue teams that are available at all times when miners are underground, or the operator must enter into arrangements for mine rescue services that ensure that two teams are available when miners are underground. Teams must be properly trained and provided with appropriate safety equipment.

Mine rescue coverage can be obtained in several ways, such as company teams, contract teams or through state agencies.

Rescue team cannot enter mine until backup team is onsite.

Rescue efforts were slow entering on foot and working by hand to remove rock and debris. Exact location of trapped miners had to be determined before a rescue method could be determined.

Three five-member teams were present, the minimum needed to set up a base and oxygen station farther in the mine, so they could start their search.

One official described the mine as a dire situation because of a mine awash in deadly carbon monoxide – evidence of fire, after an explosion.

> ### 1:00 p.m. – Monday

Consolidation Coal teams and the Tri-State teams arrive. Consol sent three of its rescue teams to aid the efforts at Sago. Teams from the Loverage Mine near Fairview, the Blacksville Mine near Wana and the Robinson Run Mine near Shinnston. Members of the units are all coal miners.

Conversation between CNN headquarters and reporter on location at Sago mine I wrote down during discussion.

Headquarters: What about the inexperienced miners – what have you heard. **Reporter:** They will tell us nothing about that. This is a close knit community – they will tell us nothing. The community is upset and angry it took so long to get rescue efforts started. A significant amount of time before a rescue team could get here. When mine owners were questioned about the time span before rescue teams arrived. They said it took time to get a team mustered together.

They said this explosion could have been caused by lightening.

> ### 3:00 p.m. – Monday

A chromatograph arrives. This is an instrument used to pinpoint gas measurements. The instrument verified measurements taken by handheld devices.

> ### 3:30 p.m. - Monday

Carbon monoxide levels had dropped to 1,400 parts per million. They made a decision to let rescue units enter the mine.

➤ **3:16 p.m. - Monday**

St. Joseph's Hospital E.R. Room prepares for the Sago mine emergencies.

➤ **5:00 p.m. - Monday**

Rescue teams are ready to enter the mine. All work has to be done by hand because they were not able to get air readings from inside the mine. The ventilation systems were knocked out by the blast. It is very dangerous because of the possibility of explosions. Rescue workers will need to move forward slowly approximately 100 yards or so at a time, establishing a fresh air base each time with a curtain to seal off the area.

The tragic story of Brookwood, Alabama, had not faded from miners' memory. In the small coal-mining town of Brookwood, Alabama, on September 23, 2001, twelve miners rushed to the site of a violent blast in Jim Walter Resources Inc.'s Blue Creek No. 5 mine to rescue a co-worker. They never came out. Thirteen persons lost their lives as a result of two large methane explosions.

Bulldozer and drilling crews arrive on site and begin survey operations to determine the best drilling location from the outside down to the miners. No communications with miners at this time.

Steve Milligan, Assistant Director, Office of Emergency Services Upshur County, West Virginia answered questions from CNN reporter:

Q.   Why the long time before a call was made?
A.   I suppose they had to walk out about one mile and call for help.
Q.   What are you doing now?
A.   Getting the Red Cross and mental health workers in to Sago Baptist Church where the families are waiting.
Q.   Is this an easy area to get medical help in and out with the country roads, etc.?
A.   In fact this mine is located on a country road which is one and one half lanes, about 10 miles from the hospital.

> **5:30 p.m. – Monday**

Nearly 12 hours after the explosion rescuers go underground to search for the missing Sago miners.

> **5:31 p.m. - Monday**

CNN reporter on site asks Bruce Dial, mining expert located in Charlotte, North Carolina, eleven hours into miners being trapped, can they survive? He answered, "They can barricade themselves by building cinderblock walls or back up a heading, seal it with brattice cloth."

> **5:51 p.m. - Monday**

An eight-member rescue team enters the mine accompanied by a coal company foreman. The team tests the air at 500 feet intervals. Power to the phones they use to communicate with at the surface are disconnected before each air test in case combustible gas is present. First rescuers entered mine 11 hours after the explosion occurred. According to officials, the lag was due to high concentrations of poisonous gas.

After experts from MSHA, the State of West Virginia, and the Company agreed that an underground mine fire was no longer likely, based on the air monitoring results, the first mine rescue team entered the mine (carrying special breathing apparatus) at 5:51 p.m. Progress had to be careful and deliberate to protect the safety of rescuers, given that many rescuers had fallen victim to secondary explosions in coal mine disasters of years past.

Consol's Robinson Run mine near Shinnston rescue unit entered the Sago. After an hour of searching, they ran into water seeping from an old, sealed off section parallel to the portal.

Rescue teams responded from Fairmont, Moundsville and Kingwood, West Virginia. Units responding from out-of-state included: 84 and Enlow Fork mines in Washington County and Bailey Mine in Green County, PA. Viper Mine in Williamsville, Indiana were also among the responding rescue units.

> ## 6:23 p.m.- Monday

First rescue team reports from 1,000 feet into the mine that carbon monoxide and methane levels are within normal range

> ## 6:30 p.m. – Monday (The Best of Times, The Worst of Times)

A second rescue team enters the mine. Several other teams remain on standby.

Governor Joe Manchin is a big West Virginia Mountaineer football fan. He traveled to Atlanta to watch his Mountaineers take on the Georgia Bulldogs in the Sugar Bowl scheduled to play on January 2, 2006.

West Virginia had finished its regular season with 11-1 record and Coach Rodriguez was on his way after four tries to a bowl game. This record was the best since 1993, so West Virginians had a right to be proud of the Mountaineers. But the Georgia Bulldogs were no slouches on the field or in the stands. Georgia had an estimated crowd of 50,000 in the stands and West Virginia had approximately 20,000 fans in the Bulldogs home territory.

The Mountaineers got off to a good start when Slaton, on his way to 105 yards by halftime, bolted on a draw on West Virginia's third play from scrimmage – slipped through the hole at left guard, cut to the left side covering 52 yards for the opening score. In just under 15 minutes, the score was 28-0 in favor or the underdogs – The Mountaineers.

But Governor Manchin missed those exciting plays. He found out at approximately 10 a.m. about the explosion at Sago mine. He was alerted that 13 miners were trapped in the mine. He immediately began making arrangements to return to West Virginia – flying in to the airport at Clarksburg. He went straight to Sago.

Governor Joe Manchin cut his visit to Atlanta and the Sugar Bowl short. As soon as he received word of the explosion at Sago mine and the uncertain fate of 13 miners trapped behind the smoke and debris, he hopped a plane and returned to West Virginia. The plane landed in Clarksburg. Governor Manchin headed straight to the Sago Church. There he embraced the families of the trapped miners, sharing in their hopes and worst fears imaginable.

West Virginia University Head Football Coach Rodriquez reminded his players of the importance of remembering the trapped miners and their families at Sago. Rodriquez is from a coal mining community not far from Sago.

A friend of mine, Bonita Bell, told me she was at the bowl game and was having such a good time. Everyone was so proud of the football team and their Coach Rodriquez. West Virginians were proud of the forensic team who had traveled to Atlanta to advertise their program. Many of the students in the forensic program were seen on CNN – national news network.

West Virginia fans knew the governor and his wife were there to watch the big game and cheer the Mountaineers on to victory. It wasn't long until the fans got word about the trapped miners. A dark cloud came over them. Bonita said, "It was the Best of Times and the Worst of Times."

When they heard that the governor had returned to West Virginia and Sago – West Virginians were proud of their governor's actions.

The major media television stations such as CNN conducted numerous interviews during the agonizing hours of waiting. One interview was with John Helms who told a CNN reporter, "My brother is trapped in that mine. He has worked in the coal mines for 15 years. I work on the rescue crew. They say they believe the miners are about 260 underground. Drilling should take about three hours. So, about 11:00 p.m. or midnight we may know something. This hole they are drilling is to establish communication. The first thing the driller will do is check the oxygen level, then, they can drop a microphone down. It will all depend on what the drillers find that will decide the next action. I was involved in a mine rescue operation in Virginia in 1972. It didn't turn out so well. No one was saved. Pray for us."

Manchin kept the public updated through interviews with major television networks, including CNN and ABC news. He appeared on Night Line.

Gov. Manchin comforted family members at the Sago Baptist Church. Manchin tells the family members and the news media, "West Virginia believes in miracles. I am from Farmington, West Virginia. On November 19, 1968, we had a mine explosion at the Farmington Mine. My uncle died in that explosion and some of my teammates on my high school football team died there also. So, I know what these families are going through."

> **7:25 p.m. - Monday**

First press conference with Gene Kitts, President and CEO of Sago. Roger Nicholason, General Counsel for International Coal Groups was also present.

CNN interviewed Bruce Dial, mine expert in Charlotte, North Carolina.
Q: If part of the mine collapses, is it likely it will continue to collapse?
A: Dial – they have roof bolts for support
Q: What else do the men have to worry about?
A.   Dial – the gas is the thing – methane – causing explosion. Carbon monoxide is another gas, very dangerous.
Q: Inexperienced miners may be in there.
A: Dial – all miners must have 40 hours training. Every miner must carry a self rescuer which allows them to breath about one hour.

Author's note: West Virginia requires 80 hours training. Federal requires 40 hours of training.

Terry Farley, an administrator with the state Office of Coal Miners' Health, Safety and Training, said that his agency had reports that the stoppings – internal walls used to direct underground mine ventilation- were blown off by the explosion.

That would tend to indicate a dust explosion, rather than a methane blast, said Davitt McAteer, who was assistant secretary of labor for mine safety and health during the Clinton administration. McAteer said dust explosions are generally much more powerful – sometimes 10 times more powerful – than methane blasts.

> **8:30 p.m. - Monday**

Drilling equipment is on site over miners' expected location, about two miles from the mine's entrance and 260 feet below the surface

CNN reporter again spoke again with Bruce Dial, mine expert, in Charlotte, North Carolina in a televised interview.
CNN reporter: Miners are 5800' feet down. That is a long way to drill.
Dial - This distance is not straight down but vertical. Concerns when drilling into this:

1. Finding a place to drill
2. Maps – maps were not always accurate
3. Even if you find a place to drill, they may not be there
4. Once they get the drill and equipment on the property – they can probably get through in several hours, probably 6 hours according to type of equipment.

By this time, I had been told at least 3 miners, probably more, from my community are employed by Sago at this mine. Their shifts were changed to weekends over the Christmas break, otherwise they would have been with this group of trapped miners. I spoke to Stephanie Nicholas whose husband, Arnett, Jr. , works for Sago. He is currently off with an injury. Teddy Johnson, lives down the road at Enon, employee of Sago. Darrell Lucas, also lives a few miles from me, employee of Sago and Martin Toler's niece, Kim Toler lives at Canvas, She works for Lowe's.

> **10:30 p.m. – Monday**

Drilling is scheduled to begin. Coal company officials said they will drill a small-diameter hole. They hoped to test the air quality through the air shaft and drop a listening device into the mine. Experts predict four to six hours to reach the miners' expected location. Drilling began at about 10:30 p.m. Rescue teams could not enter the mine until damage and air contaminants were assessed.

A V2 search robot was brought in to search for information. The robot is a 1,300 pound track machine operated by the officials of the Mine Safety Health Administration. The machine is equipped with air sampling and video capabilities. It was later learned the robot became bogged down in the mud and was ineffective.

> **10:45 p.m. – Monday**

Rescue team reports safe levels of carbon monoxide and methane levels at 4,800 feet from mine's entrance. Drilling not progressing as well as hoped.

Tuesday, January 3, 2006

Early morning news reports the miners were an experienced crew with mining experience from 3 to 30 years.

Families wait and watch all night long, many of them walking the distance from the bridge leading to the mine entrance and back to the church. Some of the family members waited in the Sago Baptist Church; some just sat in their vehicles all night long, waiting for word. The weather was misty and gloomy, visibility low. Sago hollow is divided by a narrow road with a creek and railroad tracks on the same side as the mine entrance. Trucks, cars, SUVs were parked all over the muddy road and in the field.

➢ 6:50 a.m. - Tuesday

Carbon monoxide levels in drill hole No. 1 are found to be triple the lethal limit. They were determined to be 1,300 parts per million, exceeding the 400 parts per million maximum safe level. Second and third drill holes are planned.

➢ 6:53 a.m. - Tuesday

Gov. Manchin gives a television interview - he informs the public the camera penetrated the shaft monitoring air quality; however, the lens became muddy and had to be removed.

Gov. Manchin prepares for a live interview with Good Morning America's Diane Sawyer. When the Governor was questioned about the numerous violations at the mine, the Governor simply replied, "We are in search and rescue mode right now focusing on finding these miners. We will deal with violations at a later date."

➢ 7:42 a.m. - Tuesday

Mike Ross, local driller, sank a bore hole within 200 feet of the trapped miners. They didn't know they were so close when drilling. They wanted to provide ventilation so the bad air could come out while huge fans forced fresh air in. This was a dangerous operation as anything producing friction could set off another explosion. Men were ordered out of the mine as the bit neared breaking through. Engines were shut off and they began pounding on the long pipe down in the earth.

Ross reported they got no response. A video camera was lowered but it soon became blurred. It showed no signs of life. A carbon monoxide measurement test of the flowing air showed 1,200 parts per million – a deadly combination.

No signs of life have been detected at the mine, says Ben Hatfield of the International Coal Group. A camera dropped through the completed drill hole showed little damage to the area but no survivors. Air tests returned discouraging results, with dangerous levels of carbon monoxide in the area where the trapped miners were thought to be.

> ## 10:30 a.m. - Tuesday

Rescue teams are 11,200 feet into the mine. Rescue teams find no significant changes in gas levels. No massive burned or charred areas found.

> ## 11:20 a.m.- Tuesday

Rescue teams move ahead of the search robot.

> ## 11:30 a.m. - Tuesday

I leave work and drive from Summersville to Sago, 1 hour + drive.

> ## 12:00 noon – Tuesday

Rescue units set up fresh-air base outside turn to First Left section. First Left crew made it out of this area when the explosion occurred.

Rescuers decided to push on toward Second Left section instead of using up valuable time and fresh air to explore First Left section.

> ## 1:00 p.m. - Tuesday

I arrive at Sago, park on the narrow, muddy, one lane road. I walk to Sago Baptist Church and went in. When I return home late in the evening, I wrote "Last Mantrip Out of Sago Mine".

> **4:30 p.m. - Tuesday**

Rescue unit reaches Second Left section – same area the makeshift rescue unit made up of mine superintendent, Jeff Toler, three mine supervisors and Owen Jones had made it to immediately following the blast.

The search unit finds the Omega blocks used to seal off a unit. They were all blown out from the sealed-off area.

> **5:00 p.m. - Tuesday**

Ben Hatfield, president of International Coal Group, says rescue teams are 1,000-2,000 feet from where the miners are trapped, and that distance should be closed within 5 hours. Officials say they don't know the cause of the blast, though it resembled a methane explosion.

> **5:18 p.m. - Tuesday**

Units searching from coal pillar to coal pillar find the body of fireboss, Terry Helms. He is inside another mantrip.

Search units make the left turn into the Second Left section.

> **6:25 p.m. - Tuesday**

No communication established with miners since they went into the mine almost 24 hours earlier.

> **7:45 p.m. - Tuesday**

Second Left crew's mantrip is found but no miners. Footprints were traced to the primary air intake. They were trying to get to the surface. Bottoms of the self-rescuers had been ditched.

➤ <u>8:00 p.m. - Tuesday (Body found)</u>

International Coal Group officials announced one miner's body had been found near the area where the explosion occurred. No information was available on the condition of the body located. Normal procedure is to simply tag the body, notify outside and move on to search for other miners. There was no information if the deceased tried to use his rescue equipment. The company expressed hope for the remaining 12 miners because their track-mounted car was found undamaged deeper in the mine.

Body identified as Terry Helms, "fireboss" - Ben Hatfield reported Terry Helms must have been working on the beltline. Terry Helms died from impact of the explosion near the belt line about 11,200 feet into the mine.

Only when rescue crews reached Helms' body late January 3 did they learn the explosion actually occurred in a nearby sealed mine shaft.

➤ <u>8:30 p.m. - Tuesday</u>

Governor Manchin reports, "Found, one dead miner. Tram found, still looking for remaining 12 miners."

➤ <u>10:40 p.m. - Tuesday</u>

Governor Manchin acknowledges hopes are dimming.

➤ <u>11:15 p.m. – 11:45 p.m. - Tuesday</u>

Rescue unit finally found a makeshift barricade – behind it 12 miners found in sitting or lying down positions. They were dead.

Somehow during the calling and receiving of the call, people at the surface misunderstood the message believing the 12 miners were found alive. The rescue unit was stretched back so far in the mine, the telephone service was spotty, and messages were shouted in relays which involved from four to seven links. The first rescuer shouted out what he had found, and by the time it reached the command center, the message had transformed into something devastatingly untrue.

Rescue crews signal to the surface that the 12 remaining miners have been found. Governor Manchin believed 12 miners were alive. He said, "We believe in miracles."

➤ **11:48 p.m. - Tuesday ("12 Alive!" "12 Alive!")**

Family and friends gathered at the Sago Baptist Church began getting cell calls that the remaining 12 of the 13 trapped miners had been found alive. It was reported the calls came from a central command post set up by ICG. The company did not confirm this information. The report of 12 found alive seemed plausible due in part to the mantrip found undamaged deeper in the mine.

At 11:48 p.m. Tuesday, the first inaccurate reports came from inside the mine and one emergency response team radioed another.

In the next two minutes, another call came in saying the men were alive and there's one call from an incident commander who requested any available medical units that can transport patients. The 911 supervisor said they never received a call saying the men were dead. They found that out by watching the news.

➤ **11:48 p.m. - Tuesday**

VOICE 1: "7472."
VOICE 2: "Go ahead, Matt."
VOICE 1: "You might as well just stand still right where you're at, Gary. They did find them, and they're all OK, I guess, so, I think we might be transporting them. I'm not exactly sure, but we're stuck right here."
VOICE 1: "10-4, Matt."

➤ **11:54 p.m. - Tuesday**

VOICES: (inaudible) VOICE 1: "And what am I telling them?"
VOICE 2: (inaudible) "Twelve, and they're bringing them out."
VOICE 1: "And they're all alive"
VOICE 2: "Uh, as far as I know ... (inaudible)"

➤ **11:49 p.m. - Tuesday**

Sago Baptist Church bells began ringing in a celebration for what they believed was 12 miracles. !2 miners alive. "12 Alive" "12 Alive"

Family and friends began clapping, singing and giving thanks to the Lord for saving the 12 miners.

Governor Manchin and his wife are at the church. They walk down the aisle – the Governor is hugging his wife.

One woman ran to the church barefoot in the cold January mud. she wanted to share in the celebration. Lynette Roby kept her son and daughter up late on the school night. She took them to the church before the news came the miners were alive. She wanted them to witness this historical event.

➢ **11:55 p.m. - Tuesday**

Television networks, news Web sites and radio stations begin broadcasting reports nationwide that 12 miners had survived. Newspapers had already put headline stories to bed and many printed "12 Alive" - "Miracle in the Mine" as leading stories. "Alive! Miners beat odds" was USA Today's headline with a picture of two smiling family members.

Wednesday, January 4, 2006

➢ **Between midnight and 12:10 a.m.**

The truth is learned; 12 miners are found dead, one lone survivor is clinging to life. International Coal Group officials and Governor Manchin find out the initial report claiming 12 miners survived is wrong but do not tell families.

➢ **12:34 a.m. - Wednesday**

A convoy of nine ambulances, a Buckhannon police cruiser, two mine rescue vehicles and several firefighters in personal vehicles turned into the road leading up to the mine. Earlier, Tom Hunter, Manchin's press secretary, said it wasn't clear whether the miners would be well enough physically to go to the church after they came out of the mine. When questioned about the entourage of emergency vehicles turning in to the mines, Hunter said that each miner was being assessed medically as he came out of the mine.

➢ **1:30 a.m. - Wednesday**

An ambulance carrying the unidentified surviving miner races out of the mine site entrance, across the bridge and heads for Saint Joseph's Hospital, 10 minutes away. The miner in the ambulance is identified as Randal McCloy, Jr. Randal lives at Simpson, WV.

The Sago Church crowd are gathered outside and start cheering and clapping when the ambulance speeds across the bridge and down Sago Road.

➢ **1:30 a.m. to 2:30 a.m. - Wednesday**

Family and friends in the Sago Church prepare for the miners to appear soon. They tell television news crews such as Anderson Cooper of CNN, the miners were going to be brought to the church in emergency vehicles so their love ones there could see them. They could come into the church and walk down the aisle. The miners would be fed at the church before they went to the hospital for their medical evaluation. The church was preparing by clearing the aisles and relishing the joy to come. God had given them "twelve miracles." The crowd moved to the outside of the church. They broke out in song, "How Great Thou Art."

➢ **2:00 a.m. - Wednesday**

West Virginia State Policemen were told to go to the Sago Baptist Church and tell the preachers to prepare their people to brace for "bad news." Bad news is coming. Prepare the people for the bad news before the coal operators came to the church. Spokesman for the West Virginia State Policemen told media they were not to deliver the message just tell preachers to brace for bad news.

➢ **2:14 a.m. - Wednesday**

One miner, Randal McCloy, is rescued and taken to a nearby hospital in critical condition after being trapped underground for nearly 40 hours.

➢ **2:30 a.m. - Wednesday**

A medical report is received from Saint Joseph's Hospital on the condition of surviving miner, Randal McCloy. Dr. Susan Long reported the miner was critically injured.

➤ **2:46 a.m. - Wednesday**

High hopes of the "12 miracles" family and loved ones were waiting to welcome turn to uncontrollable anger, shock and disbelief when coal officials arrive at Sago Baptist Church and tell those waiting the truth. There is only one survivor, Randal McCloy. The other miners are dead. Family members accused coal officials of lying to them by telling them the miners were alive. The 12 deaths are confirmed.

Waiting families go out of control with this bad news. They were preparing to see their loved ones. They had been told the 12 were alive and believed that for nearly 3 hours after the truth was known.Fights broke out in the church. People were screaming and cursing. It is reported that Jim Bennett's son-in-law lunged at the coal officials.

The Inter-Mountain Newspaper reported: "It was lucky they had the patrolmen they had, Daniel Merideth said."

Nick Helms, son of victim Terry Helms, said several family members had to wrestle one distraught man to the ground to keep him from hurting the coal company officials.

"I immediately took my girlfriend, my sister and everyone else out (of the church)." Helms said. "They were trying to get them. They were doing everything they could to get the officials."

The angry crowd attempted to force their way through a barrier on the bridge which led the mine site. West Virginia State Police on hand were able to control the angry crowd. The angry crowd blamed the miscommunication on the ICG officials and the news media. News media said they had not seen anything like it before.

Some of the family members fainted when they heard the devastating news.

➤ **2:50 a.m. - Wednesday**

Lynette Roby and two children rushed up to Anderson Cooper of CNN and told him the 12 miners were dead and not alive as they were led to believe.

Roby described the scene inside the church to Cooper: "The scene turned quickly to mayhem. People began screaming, "You lied to us!" and "Hypocrites!" before charging officials. She said the church turned into a "mob scene." Police intervened, she said. "They started running everywhere, and then the next thing you know we see fists flying everywhere," her son, Travis, said, "Cops and people and everything was hitting each other."

Ben Hatfield of International Coal Group gave a press conference officially announcing that 12 miners were found dead and not alive as believed. One lone survivor was critically injured and by this time had been transferred to Ruby Memorial Hospital in Morgantown, West Virginia. Hatfield blamed the confusion on "miscommunication."

ICG CEO Hatfield and Gene Kitts, Senior V-P, gave the following explanation on how the false information came to be circulated as truth:

Rescuers were working under full-face oxygen masks - through extreme stress and physical exhaustion - and communicating in code over a possibly spotty connection to the operations base on the surface. Any of those conditions or a combination could have resulted in the confusion. Hatfield said that stray cell phone calls may have been the cause of the word spreading so rapidly.

Survivor McCloy was in urgent need of resuscitation. After McCloy was found news was relayed in code to the operations base: "One item was found at break 56." Rescue teams were speaking to the command center over the mine communication system on an open system.

Hatfield said he knew within 20 minutes that the information was terribly wrong. He said that he wanted correct information before telling the families. He said, "Who do I tell not to celebrate?"

Nick Helms said that when the bad news was delivered to the families, "There was no apology. There was nothing. It was out the door." Nick's father, Terry Helms, was the first miner found dead. He was the fireboss at Sago.

Hatfield urged those devastated by the tragedy to be thankful for Randle McCloy.

Governor Manchin was inside the church in a room off the sanctuary of the church when he heard the celebration begin. He asked what was happening. He was told, "Twelve alive, Twelve alive." The Gov. asked if this information had been confirmed. The aide gave a negative response. He left the room and started toward the command center. By this time people inside the church had moved to the outside. They were in a euphoric state. He said he felt the same way. As he inched his way through the crowd, the media asked him for comments. He simply told them, "We believe in miracles."

MSHA staff incorrectly informed Senator Robert C. Byrd and J. Rockefeller that the 12 miners had been found alive. They failed to correct the error.

It was later learned through the Rev. Mark Flynn, a Methodist preacher who spent a deal of time at the Sago Church, that one preacher at the church did find out that only one miner survived, but he did not tell it to the miners' families. The ministers at the church were told by the State Policemen to prepare their members for bad news.

Dennis O'Dell, UMWA official present, recounts the story which took place at the command center. O'Dell said that he talked to the ICG employee who had told him earlier 12 alive but this time he had a different demeanor. The employee broke down. The employee told O'Dell there had been a mistake. One was alive and 12 were dead. Still, family members believed 12 were alive. Those at the command center could hear them celebrating across the river in front of the Sago Baptist Church while the truth was known. O'Dell describes it as a sickening feeling.

O'Dell, after talking with the rescue teams and officials at the command center believes he knows what happened. After the rescue workers at the fresh air base inside the mine received communication the miners had been found – they believed it meant all 12 had been found alive. When the rescue unit went to the Second Left section to help bring the miners out to safety, they were shocked the workers were trying to revive only one miner, Randal McCloy.

There, the rescue workers who found the miners and the unit from the fresh air base were able to sort out the miscommunication. The workers then returned to the fresh-air base to report there had been an error in the earlier report.

Later, after Dennis O'Dell returned to the UMWA Office in Fairfax, Virginia, he had time to think things over. He summarized it as follows: The problem was not in the miscommunication but mine rescue rules are that you never release information to anyone until it has been verified. That communication never should have gotten past the command center.

The rescue units do not want to talk about it. They are having a hard time dealing with this according to Rod Henry, part of the rescue team from Enlow Fork.

➢ **10:26 a.m. - Wednesday**

Bodies of the 12 miners were retrieved by 10:26 a.m. on Wednesday, January 4, 2006. Autopsies were scheduled for Thursday and Friday.

➢ **44 hours passed**

Kanawha County Schools conducted a lockdown at an elementary school where Ben Hatfield's wife teaches following death threats against ICG officials.

➢ **Wednesday, January 4, 2006**

John Casto, community member in a televised report to CNN reporter tells how people were handling the miscommunication about the miners as follows:

"We was looking for them to come through that door, man," a red-eyed John Casto said Wednesday as he stood beside a funeral home tent in back of the Sago Baptist Church, where the bells had tolled the "miracle" just hours before. "And it didn't happen that way. They began to holler and curse," local resident John Casto told CNN, in a voice cracked by tears. "Just a few minutes before that, we was praising God." What had been a place of united praise was now riven with furious shouting.

"Our pastor got 'em settled down and he said, 'Look to God in this tragedy,'" Casto went on. "I don't believe in cussin', but one guy said, 'What in the hell has God ever done for us?'"

"You know, I'm not kin to none of these people under that hill over there, but each and every one of 'ems a brother to me. Each and every one of them." He then looked toward the reporter and said, "Because you're my brother," and then turning to the cameraman, "and you're my brother. The way I look at it."

Memorial services and eulogies

Nelson Tinnel tells me Owen Jones is one of the best in the field of mining. Now, his brother, Jesse was trapped somewhere behind that smoke and debris in Second Left section of Sago; two miles back and 260 feet underground. Owen went back in. He could not leave Jesse in the fuming dark hole but his carbon monoxide monitor off. He had no choice but to turn around. Jesse and 11 brother miners did not make it out alive.

Today, January 16, 2006, is the first day since 6:30 a.m. on January 2 that news coverage has finally turned from Sago to other current events, but Sago will never be the same. Yesterday, Sunday, January 15, 2006, a Memorial Service was held remembering the miners. I attended. According to one of the ministers presiding, the Memorial Service gave the community a venue for healing, allowing people to gather with the families of the miners, honor the dead and let us show, that we, the public are hurting.

This nation held its breath, cried, felt anger, questioned coal operators and even God over the course of this tragic event. More than 2000 people gathered for the service. Preacher McDowell told the audience the service was originally intended for the miners' families to get together, hug each other and talk. It was felt a reunion with each other after the funerals was needed because services were held in different communities and different counties where the families lived. That was the purpose of the Memorial Service. That was last Saturday, just a week for planning. So, the service was be small and homey. The Wesleyan Chapel of Wesleyan College was chosen because that is where a holding tank was established for the families who waited their turn to go over and identify their loved one at the makeshift morgue. It seemed fitting the Memorial Service would be held in the same facility.

Somehow, word got out about the planned service, and the preacher said calls came in from all over the country. People wanted to come. He received a call from the New York Opera; an opera singer wanted to come and sing opera at the Memorial Service remembering 12 dead coal miners. The preacher told the audience, "I like opera, I guess. I don't know about those 12 miners, would they buy into it?" He made everyone laugh. Instead of opera, songs like "I'll Fly Away," "Homesick" and "When I Get To Where I'm Going" were sung. We all knew those songs would go over well with the miners who had gone on.

It was a beautiful, dignified ceremony. Sen. Robert Byrd quietly stole through a side door near the front. Sen. Rockefeller and other West Virginia State public officials attended. MSHA officers were on hand. We were all scanned for weapons as we passed through the chapel doors.

Governor Joe Manchin and his wife, Gayle, helped family members light candles; one for each miner. Small children were held high in the arms of mothers or the arms of the governor to light a candle for their daddy. Programs, with the theme "A Service of Honor, Hope, and Healing" encircled the figure of a coal miner. White ribbons and teddy bears were handed to each person as they entered the chapel and billows of white balloons were released at the conclusion resembling white Doves.

We, the public, had an opportunity to gather and honor the miners and their families and express sorrow for this tragic event. We then would resume our normal life, but the miners' families had just begun the battle of grieving. When the shock wears off and reality sets in, that is the worst kind of sorrow. They will be faced with seeing the empty chair at the kitchen table; a baseball hat on a doorknob; the new fishing rod in the closet, a Christmas present to share with a son or daughter; hearing the familiar footsteps on the stairs in the middle of the night and when you get out of bed to check, no one is there. And, seeing that face of the person you love in a crowd only to rush to it and have it vanish. Th loneliness and sorrow sets in.

Homer Hickam

"A Service of Honor, Hope and Healing"
Sago Miners Memorial Remarks
by Homer Hickam
Buckhannon, WV January 15, 2006

Families of the Sago miners, Governor Manchin, Mrs. Manchin, Senator Byrd, Senator Rockefeller, West Virginians, friends, neighbors, all who have come here today to remember those brave men who have gone on before us, who ventured into the darkness but instead showed us the light that shines on all West Virginians and the nation today:

It is a great honor to be here. I am accompanied by three men I grew up with, the rocket boys of Coalwood: Roy Lee Cooke, Jimmie O'Dell Carroll, and Billy Rose. My wife Linda, an Alabama girl, is here with me as well.

As this tragedy unfolded, the national media kept asking me: Who are these men? And why are they coal miners? And what kind of men would still mine the deep coal?

One answer came early after the miners were recovered. It was revealed that, as his life dwindled, Martin Toler had written this: It wasn't bad. I just went to sleep. Tell all I'll see them on the other side.

I love you.

In all the books I have written, I have never captured in so few words a message so powerful or eloquent: It wasn't bad. I just went to sleep. Tell all I'll see them on the other side. I love you.

I believe Mr. Toler was writing for all of the men who were with him that day. These were obviously not ordinary men.

But what made these men so extraordinary? And how did they become the men they were? Men of honor. Men you could trust. Men who practiced a dangerous profession. Men who dug coal from beneath a jealous mountain.

Part of the answer is where they lived. Look around you. This is a place where many lessons are learned, of true things that shape people as surely as rivers carve valleys, or rain melts mountains, or currents push apart the sea. Here, miners still walk with a trudging grace to and from vast, deep mines. And in the schools, the children still learn and the teachers teach, and, in snowy white churches built on hillside cuts, the preachers still preach, and God, who we have no doubt is also a West Virginian, still does his work, too. The people endure here as they always have for they understand that God has determined that there is no joy greater than hard work, and that there is no water holier than the sweat off a man's brow.

In such a place as this, a dozen men may die, but death can never destroy how they lived their lives, or why.

As I watched the events of this tragedy unfold, I kept being reminded of Coalwood, the mining town where I grew up. Back then, I thought life in that little town was pretty ordinary, even though nearly all the men who lived there worked in the mine and all too often, some of them died or were hurt. My grandfather lost his legs in the Coalwood mine and lived in pain until the day he died. My father lost the sight in an eye while trying to rescue trapped miners. After that he worked in the mine for fifteen more years. He died of black lung.

When I began to write my books about growing up in West Virginia, I was surprised to discover, upon reflection, that maybe it wasn't such an ordinary place at all. I realized that in a place where maybe everybody should be a afraid after all, every day the men went off to work in a deep, dark, and dangerous coal mine instead they had adopted a philosophy of life that consisted of these basic attitudes.

We are proud of who we are. We stand up for what we believe. We keep our families together. We trust in God but rely on ourselves.

By adhering to these simple approaches to life, they became a people who were not afraid to do what had to be done, to mine the deep coal, and to do it with integrity and honor.

The first time my dad ever took me in the mine was when I was in high school. He wanted to show me where he worked, what he did for a living. I have to confess I was pretty impressed. But what I recall most of all was what he said to me while we were down there. He put his spot of light in my face and explained to me what mining meant to him. He said, "Every day, I ride the mantrip down the main line, get out and walk back into the gob and feel the air pressure on my face. I know the mine like I know a man can sense things about it that aren't right even when everything on paper says it is. Every day there's something that needs to be done, because men will be hurt if it isn't done, or the coal the company's promised to load won't get loaded. Coal is the life blood of this country. If we fail, the country fails."

And then he said, "There's no men in the world like miners, Sonny. They're good men, strong men. The best there is. I think no matter what you do with your life, no matter where you go or who you know, you will never know such good and strong men."

Over time, though I would meet many famous people from astronauts to actors to Presidents, I came to realize my father was right. There are no better men than coal miners. And he was right about something else, too:

If coal fails, our country fails.

The American economy rests on the back of the coal miner. We could not prosper without him. God in His wisdom provided this country with an abundance of coal, and he also gave us the American coal miner who glories in his work. A television interviewer asked me to describe work in a coal mine and I called it "beautiful." He was astonished that I would say such a thing so I went on to explain that, yes, it's hard work but, when it all comes together, its like watching and listening to a great symphony: The continuous mining machines, the shuttle cars, the roof bolters, the ventilation brattices, the conveyor belts, all in concert, all accomplishing their great task. Yes, it is a beautiful thing to see.

There is a beauty in anything well done, and that goes for a life well lived.

How and why these men died will be studied now and in the future. Many lessons will be learned. And many other miners will live because of what is learned. This is right and proper.

But how and why these men lived, that is perhaps the more important thing to be studied. We know this much for certain: They were men who loved their families. They were men who worked hard. They were men of integrity, and honor. And they were also men who laughed and knew how to tell a good story. Of course they could. They were West Virginians!

And so we come together on this day to recall these men, and to glory in their presence among us, if only for a little while. We also come in hope that this service will help the families with their great loss and to know the honor we wish to accord them.

No matter what else might be said or done concerning these events, let us forever be reminded of who these men really were and what they believed, and who their families are, and who West Virginians are, and what we believe, too.

There are those now in the world who would turn our nation into a land of fear and the frightened. It's laughable, really. How little they understand who we are, that we are still the home of the brave. They need look no further than right here in this state for proof.

For in this place, this old place, this ancient place, this glorious and beautiful and sometimes fearsome place of mountains and mines, there still lives a people like the miners of Sago and their families, people who yet believe in the old ways, the old virtues, the old truths; who still lift their heads from the darkness to the light, and say for the nation and all the world to hear:

We are proud of who we are.
We stand up for what we believe.
We keep our families together.
We trust in God.

Courtesy of Homer Hickam

The Company

Author's note: In extreme contrast to the love, sympathy and understanding pouring out from our nation as a whole - The hate group headed up by Fred Phelps from Topeka, Kansas showed up for the memorial service. They came as close to the front door of the chapel as the law allowed. I was told they had obtained a permit. This protest group carried signs reading, "God hates dead West Virginia Coal Miners." They got little publicity.

Mine Has History of bad top and violations

2004 injury – 3 times greater than underground mine of comparable size
12 accidental roof falls (MSHA data) – 3 after ICG took over
$24,000 in fines for approximately 200 violations (MSHA data)
October – December, 46 citations, 3 orders for safety violations 18 of the violations "Serious and Substantial"
October – December, Sago cited for not following roof control plan and ventilation plan – cited for violation regarding emergency escapeways and pre-shift examination
July – September, 70 violations, 42 listed as "S & S" (MSHA data)
April – June, 52 violations, 31 listed as "S & S" (MSHA data)

Wilbur Ross denied his company had compromised worker safety. Company officials said safety had improved since Mr. Ross's firm took over.   Three major cave-ins have occurred since the takeover, including one on Nov. 27 that dropped a rock 70' in length, 20' wide and 18' high.

"The number of violations is sufficiently high that it should tip off management that there is something amiss here," J. Davitt McAteer said. "For a small operation, that is a significant number of violations."

McAteer said the roof fall frequency "suggests that the roof is bad and that the support system is not meeting the needs of the roof." (Data and quote from Charleston Gazette article by Ken Ward) McAteer is former Mine Safety and Health Administration Head.

Gene Kitts, Vice-President, told reporters, safety at Sago has improved 80% between the 2nd and 4th quarter of 2005.

The roof must be checked visually and then with a ball peen hammer for a hollow sound or a solid sound to determine stability. Roof bolters check the stability of the roof or top by drilling test holes – roof bolts cannot be set in test holes.

Sago's Tangled Web from Wilbur Ross to Enron to the Hills of W. VA.

The New York Times on October 13, 1997, published the story of a helicopter crash in a remote area of Upshur County, West Virginia killing John Faltis, President of Anker Energy Corporation and his wife, Kathleen Faltis, West Virginia, State Board of Education member. Also killed were the pilot and a commercial photographer. According to firefighters it took about 30 minutes to hike into the heavily wooded hillside where the helicopter crashed. The Bell 206 Jet Ranger did not burn. The team was doing commercial shots to promote Anker Energy Corporation.

John Faltis and Kathleen had not been married long. She was a former resident of my community, Summersville, West Virginia. She met John, married and moved to Morgantown after the breakup of her first marriage. Summersville now has a shelter for run-away-children named in her honor, The Faltis Shelter.

COAL Magazine in its November '95 publication profiles John Faltis and Anker Energy Corporation. "The Anker Group Positions Itself as an Industry Leader." John Faltis gets the credit for the progressive corporate profile.

Faltis was well known in Barbour and Webster Counties for buying up castoff coal reserves which were too costly for Island Creek, Peabody and Consol, etc. Faltis made his mark with a corporate philosophy which included taking on others' liabilities and turning them into assets. Just prior to this deadly helicopter crash Anker purchased the Pittston Grand Badger mine in Sago (mine which exploded on Jan. 2, 2006), the Upshur Coal/Bass Energy mine on French Creek across Route 20 from Sago and Island Creek Enoxy/Consol Tenmile Complex in northern Upshur County.

The death of 55 year old John Faltis set a series of unfortunate happenings in motion over at Anker Energy. Coal production experienced a significant drop from 7.3 million tons in 1998 to 3 million in 2000. In 2002 the company filed for bankruptcy after issuing $125 million in bonds as a funding source and three years later defaulting on more than $6 million in interest due bondholders.

The company came to a screeching halt in 2002 firing CEO William Kilgore, President Bruce Sparks and V-President Richard Bolen in charge of corporate development. Anker closed several of its mines in 2002 the year of its bankruptcy including three year old Sago. They listed poor marketing conditions as the reason for this mine closing.

Sago's present owner, former investment banker, New York billionaire, Wilbur Ross, Jr. already a member of the board of Anker, parent company of Sago, seven months prior to bankruptcy proceedings targeted troubled Anker for buyout purposes. On March 31, 2005, Ross became the owner of bankrupt Anker Campany. Instead of abandoning ship, he bought the sinking ship. Board members at the time of purchase were: Wilbur Ross, Wexford Capital's Mark Zand and two representatives from Enron Corporation coming together under the corporate name of International Coal Group (ICG). Providing management services as early as June 2005, ICG's focus turned to a productivity culture which encouraged employees to perform efficiently, safely and productively.

Sago was a small portion of the coal conglomerate amassed by Ross. On August 17, 2004, Ross acquired Horizon Natural Resources through a bankruptcy court auction. This auction was held in Lexington, Kentucky after US Bankruptcy Judge, William Howard, upheld the bankruptcy ruling in favor of the Addington Brothers of Ashland, Kentucky, owners of Horizon. Ross made a combined deal at this auction with Massey Energy – Ross's firm took Horizon's 14 nonunion mines in West Virginia, Kentucky and Illinois. Massey took the two union mines from Horizon; the Cannelton Hollow mine in Kanawha County, West Virginia and Starfire mine in Perry County, Kentucky. Massey quickly opened their new acquisitions as nonunion operations.

So, instead of joining the ranks of the retirement community, this gray-headed, 67 year old former Rothchild employee of 26 years, struck out on his own forming W. L. Ross & Company, LLC. He began buying up failing companies operating under a self-designed form of management, making good off others' misfortune.

This type of management earned him the Yale School of Management prestigious title of Legend of Leadership on December 13, 2005. This type of financial management has earned him other titles as well. Business Week online in an article on December 22, 2003, dubbed this type of financial maneuvering as "distressed investment" or "vulture investing." Paul J. Nyden reporter for the Charleston Gazette writes on January 3, 2006, the following about Ross. "After buying troubled companies, Ross typically consolidates operations, lays off people and renegotiates union contracts. Fortune magazine recently dubbed Ross The Bankruptcy King, while Business Week reported that Ross supervises growing empires of the damned. An article in New York magazine called Ross the Bottom-Feeder King."

Following Ross's takeover of Sago, coal production began again during the first quarter of 2004 but not to capacity. Sago miners were doing the work. In spite of claims of a safer work environment by owner Ross who boasted they had won several safety awards, the safety record at Sago worsened with 208 violations cited by MSHA (Mine Safety and Health Administration) in 2005; 70 federal safety citations during 3rd quarter and 45 during the 4th quarter. The mine continued to work even though 10 violations serious enough to fall under "withdrawal orders" were issued. These citations named: weak roof, improper ventilation, blocked escape passages, piles of combustible materials and improper pre-shift examinations. Also, a citation was issued for allowing coal pillars to be cut dangerously thin. (Coal pillars support the top or roof in an underground mine. A plan is designed for the mining area and must be approved by MSHA. This plan specifies pillar width, etc.)

On November 18, 2005, ICG completed acquisition of Sago and a mere two weeks before Christmas, a federal inspector gave ICG an early Christmas present in the form of a citation, "shown a high degree of negligence" by allowing potentially explosive coal dust to accumulate. A section was sealed off, bad top resulting in 31 roof collapses during 2004 and 2005. Could not get an accurate reading of methane gas in that area.

Sago Mine Company Profile

Mine ID:	4608791
Operator:	Anker West Virginia Mining Company Inc.
Mine Name:	Sago Mine
Controlling Company:	Anker Group Inc.
Ownership Date:	1/11/2002
Mine Status:	Active
Status Date:	2/11/2004
Mined Material:	Coal (Bituminous)
Type of Mine:	Underground
Location:	Upshur County, West Virginia
State:	West Virginia

Source: U. S. Department of Labor

Sago mine produced 366,043 tons of coal during 2005 with 145 employees

The United States has about a 250-year supply of coal, with the industry calling America the Saudi Arabia of coal. The biggest use for coal is as fuel for power plants, accounting for half of U.S. electricity generation.

Profile of International Coal Group officials:

- **Wilbur L. Ross, Jr. (67):** International Coal Group Chairman. Ross, a New York billionaire, has controlled the company that owns Sago Mine since at least early 2001 according to public records. Sago Mine was under management of International Coal Group. "It's a horrible freak accident," Wilbur Ross said in an interview. "Apparently a lightning bolt struck the mine."
- **Ben Hatfield (49):** Named President and Chief Executive Officer of International Coal Group (ICG) in March 2005. Bennett K. Hatfield, born in 1946, is a former Massey Energy official. Hatfield holds a B.S. in mining engineering from Virginia Polytechnic Institute and State University (Virginia Tech).
- **William D. Campbell (45):** Chief Financial Officer
- **Oren Eugene Kitts (51):** Senior Vice-President of Mining Services. Former Massey Energy official.
- **Phillip Michael Hardesty (45):** Senior Vice-President of Sales and Marketing.
- **Gene Kitts,** Senior Vice President, has announced plans to open a new underground mine near Grafton, West Virginia. Up to 350 people could be employed to produce the 4 million tons per year. This operation is headed up by New York billionaire, Wilbur Ross, the same Ross who bought up the Horizon Natural Resource Company when the Ashland, Kentucky, brothers were granted permission to declare bankruptcy by a U.S. Bankruptcy judge in August 2004.

International Coal Group has operations in West Virginia, Kentucky, Maryland and Illinois with 2,100 employees. Sold about 19 million tons of coal during 2005

Governor Joe Manchin ordered flags lowered to half-mast at all state facilities and to remain half-staff until sunset on the day of the burial of the last victim.

Notes left by miners

Martin Toler note:
"Tell all see you on the other side. It wasn't bad. Just went to sleep. I love you." Junior

David Lewis note:
"He loved her and wanted her to be courageous."

Tom Anderson put together a note to his wife and son, Ti, and other family members. He told his wife Lynda, that he loved her. He told Ti to grow up, be strong and help his family.

"We don't hear any attempts at drilling or rescue. The section is full of smoke and fumes, so we can't escape. Be strong, and I hope no one else has to show you this note. I love you both and always have. I'm in no pain, but don't know how long the air will last." George Hamner Jr.

Jim Bennett - He documented a time line. He was still writing 10 hours after the blast. His daughter said if rescue efforts had moved faster, her father could have been saved. Near the end, "He said it was getting dark. It was getting smoky. They were losing air." He, "wanted everyone to know to tell my mom that he loved her." said his daughter, Ann Meredith. "And he wanted me and my brother to know that he loved us."

Nelson Tinnel, former Sago employee speaks out

Author's note: I asked Nelson Tinnel, a coal miner with 42 years of mining experience and former employee of Sago Mine as Dispatch Officer, to read my story of the Sago Mine disaster and give me an opinion on my work - technical information pertaining to underground mining or any other thoughts relevant to the Sago Mine disaster.

I didn't expect to receive a 15 page, 8.5 x 14" itemized report with explanations and recommendations on the Sago Mine disaster. Nelson has produced his theory of what caused the explosion at Sago and recommendations to prevent future accidents. The material Nelson has prepared is valuable not only to me, as an author, but to the mining industry as well.

The Sago Mine disaster resulted in the deaths of 12 good men, loss of wages of more than 100 employees, and exposed weaknesses in our coal industry.

Nelson Tinnel comments:

1.   Prepare to Meet God. Photograph by Builder Levy - Great picture and caption

2.   Citations or violations referred to in story are not necessarily a direct link to injuries and accidents. Certain types of citations can be, but it takes a vast amount of experience and familiarity with a mine and its people to accurately make that determination.

3.   The phrase, "good bunch of men" meant several things; good, productive workers, good family men, good neighbors, but on the job a good bunch of men are the product and reflection of a good foreman or leader.

4.   "Black lung, pneumoconiosis" (term used) The "pioneer" coal miner who lived on a small farm and supplemented his meager wages with the produce of the land (hunting, gathering, gardening). I'm not sure which supplemented the other. The "transient" miner whose only activity was mining, lived a totally different lifestyle. In the 20s and 30s he spent his work shift breathing the coal dust and his off work time breathing the smoke of tobacco and the fumes of alcohol. He spent his off time in a "beer joint" or at home on the couch listening to a radio or in the 2nd half of the 20th Century, watching television. He rarely made it to the age of 65.

Not so with the "pioneer" miner. He spent his "off time" chasing a farm animal or a wild animal and working the land. Those "pioneer" miners are the ones who lived to 90 or 100 and some of the later ones are still living, for example, Lacy Hughart who is now 104 and started mining coal at the age of 14 or 15.

5. Sago was a drift mine (mines types are defined by how they enter the coalbed or vein or seam.) All underlined words mean the same thing. A shaft mine enters the coal "seam" straight down because the seam is below valley floors. A slope mine enters at an angle – a drift mine horizontally.

6. The idea that coal mining gets in your blood and that coal miners cannot do anything else is a myth. In order to be a good coal miner you have to do everything. A miner can be an electrician, a plumber, a carpenter, do anything with hydraulics, expert welder, a surveyor or all of the above. A coal miner can do anything.

7. Understanding the events that led to the explosion is a fairly complicated process. It may be beyond the ability of the average non-coal miner and perhaps even more so to the highly professional, engineer, hi-tech coal miner. I will try to explain it from a "pioneer coal miner" common sense perspective.

The Main Entries or headings at Sago were extracting the coal and advancing or proceeding in a nearly easterly direction and had advanced about 2 miles in that direction. Several months before the accident, mining conditions became adverse enough to cause them to pull back and begin developing a new area in a more northerly direction. Two sets of headings, or sections were developed in the new direction. It is a common practice in U.G. (underground) mining to seal off areas that are retreated from and abandoned like the headings that had been advancing in the easterly direction. This eliminates the requirement to travel and examine such areas.

In my opinion, it is not a good practice and does not have to be done. When the seals are built air movement and currents ceased behind them. No fresh air containing 21% oxygen necessary for life and combustion enters those areas.

Now a new process begins that changes the atmospheric environment of the sealed off area. The oxygen content begins to slowly decrease from the 21%, at a rate depending on the rate that other gases are being generated and no longer being diluted by fresh air entering the area. The methane content is rising and oxygen is falling. When the Oxygen - Methane mixture of the atmosphere reaches a mixture range of 5 to 15% it is most explosive.

Three things have to be present for a fire or explosion to occur: (1) fuel, (2) Oxygen, (3) source of ignition. Items 1 and 2 (fuel and oxygen) are not in question. The source of ignition is. If that source had occurred early in the process of oxygen depletion and rising methane, before it reached the deadly 5 to 15% mixture or after the oxygen had been reduced to a much lower content, nothing would have happened. Indeed that may have occurred and we never knew it. But at the right time, and no one knows when that time began and when it would have ended. It depended on the rate that methane gas was being liberated and now reducing the unregenerated oxygen content because of the lack of a fresh flow of air.

But what was the source of ignition? The common theory being projected by the industry and state and federal agencies is that a lightening strike was the source of ignition. There was a severe storm occurring at the time of the accident. In my opinion, and based on my background as a "pioneer" miner, and amateur naturalist, and as a professional electrician, I am convinced that for lightening to penetrate 250 feet or more of earth strata and enter the now highly explosive atmosphere of the sealed off areas, it has to have a path or conductor. We have to ask what could that path or conductor have been? Tree roots? Well casings? Bore holes for electric conductors to the enter the mine?

Tree roots do not penetrate even the subsoil and iron deposits. The roots would not provide paths 250 feet or more into the earth. No wells or casings or bore holes are known to be in a proximity close enough to have been the culprit.

So, what is left?

Curiously, old miners believed that major roof falls occurred in the early hours of the morning. Certainly, whenever they occur tremendous pressure is exerted at the point that the rock shears and slides along the sear as it falls, especially in sandstone. Most miners who have worked in the extraction of pillars have observed the streak of fire and sparks produced by the abrasive action of shearing strata. When a shear occurs at a roof bolt hole, the bolt can be pulled along the shear wall producing sparks. This action in my opinion caused the explosion at Sago.

Did the atmosphere, lightening and thunder storm play any part? It is possible, I think that thunder claps may have produced very slight tremors, vibrations that triggered a fall that was about to occur anyway.

I strongly recommend a review of the practice of sealing off areas in a mine. This needs to be reconsidered.

Every time abandoned areas are sealed the potential for the event is created. If the practice is to be continued and at present it certainly is, then, other steps need to be taken.

Some possibilities that need to be explored are:

a.   Drilling bore holes above the area to vent the gases

b.   Introducing a non-explosive atmosphere to the area, perhaps with exhaust of an internal combustion engine

c.   Flooding the area.

8.   Conventional shifts were not worked at Sago which may not be a factor in the explosion, but perhaps a contributor to other accidents and injuries due to long hours that produces a lack of environmental awareness necessary for safety. This is no different than driving your auto for too many hours.

9.   There is no indication that there were any inadequacies in the performance of fireboss duties relating to the accident.

10.   The condition of detectors or methane liberated where roof bolting was being done, had no bearing on what was occurring behind the seals.

11.   Backward "F" - The vertical base of the "F" extends into the abandoned sealed area, hence the force of the explosion took the only path available - down the main line. The vertical base of the "F". Siglers' Mine Company was not connected to the Sago Mine and had no relevance. (Sigler Mine Company had mine the area at an earlier time.)

12.   "Thunderstorms and lightening hit the area during Sunday, January 1, and all through the night into Monday. Ron Grall, member of the First Left crew, commented on the odd weather for West Virginia in January, rain pouring down, when the mountains are usually covered in snow during this winter's month."

This will no doubt lead some to believe the lightening strike theory, but I am not convinced as indicated earlier. Perhaps tremors induced by the storm hastened a roof fall already in progress. Lack of evidence of a conductor or path for the lightening to travel to the mined area is evidence that the ignition source was a roof fall, not a lightening strike.

The issue now is not what caused the explosion, but why. It is my belief the potential for it to happen again is behind every sealed area that exists in any mine. Certainly we understand how, when, and why explosive atmospheres are created behind seals and there are more than one out there. Perhaps another is being created right now, this very moment. This issue needs to be addressed.

13. The likelihood that the velocity of the explosion was less in the fingers of the backward "F" is real. Was there a rescue storage station on the section? Were there oxygen tanks on the section that they could have used?

14. Neither the financial shenanigans nor the citations issued had any bearing on the explosion. The mining practice that results in too small of blocks of coal pillars is caused by center line not being drawn (painted) on the roof for the miner operator to follow.

    Many times these people visit the working section only for production issues   and don't even address serious issues like center lines!

15. Many times these problems areas are a personnel issue. Some lack the expertise to test and maintain some of the equipment. Checking and calibrating methane detectors, self rescuers and other hi-tech equipment may be over the head of chief electricians and safety people assigned to these items.

16. We need to look at the long hours men spend underground. Just as driving a big rig over the highways affect the safety and the other people on the roads, a tired miner is unattentive to his job and a risk to himself and his fellow workers.

17. Safety will never be achieved in any industry through legislation. Rules and regs are important and we must have them, but safety is a result of knowledge and constant awareness of our environment. (You covered these issues well, I think)

18. If self rescuers are used properly and are working properly, carbon monoxide is not dangerous property. He was almost there according to stories, but MSHA nor state officials could not make it in the next 36 hours?

19. The CO was likely found in the return air at the mine portal indicating that fire and depletion of O2 had occurred, not necessarily that it was then goingon or ongoing.

20. I am not that familiar with the Brookwood event but the problem at Sago was trying to re-establish ventilation, which in fact, could have caused an ignition.

21. Poisonous gas is overcome by use of self-contained (oxygen producing) rescuer devices!

22. All miners under West Virginia law have 80 hours training. MSHA reg is 40 hours.

23. Were the safe 02 & CH4 levels reduced by the rescuers in the intake and were levels still high in the return? We need to know when and where air tests were made. These times and places can be manipulated, and they are critical.

24. Again, we need to know where the hole was in relation to a precise location u.g.

Again - CO poses no threat to an experienced rescuer with a self-contained rescuer.

25. "Air tests returned discouraging results with dangerous levels of carbon monoxide in the area where the trapped miners were thought to be."

26. Selection from Homer Hickman is good choice.

27. "Hamner said he was "still OK at 2:40 p.m." but couldn't hear "any attempts at drilling or rescue."

At 2:40 p.m. it is likely that all the oxygen in the SCSR has been used up for several hours. They have survived on what oxygen they trapped in their barricade. If any of the group had passed away at the time George Hamner would likely have noted it.

Your story is well written and reconstructs the events very well.

There is no need for me to comment further on these events. Hopefully, my criticisms are constructive. If we are to learn from the past and prevent such occurrences in the future, we must face facts as we perceive them.

I fear the potential for such an event exists anywhere new seals are constructed in underground mines. Technology has always existed to prevent such an event.

Nelson Tinnel

The Charleston Gazette

April 28, 2006 article
McCloy: Sago miners hit gas pocket 3 weeks before blast

Survivor says 4 rescuer devices failed trapped men

By Ken Ward Jr.
Staff writer

Workers at the Sago Mine hit a pocket of explosive gas three weeks before the Jan. 2 blast that killed 12 workers, the sole survivor of the disaster said this week.

Randal McCloy Jr. described the incident — and the final hours of his co-workers — in a letter to the families of Sago disaster victims.

McCloy reported that four of the emergency breathing devices issued to the Sago miners did not work, forcing the trapped miners to share them in a desperate attempt to survive.

"I shared my rescuer with Jerry Groves, while Junior Toler, Jesse Jones and Tom Anderson sought help from others," McCloy wrote. "There were not enough rescuers to go around."

McCloy also said that Anderson and Toler made a last-ditch effort to find a way out of the mine.

"The heavy smoke and fumes caused them to quickly return," McCloy wrote. "There was just so much gas."

McCloy's three-page letter, marked "Confidential" and dated Wednesday, was given to Sago families during a private meeting Wednesday. Family members have been meeting periodically with state and federal officials to hear updates on the Sago investigation, and privately with a team of lawyers representing the various widows, children and other loved ones.

Despite an agreement among the families to keep the letter private until the start of a public hearing next week, copies were leaked to the media and received widespread coverage via The Associated Press.

The families of victims Anderson, Jim Bennett, Alva Martin Bennett, Groves, George "Junior" Hamner, Terry Helms, David Lewis, Fred Ware Jr. and Marshall Winans released a statement through Morgantown attorney Jane E. Peak late Thursday that they do not wish to comment during "a very difficult time" and hope to have their privacy respected before the public hearings next week.

Several families will release a statement next week after the hearings, Peak said.

One worker was killed by the Jan. 2 explosion and 11 others perished before rescue teams reached them more than 40 hours later. McCloy was trapped with the 11 other miners, but somehow survived and is continuing what his doctors say is a miracle recovery from serious carbon monoxide poisoning.

The accident was the worst coal-mining disaster in West Virginia in nearly 40 years, and has spurred numerous calls for improved mine safety enforcement and tougher regulations.

In the first paragraph of his letter, McCloy recounted that three weeks before the disaster, he and Toler, "found a gas pocket while drilling a bolt hole in the mine roof."

"Our detector confirmed the presence of methane," McCloy wrote. "We immediately shut down the roof bolter [machine], and the incident was reported up the line to our superiors. I noticed the following day that the gas leak had been plugged with glue normally used to secure the bolts."

It was not immediately clear if the incident McCloy described meant anything for investigators trying to determine the cause of the Sago explosion.

So far, investigators have said that they believe that a spark ignited methane that had built up behind the seals installed in an area of the mine that was closed because of repeated roof falls. McCloy did not say where in the mine he and Toler found the methane pocket.

In his letter, McCloy said that the trapped miners pounded a sledgehammer on mine bolts and plates to try to signal rescue teams. When they received no response, the miners gave up.

The air in their makeshift shelter "grew worse, so I tried to lie as low as possible and take shallow breaths," McCloy wrote.

"We were worried and afraid, but we began to accept our fate," he wrote. "Junior Toler led us all in the Sinners Prayer.

"As time went on, I became very dizzy and lightheaded," McCloy wrote. "Some drifted off into what appeared to be a deep sleep, and one person sitting near me collapsed and fell off his bucket, not moving.

"As my trapped co-workers lost consciousness one by one, the room grew still and I continued to sit and wait, unable to do much else," he wrote. "I have no idea how much time went by before I also passed out from the gas and smoke, awaiting rescue.

"I cannot begin to express my sorrow for my lost friends and my sympathy for those they left behind," McCloy concluded. "I cannot explain why I was spared while the others perished. I hope that my words will offer some solace to the miners' families and friends who have endured what no one should ever have to endure."

On Thursday, Davitt McAteer, Gov. Joe Manchin's adviser on mine safety issues, said that McCloy's comments about the failure of the breathing devices — called self-contained, self-rescuers, or SCSRs — will be addressed during the hearing.

"This raises questions about the devices and about the training miners receive," McAteer said. "We really need to work on this system to make sure these work for the miners."

In his letter, McCloy said that, after the explosion, "The first thing we did was activate our rescuers, as we had been trained."

McCloy said that four of the devices did not work, but did not describe the problems in any detail.

In a prepared statement, ICG said that it provides workers with SCSRs made by Pittsburgh-based CSE Corp. The company said that they are "widely used in the coal industry and are approved for use by MSHA."

ICG said that all of the rescuers were within their manufacturer-suggested life.

According to the company, the devices found with the Sago miners "were deployed and showed varying degrees of usage. The federal investigators did not note any defective SCSRs and all SCSRs appeared to be in working order."

In a prepared statement, MSHA spokesman Dirk Fillpot said that his agency, "would like to reassure all underground coal miners that the SCSRs used in U.S. mines have proven to be reliable and effective rescue devices.

"Initial testing conducted by MSHA and NIOSH on all SCSRs recovered after the explosion at the Sago Mine found that those that were activated would have functioned properly," Fillpot said. "MSHA is looking at whether the miners received adequate training in the use of the SCSRs. MSHA is also initiating an effort with state agencies to ensure that miners are properly trained in SCSR use nationwide."

Staff writer Ken Ward Jr.'s continued reporting on the Sago Mine disaster and mine safety is being supported by a fellowship from the Alicia Patterson Foundation.

Article: Courtesy of the Charleston Gazette

Sole survivor of the Sago Mine disaster, Randal McCloy, Jr. wrote the letter below to the families of the 12 miners who died in the January 2, 2006 explosion.

The letter is two pages, typed, addressed, "to the families of the loved ones of my co-workers."

McCloy describes in haunting detail the miners' desperate attempts to signal the surface for help using a sledge hammer, and how some of their breathing equipment failed.

Randal McCloy, Jr.'s letter
The Charleston Gazette

April 28, 2006
Text of Randal McCloy Jr.'s letter

Randal McCloy Jr., the lone survivor of the Sago Mine disaster, wrote this letter to the families of the 12 miners who died in the Jan. 2 explosion. In the letter, he refers to a "man-trip," which transports miners into mines; "rescuers," which are emergency air packs; and a "rib," which is the wall of the mine.

To the families and loved ones of my co-workers, victims of the Sago Mine disaster:

About three weeks before the explosion that occurred on January 2, 2006, toward the end of our shift, Junior Toler and I found a gas pocket while drilling a bolt hole in the mine roof. Our detector confirmed the presence of methane. We immediately shut down the roof bolter, and the incident was reported up the line to our superiors. I noticed the following day that the gas leak had been plugged with glue normally used to secure the bolts.

The explosion happened soon after the day shift arrived at the mine face on January 2, right after we got out of the man-trip. I do not recall whether I had started work, nor do I have any memory of the blast. I do remember that the mine filled quickly with fumes and thick smoke and that breathing conditions were nearly unbearable.

The first thing we did was activate our rescuers, as we had been trained. At least four of the rescuers did not function. I shared my rescuer with Jerry Groves, while Junior Toler, Jesse Jones and Tom Anderson sought help from others. There were not enough rescuers to go around.

We then tried to return to the man-trip, yelling to communicate through the thick smoke. The air was so bad that we had to abandon our escape attempt and return to the coal rib, where we hung a curtain to try to protect ourselves. The curtain created an enclosed area of about 35 feet.

We attempted to signal our location to the surface by beating on the mine bolts and plates. We found a sledgehammer, and for a long time we took turns pounding away. We had to take off the rescuers in order to hammer as hard as we could. This effort caused us to breathe much harder. We never heard a responsive blast or shot from the surface.

We eventually gave out and quit our attempts at signaling, sitting down behind the curtain on the mine floor, or on buckets or cans that some of us found. The air behind the curtain grew worse, so I tried to lie as low as possible and take shallow breaths. While methane does not have an odor like propane and is considered undetectable, I could tell that it was gassy. We all stayed together behind the curtain from that point on, except for one attempt by Junior Toler and Tom Anderson to find a way out. The heavy smoke and fumes caused them to quickly return. There was just so much gas.

We were worried and afraid, but we began to accept our fate. Junior Toler led us all in the Sinners Prayer. We prayed a little longer, then someone suggested that we each write letters to our loved ones. I wrote a letter to Anna and my children. When I finished writing, I put the letter in Jackie Weaver's lunch box, where I hoped it would be found.

As time went on, I became very dizzy and lightheaded. Some drifted off into what appeared to be a deep sleep, and one person sitting near me collapsed and fell off his bucket, not moving. It was clear that there was nothing I could do to help him. The last person I remember speaking to was Jackie Weaver, who reassured me that if it was our time to go, then God's will would be fulfilled. As my trapped co-workers lost consciousness one by one, the room grew still and I continued to sit and wait, unable to do much else. I have no idea how much time went by before I also passed out from the gas and smoke, awaiting rescue.

I cannot begin to express my sorrow for my lost friends and my sympathy for those they left behind. I cannot explain why I was spared while the others perished. I hope that my words will offer some solace to the miners' families and friends who have endured what no one should ever have to endure.

April 26, 2006

Randal McCloy Jr.
Article: Courtesy of The Charleston Gazette

Author's note: Owen Jones was foremen of 1ˢᵗ Left Crew and the brother of Sago disaster victim Jesse Jones. This interview with Owen Jones was conducted on January 17, 2006.

STATEMENT UNDER OATH
OF
OWEN MARK JONES

Taken pursuant to Notice by Miranda D. Elkins, a Court Reporter and Notary Public in and for the State of West Virginia, at Clarksburg Bankruptcy Court, 324 West Main Street, Clarksburg, West Virginia, on Tuesday, January 17, 2006, at 11:55 a.m.

A P P E A R A N C E S

DOUG CONAWAY, DIRECTOR
Office of Miners' Health, Safety and Training
1615 Washington Street, East
Charleston, WV 25311

JAMES BROOKS CRAWFORD, ESQUIRE
Senior Trail Attorney
Mine Safety and Health Division
U.S. Department of Labor
Office of the Solicitor
1100 Wilson Boulevard
Suite 2231
Arlington, VA 22209-2296

JOSEPH R. O'DONNELL, JR.
Supervisory Coal Mine S&H Inspector
U.S. Department of Labor
Mine Safety & Health Administration
District 11
3667 Pine Lane, Suite 205
Bessemer, AL 35022

R. HENRY MOORE, ESQUIRE
Jackson Kelly, PLLC
Three Gateway Center
401 Liberty Avenue – Suite 1340
Pittsburg, PA 15222

SAM KITTS
6002 Pinnacle View Road
Hurricane, WV 25526

P R O C E E D I N G S

MR. O'DONNELL:

My name is Joe O'Donnell. I'm an accident investigator with the Mine Safety & Health Administration, an agency of the United States Department of Labor. I'd like to introduce the State. With me is James Crawford, Solicitor's Office; Doug Conaway, with the West Virginia Office of Miners' Training. And representing the International Coal Group is Henry Moore.

I've been assign to conduct an investigation into the accident that occurred at the Sago Mine on January the 2nd, 2006, in which 12 miners died and one was injured. The investigation is being conducted by MSHA and the West Virginia Office of Miners' Health, Safety & Training to gather information to determine the cause of the accident, and these interviews area an important part of the investigation. At this time, the accident investigation team intends to interview a number of people to discuss anything that is relevant to the cause of the accident.

After the investigation is completed, MSHA will issue a written report, detailing the nature and causes of the accident. MSHA's accident reports are made available to the public, in the hope that greater awareness about the causes of accidents can reduce their occurrence in the future.

Information obtained through witness interviews is frequently included in these reports. Your statement may also be used in other enforcement proceedings. I'd like to thank you in advance for your appearance here. We appreciate your assistance in this investigation. The willingness of miners and mine operators to work with us is critical to our success in making the nation's mines safer. We understand the difficulty for you in discussing the events that took place, and we greatly appreciate your efforts to help us understand what happened.

This interview with Mr. Owen Jones is being conducted under Section 103(a) of the Federal Mine Safety & Health Act of 1977, as part of an investigation by the Mine Safety & Health Administration and the West Virginia Office of Miners' Health, Safety & Training into the conditions, events and circumstances surrounding the fatalities that occurred at the Sago Mine, owned by International Coal Group in Buckhannon, West Virginia, on January 2nd, 2006. This interview is being conducted at the U.S. Bankruptcy Courthouse in Clarksburg, West Virginia, on January 17th, 2006.

Questioning will be conducted by representatives of MSHA and the Office of Miners' Health, Safety & Training. After MSHA and the state officials have finished asking questions, the representative of the mining company and the representative of the miners may ask clarifying questions only. This is not an adversarial proceeding, therefore cross examining will not be permitted.

Mr. Jones, the interview will begin by asking you a series of questions. And if you don't understand a question, ask me to rephrase it. Feel free at any time to clarify any statements that you make in response to your questions. And after we finish asking questions, you will have an opportunity to make a statement on your own and provide us with any other information that you believe is important.

If at any time after the interview you recall any additional information that you believe may be useful in this investigation, please contact Richard Gates at the phone number or e-mail address provided to you. And those are on the cards there that we just gave you. Your statement is completely voluntary. You may refuse to answer any question and you can end this interview at any time. If you need a break for any reason, let me know.

A court reporter will record your interview and will later produce a written transcript of the interview. Please try and respond to all the questions verbally, since the court reporter cannot record nonverbal responses. Also, please try to keep your voice up. Copies of the written transcript will be available at a later time. If any part of your statement is not based on your firsthand knowledge, but on information that you learned from someone else, please let us know. Please answer each question as fully as you can, including any information you have learned from someone else. We may not ask the right questions to learn the information that you have, so do not feel limited in the precise questions that are asked. If you have information about the subject area of a question, please provide us with that information.

At this time, Mr. Conaway, do you have anything you'd like to add on behalf of the Office of Miners' Health, Safety & Training?

MR. CONAWAY:
Yeah. Owen, we appreciate you appearing before us here today. And as was mentioned, we want you to be as comfortable as possible. And at any time you need to take any break, please let us know. But I've got a statement. The West Virginia Office of Miners Health, Safety & Training is conducting this interview session today jointly with the Mine Safety & Health Administration. And we are in agreement with the procedures outlined by Mr. O'Donnell for these interviews that

will be conducted here today. But the Agency reserves its right, if necessary, as outlined in the West Virginia Code, to call and subpoena witnesses or require the production of any record, document, photograph or other relevant materials necessary to conduct this investigation.

So right now Mr. O'Donnell will go ahead and he'll proceed with the main line of questioning.

BY MR. O'DONNELL:

Q. Mr. Jones, you are permitted to have a representative with you during this interview, and you may consult with your representative at any time. You may designate any person to be your representative. Do you have a representative with you?

A. No, I'm not --- I don't have a representative

Q. You don't have a representative? Do you have any questions regarding the manner in which this interview will be conducted?

A. No.

MR. O'DONNELL:

Will you please swear in Mr. Jones?

OWEN JONES, HAVING FIRST BEEN DULY SWORN, TESTIFIED AS FOLLOWS:

BY MR. O'DONNELL:

Q. Can I address you as Owen?

A. Yeah, that's fine.

Q. You can call me Joe.

A. Okay.

Q. Owen, could you please state your full name and spell your last name for us?

A. Owen Mark Jones, J-O-N-E-S.

Q. And please state your address and telephone number, if you would.

A. Route 2, Box 143, French Creek. The ZIP is 26218. And what else?

Q. Do you happen to have an e-mail address?

A. We do, but I don't know what it is.

Q. Are you appearing here today voluntarily?

A. Yes.

Q. And how many years have you --- how much mining experience do you have?

A. Starting on 17 years.

Q. And what have you done since you've worked in a coal mine?

A. Run just about every piece of equipment that you can run, except running longwalls. I've never worked on that. And I've been a section boss since 1998, I think. I think that's what it is.

114

Q.   That's long enough. And how much time have you been a boss at this mine?

A.   This March would make three years.

Q.   So your whole time you've been a boss and ---?

A.   Yeah.

Q.   Okay. And is that what you were doing on January the 2nd, you were a foreman?

A.   Right.

Q.   And what were your assigned duties for that day?

A.   Just to go in and to run coal like we always do.

Q.   What section are you a foreman in?

A.   One Left.

Q.   You're One Left foreman. And how long have you been the foreman in that section?

A.   Ever since we started that panel.

Q.   Have you done anything else other than face boss in the mine, at this mine?

A.   No.

Q.   No? What kind of certificates do you have in West Virginia and any other states that you may have worked in?

A.   I got my shop fireman paper and my dust sampling card. And as far as I know, I just got my EMT cared, or I passed the test.

Q.   And your Foreman Certification?

A.   Foreman Certification.

Q.   In West Virginia?

A.   In West Virginia.

Q.   And no other states?

A.   No.

Q.   And who is your supervisor, Owen?

A.   In which way do you mean? Superintendent?

Q.   Who's your boss?

A.   Jeff Toler. He's the superintendent.

Q.   He's the superintendent?

A.   He and Carl Crumrine (phonetic), he's the mine foreman.

Q.   Okay. What time do you normally start your shift each day?

A.   Six o'clock.

Q.   Six o'clock. And do you rotate shifts or ---?

A.   Rotate out at the face. I mean, not seat at the face.

Q.   You hot seat at the face?

A.   Right.

Q.   And do you work three shifts or do you work just ---?

A.   Three shifts, day, evening and hoot owl.

Q.   Okay.

A.   I mean, my crew, we only worked dayshift.

Q.   Oh, you're steady daylight?

A.   Steady daylight. That's a misunderstanding.

Q. That's okay. And you were working at the day of the accident?

A. Right.

Q. Now, I'm just going to let you tell your story. And I want you to start at the time you arrived at the mine. Please tell us everything that you did until you left the property that day. Include as may details as you can recall, including any times you might remember. And I'm not going to stop you. Just start rom the beginning and work through the whole time.

A. Okay. We take our pre-shift call, which was --- mine was called out by Terry Helms himself. So I took it, wrote it all down. So we go off the hill, me and my brother always went off the hill a few minutes earlier to get the mantrips ready. And he --- we always let them go first because they was inby. So as I pull up behind them there, they are getting loaded in their mantrip, and some of them started getting in my mantrip. But I realized that some of the men that done got in mine, that it was too small to hold all of us. So everybody gets back out and I take it back out in the yard there, switch out, get a bigger mantrip. Then we reload everybody and we take off. I'm going to say five after 6:00 we probably started. I'm guessing we're eight to ten minutes behind the other crew. And we travel all the way in to, I think, the first right. Then I let John Boni off, and he's off there to do something. Then I get on up to Four Head and I let Pat Boni off, because he's a beltman, and we pull up to our switch. Right at the switch my miner operator gets off to throw the switch, gets back in, and just as son as he sits back down, it hits us.

I mean, more wind and dust than you could even think about. There was no warning, no nothing, just it was right there on us. And at first I thought it was a waterline blowed up in my face for a split second, but then I knew what it was from being in an ignition once before. So I get up on top of the mantrip to try to run it to get out of it somewhere, somehow, and it blows me off the top of the mantrip, the wind does. And I'm standing there and it's pushing me forward. It's making me walk. And I'm thinking it's going to absolutely pick me up and throw me, I mean, and then it quits. Then one of my guys, which I'm pretty sure it was my miner operator, screams, the mine's just blew up. Then we're all hollering ateach other, everybody all right, everybody all right. And everybody is saying, let's get to the intake immediately. And I'm looking around for my hardhat because it blowed it off my head somewheres, but I can't find it. So we all take off. It's so dusty that you can't even see the ground. You can't even see your feet. We're following the track the best we can down through there, going through the mud and the slop, stomping. Some of them is ahead and I'm screaming at them all to stick together, stay together. And I know I'm ahead of some of my men even because we're all going, I mean you know we all took off there. And two of them I think it's Ron Grall and Paul Avington, and I might be wrong about this because it's so dusty and dark, but go to the first man door that we come to, and they say it's too dusty here. We can't see, can't breathe. As we go on down through there, they holler --- they get to the second man door and they say, we can see and breathe a little bit in here.

But I only stopped there for a second because my miner operator had fell down behind me, where he had so much dust in his eyes. And my one bolter operator, Randy Helmick, comes along and I say, help me pick him up so we can get him to the man door. And I say, where's everybody else at, and he said, they're coming. And they was, but you couldn't see them from ten feet away. You couldn't even see their lights, it was still so dusty. And I say --- and everybody gets there. And some of them, the reason they wasn't there, they had stopped and donned the rescuers. And I asked the, I said, is that everybody behind you, and they all said yes. So we proceed forward and go to that door and then get everybody in. I said --- I'm looking to see that we got everybody. I'm telling my men, I said, you men get out of here immediately. Get going down the intake. I said I'm going to stay in here and see what I can do because I got a brother up here. And I know --- you know what I mean, I'm knowing that they're still trapped up there somehow, someways. And my men begs me to go with them, but I said, no, you all go. I said, I got to go see if there's anything I can do.

But I do --- let me take this back. As we're walking down through there, I do come upon a mine phone up where we get to that second door, and I call out and said, we've had something happen in the man, an explosion or something, I said, get the people in here. I did call that out.

And they're going down trough there, I think to myself --- my carbon monoxide detector went off immediately after the explosion, whatever. I'm thinking to myself, after men take off down through there, I start to go up that way. I didn't even go up a half a break and I'm thinking to myself, all this carbon monoxide, if I go, I'm going to be dead with them. So I just went back, back and forth from the track, the intake, watching them guys. And they come in on the rails to get them, to get my men. I don't know, one of them, I looked through the man door and seen them --- seen the mantrip and flagged them off. The chief electrician, Dick Wilfong, hollers to me from a phone down there and says, get your --- I won't say the cuss word he said, but get down here. And I said okay. But he goes on without them. And by that time, Jeff Toler and some of them rode in to come in, and had rode in with him to get the men. And they come up to me where I'm at.

So we started going up through there. I seen them putting up curtains. I'm sorry. Let me rephrase that.

Q.   Take your time. No hurry.
A.   Okay. We're there, looking things over, and he hollers on the phone and tells --- I can't remember who it was, Dick or Vern Hofer, one of them to bring in lots of curtains, fly boards, nails, extra detectors and get back in here immediately. So

we're back and forth. They were looking. And I can't tell you how long it was in between the time that they got in and out. But when they get up there, we start going through there, putting some curtains up. My superintendent tells me, he says, you stay here. He says, I don't want you going up there. I know why. He's saying that in case my brother is up there and he don't want me seeing. So I do sit there. I'm thinking to myself, I don't want to see this either. But he goes on up and gets to another phone. And I help him put up some curtains, but he told me, too, to stay there and answer the phone in case somebody hollered.

So they get up there a ways to the next phone and he hollers and says, come on up here. And I go up and help him hang a few more curtains. But the one block break we made it to, I know we inby our switch up there for a ways, and he looks at me and says, you and Vern, because Vernon Hofer went back to get a new roll of curtain from probably 37 break, where they parked the mantrip, up to where we was, and he looks at me while we're up there and he says, how about you and Vern getting a new roll of curtain and heading out, put a curtain across it. I said okay. So we walked down there, checking all the stoppings. And we get Two Right and the overcast wall there is blowed over. I told Vern, I said, this is where the air is short circuiting because there wasn't much air going up the intake at all. So I said, we need to put this curtain up across where the overcast was. So we put the curtain up and, I mean, you feeled air, I mean, going up through there immediately then. By that time, Vern had walked over there and looked up the intake for some reason, just --- he said that he sees lights acoming. so it's Dick Wilfong and the guys coming down there and they said we need to get out of here because there's fresh air going back up there. It's liable, if there's gas --- if there's a fire, it'll push that gas back over top of the fire and blow it up again. So we walked out then. We got out. I don't know what time we got outside for sure or nothing. Just we walked upstairs, I mean, to the offices.

You could see where it blowed out stoppings. As we was reventilating, you could see where it blowed out on the intake stoppings, even some return stoppings.

Q.   What time did you go to the mine that day?
A.   That morning?
Q.   Yes.
A.   I'm going to say right around 5:00
Q.   And what time do you usually start?
A.   On that hill, at 6:00
Q.   Do you remember what you did before you went underground that day, after you got dressed and your procedure that you ---?
A.   Usually I just sit back there in the office, take my pre-shift and we talk and --- you know, like everybody does, about what's going on and ---.

Q.   Was your pre-shift called out that day?

A.   Yeah.

Q.   And who called it out to you?

A.   Terry Helms.

Q.   And do you recall what he reported to you?

A.   Can't remember. All I know is no CH on the faces and gave me my air reading and maybe a place or two down on bolting, I think, but I can't remember for sure.

Q.   But any hazardous conditions?

A.   I don't think. No.

Q.   And did anyone go in the mine before you that day?

A.   That morning?

Q.   Yes. You said that ---

A.   No.

Q.   --- you --- the other mantrip ---.

A.   Oh, yeah. I'm sorry, the other mantrip, yeah, went in before.

Q.   Let me ask you this, when you guys went in the mine that morning, was anybody underground or was everybody out?

A.   Terry Helms would have still been in there somewheres.

Q.   Terry Helms stayed in?

A.   As far as I know.

Q.   Do you know where he stayed at? I mean, do you know where he called you from?

A.   No, he did not give us ---.

Q.   But he did not exit the mine?

A.   No, not that I know of.

Q.   So then he would have been the only one underground?

A.   Right.

Q.   Okay.

A.   Unless --- don't get me wrong, now unless he did exit the mine and went back in with my brother and them, the first crew.   Because like I say, they got off before we did, so I don't --- but I'm assuming that he stayed under there.

Q.   Okay. And you say that the other crew went in ahead of you then. And how long --- and you say that you had to change mantrips?

A.   Right.

Q.   What was the reason?

A.   The one we had was too small to hold all the men. It didn't have enough room.

Q.   And what kind of mantrip do you usually go in on? Is it an open mantrip?

A.   Well, they got a top on them and wire screen in front of you where men sit.

Q.   Was it a diesel or electric?

A.   Battery.

Q.   Battery. And so that crew, that was the Two Left crew then. Did you ever hear from them after that? Did you have any contract with them at any time?

A.   No.

Q. None. Once they went in the mine, then ---?

A. Right.

Q. Okay.

A. That's one thing, I thought you might hear a little noise, you might see a light or something or anything.

Q. So how many people did you have in your mantrip?

A. I'll have to figure it up. You mean everybody, all together?

Q. What you can recall.

A. There would have been 14 or 15 of us.

Q. Fourteen (14) or 15. Do you remember who they were?

A. Yeah, my whole crew. Gary Rowen, Randy Helmick, Alton Wamsley, Joe Ryan, Roger Perry, Denver Anderson, Chris Tenney, Ron Grall and Pat Boni, John Boni, Eric Hess. Let's see who else I'm missing. I said Gary Carpenter, didn't I .

Q. No.

A. Paul Avington. And Chris Tenney, I said him. I think that's pretty well everybody. Oh, my mechanic, Hoy.

Q. Okay. Was that a normal number of people you usually go in with or ---?

A. John Boni, not every day, no. And Ron Grall, not every day.

Q. Okay.

A. It depends on where they're going and what they got to do all day.

Q. But you mentioned Pat Boni and John Boni. Where did you drop those guys off?

A. I think John Boni got off at One Right. I might have said Two Right, but it was One Right. And Pat Boni got off at Four Head.

Q. What I want you to do now is could you take this green marker and go to the far right map, and we'll call that Jones Exhibit One, and just in your --- draw a line and describe where you went in the mine and where you stopped with the mantrip. And also here's a black marker, if you could mark where you dropped Pat and John Boni off, too.

(Jones Exhibit Number One marked for identification.)

A. Do you want me to color this the whole ways from outside with this?

BY MR. O'DONNELL:

Q. Yes.

A. That's where we stopped in there.

Q. Could you describe where you stopped your mantrip?

A. Right at the switch, just enough for a man to get out and throw the switch.

Q. Okay. And could you please draw it on the map?

WITNESS COMPLIES

A. He got off right here.

BY MR. O'DONNELL:

Q.   And you're saying that that is at First Right?

A.   Yeah.

Q.   And is that a switch?

A.   Yeah, there's a switch there.

Q.   Okay. And what person exited there?

A.   John Boni.

Q.   Could you mark --- put an arrow to it and mark ---?

A.   Right here?

Q.   Yes. That's fine. You can draw.

Q.   So the location is ---?

A.   Pat Boni.

Q.   Pat Boni. What crosscut is that; do you know? What do you call that location?

A.   It would be right at 39 block, on the three --- three belt, really. That's right where he went out.

Q.   Okay. Thank you. Do you know what their assignment was that day, why you were dropping them off along the track?

A.   John Boni is a --- he walks airways, plus keeps the pumps agoing, checks pumps. And he might have got off that day and be checking a pump right there.

Q.   Okay.

A.   And Pat Boni is a beltman. He works on the belts.

Q.   So it's just a normal occurrence that you pick up a couple of the belt boys or ---?

A.   Right. They catch one of the two crews in. They see which one's got enough room and get in and ride with us.

Q.   Owen, did you see Pat or John any time after that?

A.   No.

Q.   So if they exited the mine, they exited before you?

A.   Right. They would have caught --- I think they caught the mantrip out, ---

Q.   Okay.

A.   --- as far as I know. That's what I was told.

Q.   And the furthest point of travel that you said was then the switch at One Left?

A.   Right.

Q.   And you never made the turn in or traveled any further inby?

A.   No.

Q.   Okay. I have to go back to the time that you felt that rush of air. Now, the miner operator's name was?

A.   Roger Perry.

Q.   And Roger got off to ---?

A.   Throw the switch.

Q.   Okay. And did he complete throwing the switch?

A. Right. And there was an old ladder --- or not an old ladder, but a new ladder there. I said, get that ladder and throw it on our mantrip, Roger. I said, I don't know whose it is, but I said we're going to take it. So he throws it on there, and then he gets in the mantrip.

Q. Okay.

A. And like I say, he just sits down. And I don't even think I got to hit the tram, and it just --- immediately right on top of us. You know what I'm saying? There was no noise, no nothing. It just ---.

Q. Did you feel your ears pop, too?

A. Nothing.

Q. Nothing. Just a gush of air?

A. Right now.

Q. Was it dust?

A. Yeah, there was stuff flying, air. And it was hitting my back so hard --- I had a flannel coat on with a lining in and my coveralls and a T-shirt. The air was hitting my back and stuff so hard, that I could feel it stinging me.

Q. And you say it knocked your hat off?

A. I'm sure it did. I mean, as I got up on the mantrip, it just --- I couldn't find it, so I don't know where it went. You couldn't see.

Q. You say you got up on the mantrip?

A. To try to get --- I was going to run it if I ---.

Q. Oh, you were just ---?

A. Yeah. I was ---.

Q. What about the rest of your crew, what were they doing when this happened, too? I mean, ---.

A. I thought I heard one of them yell, but I don't know because just a lot of noise. But they was trapped sitting in a mantrip. I mean, they was --- the force was right against them and they was --- so they were stuck there until it quit blowing.

Q. And how long did that air continue?

A. I'm going to guess eight seconds maybe.

Q. Did anybody get hurt?

A. Not critically or bad, but the one, my scoop operator, his back was peppered and stung pretty good. And Denver Anderson's face had little skin pieces all over it. It stung everybody's face. It didn't matter what direction you was sitting, forwards or away, everybody got stung.

Q. So it was just mostly force. What about smoke? Did you smell anything?

A. Not at first, no. But you could --- after we got in the intake, you could smell it then.

Q. What did it smell like?

A. I can't describe that for you. Like oil, like a coal burning.

Q. It smelled like coal burning?

A. Right.

Q. Okay. But we kind of know what that smells like.

A. Right.

Q. And you say that you didn't hear anything. You didn't hear an air rush or ---?

A. No.

Q. Nothing?

A. It was so quick. Like I say, I just --- I mean, we were just getting ready to hit the tram and take off, and I mean it was immediately on top of us. There was no split second or nothing, no little noise or nothing, it just, right now.

Q. You don't know if you had any damage to that mantrip, do you?

A. Don't know.

Q. Now, how about your detectors, did they go into alarm immediately?

A. Mine did.

Q. Yours did?

A. Right. The other --- the regular men's, it just checked methane for them. And mine was carbon monoxide, oxygen and CO.

Q. Did you notice what those readings were?

A. It was so covered with dust at the time. And you couldn't have seen anyhow because --- then when I got in the intake, it was so covered with dust. I just knew it was beeping, I mean steadily beeping.

Q. So this lasted, you said, six to eight seconds?

A. I'm going to say that, guess that.

Q. And then what was it like after that happened, I mean ---?

A. It was so dusty. That's why I say so much dust that you couldn't see your feet.

Q. I mean, did the air reverse? Did it go back in or come out?

A. We couldn't tell because of all the dust. It was just ---.

Q. Just hanging?

A. Yeah, hanging.

Q. And did it happen any time after that again? Did you feel any popping in your ears or a pressure change? What we're trying to ---.

A. Right.

Q. Did you get another one?

A. No.

Q. So there was no evidence that anything happened after that initial?

A. Right. There was nothing.

Q. Okay.

A. And the dust was --- as we got in the intake and stuff. When I went back on the track, the dust was settling real fast in the track entry.

Q. So Owen, you're saying it was dust and not smoke?

A. Right.

Q. Okay.

A. Just your rock dust, your little --- you all know how it is in the mine.

Q. Yeah.

A.   All your little pebbles and everything, just --- I do remember seeing a Omega block further down the track, looked like, I don't know, a couple hundred feet, a half of an Omega block.

Q.   And you saw that go by you?

A.   No. We just seen it laying down on the track.

Q.   Oh, you saw it?

A.   So we knew that it had blowed down through there.

Q.   Now, after this --- you're standing there and it's dusty and you can't see, and you rounded your men up?

A.   Yeah. We're all --- everybody --- not only me, everybody was screaming, let's get to the intake.

Q.   Okay.

A.   So we all come out of there and we all take off at the same time, walking through.

Q.   If you would, could you --- I have a marker here. And what I want you to do is to mark with this marker, mark it with the pink, where you left your mantrip and explain it and where you got into the intake. Okay?

A.   All right.

MR. O'DONNELL:

This would be Owen's Exhibit Two. (Jones Exhibit Number Two marked for identification.)

WITNESS COMPLIES

BY MR. O'DONNELL:

Q.   And could you describe where that was?

A.   At the One Left switch.

Q.   Okay, One Left switch. Draw a line and mark the One Left switch.

Q.   So go ahead and explain where you traveled to.

A.   Where we traveled to?

Q.   Yes.

A.   You mean walked?

Q.   Yes. That's what you did, you walked?

A.   Right, we walked.

Q.   You left your mantrip parked on the track?

A.   We were in a hurry to get out to get the fresh air. We had to.

Q.   Okay.

A.   Do you want me to color it in?

Q.   Yes, please.

A.   I can't tell you exactly where the man doors are. So we come in wherever the first man door was along there.

Q.   Okay.

124

A.   It goes up here.

Q.   If you think that's where it's at, just go ahead and mark it.

A.   I think we come down --- I don't know.

Q.   You walked the track down?

A.   Right.

Q.   Okay. That's fine.

A.   Right there, too, I could be looking at it. It was still so dusty. We couldn't see, so we needed to go in there, so we came back and went down there --- and then to right in here. I'm assuming that's a door. Because I know for a fact from years ago at 37 Crosscut.

Q.   And that is 37 Crosscut on?

A.   Four Belt.

Q.   Four Belt. Okay. Now, Owen, when you went through that --- when your men went through the --- they went into the Number --- is it Eight entry?

A.   Seven entry.

Q.   Number Seven entry. Tell us what happened then.

A.   When we were all down there, I think we had everybody.

MR. CONAWAY:

For the record, turn around this way, so the court reporter can hear. And Joe, you may want to turn around so that the voices go towards the court reporter.

A.   After we got in the intake, I told my men, I said, get outside immediately. I said, I'm going to stay. And some of my men were begging me to go with them. I said, no, I got my brother in here, I'm 1 going to stay. Ron Grall tells me, come on, Owen, he said, think of yourself. I said, no, I got a brother up there. I'm going to stay and see if I can do anything. I said, you all go. And they proceeded to go on down through. Do you want me to draw it?

Q.   Yes. Just mark it in pink, where they traveled.

A.   They would have traveled down like this. And I think they got picked up in here somewhere by a mantrip.

Q.   And you marked down the Number Seven entry. Do you know where they were picked up along ---?

A.   No.

Q.   You don't know?

A.   No.

Q.   They were picked up by whom?

A.   I think it was Dick Wilfong.

Q.   And then they rode out the rest of the way?

A.   Right.

Q.   Okay. Do you know if any of them had put on their SCSRs?

A.   They did.

Q.   They did? When did you guys put them on?

A. They --- some of my men put them on before they --- when I said my --- remember me saying my miner operator fell down ---

Q. Yes.

A. --- and I said I knew some of my men was behind me? I said, where is everybody at, and one of them said, they're up there --- they had stopped to put their rescuers on. So they come down through there and, yes, some of them had stopped and put on their rescuers.

Q. So they put them on at different times, is that what you're saying?

A. Probably.

Q. You had some that were up at the mantrip ---?

A. Some of us going down, never even stopped, just kept right on getting ahead of me to the man door. And some of the ones that were behind, there was about three that was behind, that had stopped and donned the rescuers. Now, I don't know if they put them on at different times there together and done it.

Q. Did you have to put yours on?

A. I should have, but I didn't.

Q. Do you know if they had any difficulty putting them on or did everybody ---?

A. I never ---.

Q. Don't know?

A. Didn't ask them. I was too worried about getting us all in the intake.

Q. Did anybody have any trouble with their SCSR?

A. I don't know that either. Because like I say, I was just too worried about getting everybody in the intake.

Q. When you said that you poked in at that one door and it was still pretty dusty, when you got outby had it cleared?

A. To the next door? It was still dusty in there, but it was breathable at least. The first door, it was just like it was on the track.

Q. Now, was your CO detector still on alarm there?

A. Yes. It went clear to failure.

Q. So at what point did it fail?

A. I think it done it when it first went off. Even after I went in the intake and I set there a little bit, back and forth by myself, after the men left, it never did quit beeping. And I had wiped it off then, at some time in there, and it showed failure.

Q. Okay. And did you shut it off or ---?

A. No.

Q. Just left it on because it was cooked?

A. Right.

Q. Okay. So then your men are in the intake escapeway and they travel out. Now, what did you do next?

A. Like I say, I thought to myself, I'll go up in there and see if I can get to them. I started --- I went up the same entry and the intake that we got to, so I started to go up through there. I went about a half a break and I got to thinking to myself, if I go, I'm going to be dead, too, from knowing that that detector went off.

Q. Sure.

A. And I knew what was in there, carbon monoxide. So I just went back to the phone and waited there.

Q. Now, what phone did you go to?

A. The one that I said I found coming down through there, you know, real close to that man door somewheres. I can't tell you where.

Q. That would be outby where the men went into Number Seven. So that would be around 37?

A. There's a phone close to that area in there somewhere, yes.

Q. And who did you call and what did you say?

A. When we first found the phone walking in through there or ---

Q. Yes.

A. --- after I stayed, you mean?

Q. When you first made your first phone call, the crew was still with you?

A. Yes. I called out and I said, we've had a mine explosion in here. I said, get mine rescue team here now. That one?

Q. Yes. How soon was that after the rush of air? I mean, ---.

A. Long enough for us to just walk down through there.

Q. Five minutes, ten minutes?

A. Five minutes maybe.

Q. And you got on that phone, and do you know who you talked to?

A. Not for sure. I just said something --- I said something bad has happened. I said, we've had an explosion in here. I said, get mine rescue team here.

Q. What was your call, outside, outside?

A. Yeah.

Q. Just to anybody?

A. Yeah.

Q. You don't recognize who that was?

A. Not for sure, no, because of panic, I mean.

Q. Right. Did they acknowledge your call?

A. Yeah.

Q. And what did they say?

A. They screamed --- I ain't sure what they were answering back, but they said, what's going on. I said, we've had some kind of an explosion in here. I said, get people in here now.

Q. Okay. And then you traveled with your men?

A. No.

Q. You stayed there?

A. That's what I say, I stayed --- this is before we got in the intake I'm telling you.

Q. Okay.

A.   And the men --- after I got my men going down the intake, I went back and talked to them a little bit. And what I said to them, I don't remember.

Q.   So you did make a second call at the same location?

A.   Yeah. I talked to them. I can't remember what all I said.

Q.   Okay. And then about how long were you there before someone met you?

A.   I don't know. Fifteen (15), 20 minutes, I guess.

Q.   You still had your SCSR off?

A.   Right. But the dust was settling pretty good on the track. And I was back and forth on the intake, too, where I could breathe. I went back in the intake to get fresh air.

Q.   Were you injured in any way yourself?

A.   No.

Q.   And were you sick from the CO?

A.   I got a bad headache.

Q.   Did you?

A.   And my wife made me go to the doctor on Tuesday of the second week, and I let them --- because I was having a funny feeling in my chest. And they did take blood and they did tell me that I had a high level of carbon monoxide in me.

Q.   So you stayed there until the other people got in the mine. Now, how did they get to you? Did they drive in?

A.   I think when the mantrip come in to get the men, that I think then when --- that Jeff Toler and Al Schoonover had rode in with him, and then they come on up there to me.

Q.   So how many men met you?

A.   Just two at the time.

Q.   It was Schoonover and ---?

A.   And Jeff Toler.

Q.   Toler. That's the safety director and the ---?

A.   Superintendent.

Q.   Okay.

A.   But I will say this, Wilfong had hollered at them to get blankety- blank down there with them. But then he had took them --- went ahead and took the men and went on outside. Because Jeff and them seen me sitting up there, so they came up there with me.

Q.   Now, the three of you are together. And what did you do then?

A.   Just walked up the track some and looked at the stoppings blowed-out and stuff. Jeff hollered outside then and told them to get fly boards and curtain and nails and extra self-contained rescuers and stuff in there. And we more or less, sat around there in the air, waiting on them to bring a mantrip in with that stuff.

Q.   So you noticed a lot of damaged controls?

A.   Yes.

Q.   Do you recall where they were damaged?

A.   I'm thinking --- if it went back as far as I'm thinking, that's back as far as 37 block.

Q.   Okay. We're going to --- if you could --- or would you, would you start from the outside, not from the outside of the mine, but from where you first noticed the first damage control and explain to us, if you can, how it was damaged, and work your way into the furthest point that you were. That would be --- I think you're going to have to start over on the far right. Or no, you can go on Exhibit Two, can't you. There were no damaged controls outby?

A.   That's the reason I say I don't know for sure where them doors I was because I think this is where the last stopping was blowed out, outby. So I ain't sure. That's what I was trying to get across to you a minute ago. I ain't sure exactly where the man doors are.

Q.   Now, were those doors open or are you just talking about ---?

A.   We crawled through a stopping with a man door in it.

Q.   Go ahead, explain it.

A.   I'm thinking that we found our first stopping blowed out here. I'll say here.

Q.   Now, was it completely blown out?

A.   Your edges were still there, the sidewalls, but pretty well your whole stopping's gone. The blocks ain't blowed out far, but they're just blowed out.

Q.   They were blown over?

A.   Yes, laying down there. And I can't remember if like it blew out one, maybe skip one or two, then blew out another one.

Q.   Now, when you say blown out, were they blown towards the intake or towards the track?

A.   Some of them I seen were blowed in this way.

Q.   You're pointing towards the ---

A.   The track.

Q.   --- toward the track?

A.   Right.

Q.   Okay. And you can't --- well, ---.

A.   But I can't remember what all walls it is, is what I'm telling you.

Q.   Okay. That's fine. But they were both directions, you're saying?

A.   Some of them I think was.

Q.   If you can --- well, go ahead.

A.   Do you want me to just ---?

Q.   Mark which ones, if you can remember, that were damaged.

A.   Let's see. I would say this one, probably this one. It looks like it might have skipped one or two, maybe three, then maybe blowed this one out.

Q.   So all of them weren't out?

A.   No. It's blow out a couple, skip one, blow out a couple, skip one or two, blow out a couple.

Q.   And the first one you marked was 48 crosscut?

A. I'm just guessing. That's what I'm saying, I can't remember.

Q. So around 48, 47?

A. Right. It might have even took this one out, but I couldn't see.

Q. Forty-three (43), 37 along the Number Four belt?

A. Right. The reason I knew some of these, we couldn't see this when we first walked out. This is after we stayed and ventilated some of this back up through there.

Q. Okay. And we'll just talk about from the Second Left switch. So you and the other two men then started to curtain up the ---?

A. Well, that's what I said, they waited until we got the curtain that was in there. We waited there and talked on the phone and I don't know what all we did talk about.

Q. Who was directing the rescuers? Who was in charge?

A. Jeff.

Q. Jeff was? And so he was pretty much telling you guys what needed done. Okay. Where did you start repairing the controls?

A. I think right here, at the 37 block.

Q. How did you do that?

A. By covering the perimeter. And we put blocks on the bottom of it 18 that remained.

Q. Spad or ---?

A. Spad them, the blocks in. And like I say, they go through there. And I can't remember where the phone is. But like I say, Jeff told me sit there, Jeff said, you sit here, you stay here.

Q. And you stayed?

A. Until we got through here, somewhere up in here, and it reventilated and I put up a couple curtains.

Q. So he told you to remain back in about what area? That would be around 37 ---?

A. Yeah, 37 or 38 block where the phone was.

Q. So you stayed there and they went inby and did what, now?

A. They were hanging curtains. And they got up here to another phone somewheres and hollered to me to come on up.

Q. And then you traveled back into the mine.

A. From where I was.

Q. Where you were.

A. I walked up the track. It was pretty clear then.

Q. It was?

A. I mean, you know, there was ---.

Q. About how much time has gone by now since the first --- since the explosion?

A. I'd say an hour maybe.

Q. An hour? So in an hour's time this kind of cleared?

A. Yeah.

Q. Do you remember what direction the air was going? Which way it cleared? Did it clear to the short circuit side or ---?

A.   I couldn't tell, because there wasn't that much air going up the intake either, just enough to barely --- it was pushing up slowly. So I'm going to say that my guess is just going both directions. Whatever you can squeeze over, maybe --- I knew I seen it blowed the return wall out here or there or somewhere in there.

Q.   So not only were there intake walls blown, but there were also some return walls out?

A.   Uh-huh (yes). I couldn't tell you how many. I just caught a glimpse of one or two of them.

Q.   Where do you think they were at, closer to ---?

A.   Around in here somewhere.

Q.   Could you mark those, if you would, and identify them?

A.   I might be wrong about this.

Q.   This is just the best you can --- you're doing very well. So you are marking it spad number 3848 and 3829 and 3828 and 3847. That would be the walls between those spad numbers. And those were return walls. And do you know --- you don't remember which way they were blown out?

A.   I couldn't tell you.

Q.   But they were out?

A.   I seen holes through them at least.

Q.   Okay.

A.   I can't say they were blowed out, but I seen holes through them.

Q.   Did you repair any over on that side?

A.   No.

Q.   Just this intake side. And now did you make your way to the First Left switch?

A.   Yes, that was the intake. I'm sure Jeff and them went up there a different way, but I went over into the intake and I went up through here.

Q.   Did everybody go into the Number Seven entry?

A.   Yes, I'm assuming after we got up to --- in here somewhere. I don't know where they went because, like I said, he told me to stay back and then he hollered at me. When he hollered at me ---.

Q.   How about marking that one in green?

Q.   Now, we're going to go from where you --- from One Left switch to where you made the jump into Seven and tried to go inby.

A.   I'm going to say whatever stopping it was --- the intake right here.

Q.   Okay.

A.   Do you want me to mark it?

Q.   Yes, please.

A.   I'll just call it the intake. There's some water holes in here. I might have crossed back and forth here and there, to get ---.

Q.   But you stayed in the intake side?

A.   Right. Right. And I'm going to guess that we got up to --- I'm going to say I think I made it up about right here.

Q.   And you're saying that's ---

A.   That's where Jeff and all was.

Q.   --- 56 crosscut of Number Four?

A.   I'm going to say yeah, I think that's about where ---.

Q.   So you got that far. Did you repair any controls?

A.   Yes. We put the curtains up.

Q.   Besides these ones. But the ones that were inby, One Left?

A.   No, just --- yeah. There was a stopping or two blowed out through here that they -- Jeff and them had hung curtains across.

Q.   And do you remember where those were?

A.   I can't remember.

Q.   How many would you say?

A.   Maybe two.

Q.   Two?

A.   Three at the most. This one right here, he told me to go find Vern back in here because Vern went back in ---.

Q.   You mean Vern Hofer?

A.   He said you go in and get Vern and take another curtain and hang in up.

Q.   Okay.

A.   Finally stopped and put a curtain up.

Q.   And what did they do? Do you know what they were doing?

A.   I don't know.

Q.   So they remained here. And what was the air like there?

A.   The last stopping I looked through here into the track you could see the yellow smoke just floating around through there real bad.

Q.   Yellow smoke?

A.   Uh-huh (yes).

Q.   And you smelled the same odor that you did before, the burning coal?

A.   Yeah.

Q.   Do you know if they had taken any readings?

A.   I do know that they brought their COs, four new ones in with them. And every time they took one out of the intake it went to failure.

Q.   So everything went over?

A.   Yes.

Q.   Do you know if --- what about methane? Do you remember if there were any methane readings?

A.   No.

Q.   There was no methane.

A.   I will say this, I think when I did look at my spotter after the first time I got in the intake, think it showed 0.2.

Q.   Where do you think you looked at it at?

A. Probably after I got in the intake here and went back and forth while I was talking to them on the phone. I did take it out and look at it, and it was showing 0.2.

Q. And you're pointing around 43 crosscut?

A. Well, wherever we got --- down here, wherever we went into the intake.

Q. Did you repair any --- you say you did repair some damage controls on your way out? Mr. Jones, on Exhibit One.

A. This is Two Right right here, me and Vern Hofer come down the intake. No, right here is Two. Here's Two.

Q. Okay.

A. And we was coming down through here.

Q. So you're traveling down the Number Seven and Eight entry?

A. We followed our intake wherever. We're watching our stopping. Wherever they was down here, we watched and seen those blowed out. When we get to this overcast, which is right there, I assume.

Q. And what overcast do you call it?

A. I don't know what they call it.

UNIDENTIFIED SPEAKER:
The mouth of Two Right.

BY MR. O'DONNELL:

Q. The mouth of Two Right?

A. So we get to right here and I show Vern, I said, that overcast right there has been damaged.

Q. How bad was the damage on it?

A. It was blowed clear over, not the underfire (phonetic), but the wall on top.

Q. You can put an arrow up there.

Q. Do you remember which way it was blown out?

A. It was blowed towards the return.

Q. Towards the return?

A. Right.

Q. And it was completely out --- what kind of --- what did you do there?

A. Like I said, you got your bottom wall, you had Omega blocks on top of it. So what did I do? There was a piece of curtain laying there. Me and Vern picked it up on the first overcast over here and we drug it over to there and we blocked it off. We got on there, a spad or two, and we put blocks on the bottom of it.

Q. Did you notice any difference in the air when you did that?

A. Oh, yeah. I knew all the air was short circuiting, it had to. It all had to go over and straight back outside. So I told Vern, I said, this is where all the air is going, straight over. So I put that up. By that time, Vern had looked back somewheres and seen them guys with their lights coming down, like I told you.

Q. And those were the other two men in the mine?

A.	Would have been Dick Wilfong and Jeff Toler. So me and Vern were there fixing to put that up. That's when they said all that fresh air is, if there's a fire burning, it's going to push the gas over top the fire and blow it again, so let's get the hell out of here.

Q.	Who told you that?

A.	I think Dick Wilfong.

Q.	Did you wait for them?

A.	Yeah. By the time we got back over in the intake, they was right there with us by then.

Q.	And how did you get out of the mine?

A.	Followed the intake escapeway the rest of the way.

Q.	And you walked the entire length?

A.	Yeah.

Q.	Did you at any time or any of the people that you were with don your SCSRs?

A.	No, because it was all fresh, clean air there.

Q.	Did you put it on at all, Owen?

A.	No.

Q.	What about the other guys?

A.	Yes. That's what I said a while ago, some of my men ---.

Q.	No, no. I mean, the other guy, Wilfong and those guys?

A.	No.

Q.	None of them put it on?

A.	Uh-uh (no). The air that we was breathing up there where we was at doing that, you could breathe. But I'm saying the carbon monoxide was setting the detectors off.

Q.	And do you recall how much that was?

A.	No. I don't know what they go up to before they go to failure.

Q.	While you were underground, was there any other contact that you made with anybody on the outside?

A.	Jeff Toler had talked with some people, but I don't know what he said.

Q.	Okay. Now, someone from the outside --- when you told them you had an accident underground, they, in turn, told you --- did they tell you anything else, just that ---?

A.	I told them to come in and look.

Q.	You told them what you were going to do? You told them you were evacuating; is that right?

A.	I told them that my men was in the intake headed out.

Q.	And you didn't see either Pat or John Boni at all?

A.	Uh-uh (no). They would have been --- Pat Boni would have been however long that beltline is, 4,000 feet, whatever it is, outby us.

MR. O'DONNELL:
Do you want to take a 5 ten-minute break?

134

SHORT BREAK TAKEN

MR. O'DONNELL:

I'd like to go back on the record. Doug, do you have any comments you'd like to make now or some questions?

MR. CONAWAY:

Yes. I've just got a few questions.

BY MR. CONAWAY:

Q.   You guys, how do you switch --- on the sections, how do you switch your --- do you do a hot seat change normally?

A.   Yes.

Q.   How long was your production activity down on One Left? Do you remember when the last shift that worked on One Left was, before you went in on Monday morning?

A.   I'm thinking that was on that Friday.

Q.   Friday. And you were down then Saturday?

A.   Sunday.

Q.   Sunday, and started back Monday.

A.   The weekend crew would have worked Friday.

Q.   But ordinarily, if they were working, you would have done a hot seat change --- you would have went in ---

A.   With the hoot owl.

Q.   --- with the hoot owl. Yes, if they would have started ---?

A.   They would have been in there at the sections and we would have switched.

Q.   You would have switched at the face?

A.   Yeah.

Q.   Do you recall --- on your type of detectors, do you know what type of detectors they were, what the name, what they were?

A.   I don't know. I never did.

Q.   Do you know what your alarm settings were on ---?

A.   How high they went?

Q.   Yes.

A.   I don't know. That's why I say ---.

Q.   They were just pre-set?

A.   I guess at some range. I just know they were, like I say, after I scraped the dust off of it finally, it showed failure.

Q.   Okay. You mentioned Omega blocks. Are they used --- you mentioned at the overcast. Are they used for stoppings at some times or ---?

A.   Yes.

Q.   So they're used a lot of places in the mine?

A.   Right.

Q. Not just for seals or ---?

A. Right. They're used for ---.

Q. Just ordinary --- your stopping line and so forth?

A. Right.

Q. When you felt the rush of air that you talked about, did you feel any heat with that?

A. A little.

Q. A little heat?

A. I felt some heat. And some of my men told me that they feel heat, too, so ---.

Q. Okay. And then you mentioned the smoke. You saw smoke, this was later, ---

A. Uh-huh (yes).

Q. --- as you got further up there and you looked back into the track entry?

A. Uh-huh (yes).

Q. And you said it was a yellow smoke?

A. To my eyes.

Q. To your eyes, it looked like yellow smoke. What about the dust? You're saying it was just --- initially it was just a blinding dust, but it was more rock dust, coal dust?

A. Yes. Whatever, yeah.

Q. Okay. Just ---?

A. Just it was so thick, you couldn't see.

Q. And everything was covered?

A. Right.

Q. The mantrip and everything was covered with dust?

A. Right.

Q. Do you recall if there was any electrical disruptions or did you lose any power or anything at any time?

A. I couldn't tell if the belt was running that morning on the way in or not, but I --- that's all I remember.

Q. You don't. If you remember, that's fine. If you don't, ---.

A. I don't.

Q. You mentioned that you made how many calls outside? Two calls outside?

A. I think. One to tell them that we've had an explosion.

Q. That was initially. And that was just within five minutes of ---?

A. Right.

Q. And then your second call was ---?

A. I can't remember what all was said, just talking to them and telling them that ---.

Q. Pretty much the same thing you said before?

A. You need to get people in here.

Q. Do you have any idea --- and I know times, you know --- but any feel for when Jeff Toler called outside and asked for fly boards and curtain and so forth? Do you have any feel what length of time had passed when that call was made?

A. After they came up to me?

Q. Yes.

A. Ten minutes maybe.

Q. After they approached you, ten, okay.

A. Yeah.

Q. You don't know who he talked to at that time? He was just hollering outside to somebody ---

A. Right.

Q. --- to bring the materials?

A. To make sure that Vern and Dick and them bring in fly boards and curtains and nails and tester spotters and extra self-contained self-rescuers.

Q. Sure. Any of the readings ---do you recall any --- you may have answered this, but I just want to make sure. You don't recall anybody at any time between Dick and the other guys that came in, Al and those guys, did anybody say any readings of CO or anything at any time? Did anybody mention their detectors? Were there alarms going off?

A. Not in the track entry.

Q. They stayed in the track entry?

A. We --- that's where we was. Because like I say, the dust settled ---

Q. Right.

A. --- quite fast where we was in the track entry.

Q. Okay.

A. But when we went in the intake, up through there, that's when they was going to failure.

Q. So their detectors, you're saying, were going to failure when they went over in the intake. And those were the guys that came in to assist and help you, ---

A. Right.

Q. --- their detectors?

A. Right. Because mine ---.

Q. Yours was gone?

A. Right. It done burned up I guess.

Q. When you say burned up, did the alarm --- do you think --- did the alarm just go off to the point to where you lost the battery or it just was reading failure?

A. Reading failure. I'm assuming that it was so high that it just burned that up. I mean, it wouldn't clear itself no more. Even in fresh air it wouldn't go back.

Q. When you looked at it physically, there was a reading on it, you're saying, that said ---

A. Failure.

Q. --- failure?

A. Yeah.

Q. Okay. And no one mentioned any other readings on the other detectors, but they did go off when you went over into the intake?

A. Right.

Q. They would get alarms?

A. Right.

Q. Where was the vehicle that Dick and those guys brought in, Owen? Where did they park the vehicle initially; do you recall that?

A. I think it was right there at the first stopping that blowed out.

Q. That would have been ---?

A. If I remember right, like I say, it was at 37 block.

Q. And that's where they parked their vehicle. And the vehicle stayed there the whole time?

A. Well, we did unplug the batteries on it.

Q. But you left it there? I mean, they didn't advance it --- as you advanced further on in, you did that on foot?

A. Right.

Q. Okay. Any reason why the vehicle stayed --- why did you walk out? I'm just curious.

A. Well, like I say, me and Vern was going in through there checking stoppings.

Q. Okay.

A. And I'm assuming that they got worried about that fresh air pushing that gas and probably figured we was better off to --- I'll tell you why, because you got that carbon monoxide that's in there, and they done unplugged the batteries on that mantrip, so you didn't want to ---.

Q. They didn't want an ignition source?

A. Right.

Q. That's why they left it and decided to walk out?

A. Right.

Q. When you made the first call outside --- and I just want to be clear. I mean, what I heard you say is you said the mine has exploded, get people in here, get us help right away, get somebody in here?

A. Right.

Q. That was your --- there's no question about that?

A. Right.

Q. One other thing, you were operating the mantrip?

A. Right.

Q. Your man bus was the one that they're closed on both ends and the middle is open for the operator?

A. Like I'm driving around here like this. The rail goes this way, ---

Q. Yes.

A. --- the driver is open, but your top is covered. You got a little gap in there about that far where your men sit looking out to the track.

Q. Sure.

A. But your --- towards the beltline side, that wall it's closed in. Just one way in and out.

138

Q.   Okay. And you were the operator?

A.   Yeah.

Q.   Okay.

MR. CONAWAY:

Joe, do you want to ---?

MR. O'DONNELL:

Okay. Thank you.

BY MR. O'DONNELL:

Q.   I just want to go back on a couple of the stopping questions. Now, you said the stoppings were blown out. What kind of block?

A.   Solid on the intake side.

Q.   They were solid. Were they four, six or eight-inch block; do you know?

A.   They were 12-by-8, I think, but they're --- they're solid, but they're hollow inside.

Q.   Okay. Now, you mentioned an Omega block that was down the track, and you kind of referred that it may have come from an area that was inby the mine.

A.   Well, there was some return stoppings on the other side that had been Omega blocks.

Q.   So you don't know where that may have come from, or do you?

A.   Not for sure. And there were some blocks that sit there right around our belt drive there somewhere, but I can't remember where, almost a whole pile of them laying there loose.

Q.   Okay. Did you happen to unplug your mantrip?

A.   No.

Q.   Your mantrip was still on. It was the outby one that you unplugged?

A.   Right.

Q.   Okay. Other than the ventilation changes that you made on the overcast, did you make any more on the way out?

A.   No. Everything from there the rest of the way out was intact.

Q.   Was intact, okay. So Owen, how long would you think you were underground from the time that you

       went in the morning, at six o'clock, until you got out?

A.   I'm going to guess something 'till 10:00.

Q.   Around 10:00?

A.   Yeah. Something 'till. I don't --- I can't --- I never did look at my watch that morning when we got out. I was glad to see daylight, though. I'll say that.

Q.   Did you play any role in the rest of the operation that transpired the rest of the day?

A.   No.

Q.   What did you do the rest of the day?

A.   Me and my men all just kind of stood there and walked around and stuff. And eventually they asked us to leave because --- the carbon monoxide was coming out so bad, that they asked us to leave. So we left, except the people they needed there.

Q.   Who asked you to leave?

A.   Some of the inspectors told us 16 to leave.

Q.   Okay. And did you leave the property then?

A.   Yes. I went to the Sago Church.

Q.   Okay. How familiar were you with any of the --- have you ever gone up to the Two Left?

A.   I have never made it up there. I helped drive the mains up through there.

Q.   So you were up --- you're talking about the mains towards the old Three Left?

A.   Before they even started the old Three Left. I helped finish the mains up. They had a super section up in there at the time. But then I've been on One Left ever since. So no, I wasn't up there ever again.

Q.   Did you ever examine up that way?

A.   No. All my walking has been on One Left.

Q.   What about methane liberations in the mine, did you ---?

A.   No. There's --- you might pick up .2, .4 here and there at your faces every once in a while, but nothing to ever worry you any.

Q.   Do you have any knowledge of increased levels of methane when they did mine the Three Left area?

A.   No, I did not.

Q.   Do you know who was in charge of building the seals in that area?

A.   I don't know, just outby bosses.

Q.   And do you know any of the people that were maybe involved in the construction?

A.   They call him Skip, but I can't think of his first name. He was one of the bosses that would have done that. I think maybe Jeff Snyder may have worked on it.

Q.   Is Jeff a supervisor?

A.   He was a section boss, but they put him to be an outby boss.

Q.   And who was Skip?

A.   He has been a contractor boss there for a long time.

Q.   Contractor boss? You mean there's contract miners that also work in the mine?

A.   Just the boss, just that boss.

Q.   But what about his crew?

A.   As far as I know, they was 24 Anker employees.

Q.   So there was a contract foreman, okay.

A.   And he might ---.

ATTORNEY MOORE:

    Skip is James Scott, for the record.

A.   I couldn't think of his name.

BY MR. O'DONNELL:

Q.   Okay.

A.   That's all I've ever called him.

Q.   Skip. Now, do you have any involvement, any idea of the construction of the seals?

A.   No. That's why I say I have no idea how they build them, what they was built out of or nothing.

Q.   Okay. We'll scratch that whole bunch of questions then. And you never examined in that area?

A.   No.

Q.   You never made it to the section; right?

A.   Right.

Q.   So there you made no examinations at all?

A.   No. The only thing I can tell you is I had my protector on on the way in.

Q.   Any time when you were mining anywhere in this mine, do you recall ever cutting into boreholes or wells or --- whether they were charted or uncharted?

A.   Not on our section, no.

Q.   Did you know of anybody that did? Was there any occasion that you had any knowledge of that?

A.   No.

Q.   Okay. Has anyone ever searched you for smoking articles?

A.   Yeah, I've been searched before.

Q.   And have you ---

A.   Yes.

Q.   --- observed anyone smoking --- have you ever observed anyone smoking underground?

A.   No.

Q.   When you've done smoke searches on your crew, have you ever found any?

A.   No. Some of the men do smoke, but they always leave it in their baskets or in their clothes.

Q.   Has anyone offered you anything or made a promise for you in exchange for your appearing here today?

A.   No.

Q.   Owen, do you have anything that you'd like to add that may be relevant to this investigation? Just take your time and say what you want.

A.   (Indicates no).

Q.   I have a few more training questions.

A.   Okay.

Q.   Do you remember when the last time is you had annual re-training?

A.   It wouldn't have been that long ago, but I can't remember when.

Q.   Was it this year?

A. This is the new year, so ---.

Q. 2005, '05.

A. I can't remember when, but we've had it.

Q. Okay. And do you remember what was covered in those training classes?

A. Your typical thing. They teach you how to don your rescuer each and every year and ---.

Q. You have hands-on training then?

A. Yeah. They show you --- every time you have your annual re-training, they go over that with you each time.

Q. Do you remember who the trainer was?

A. Al Schoonover.

Q. Al Schoonover. Okay. He's the safety director; right?

A. Right.

Q. And he signs your 5023?

A. (Indicates yes).

Q. And do you know if he did this time?

A. He gave us our little pink slip.

Q. Okay. And do you go over your evacuation plan during that training?

A. Well, we go over the maps and things and stuff, yeah, and then we do it --- I do it at work with the men, too.

Q. Who's the responsible person that's in charge of the evacuation; do you know?

A. I don't know.

Q. Do you know where the emergency firefighting materials are located in the mine?

A. Barricade supplies and such? 15 Yes, I do. What block, though, I can't remember. I'm thinking --- it's just outby where some of them stoppings were blowed out, but I can't remember what block for sure.

Q. Somewhere around 37 on Number Four belt, is that what you're saying?

A. Thirty-some (30-some) block I'm thinking.

Q. Is there a switch there with the material or ---?

A. No. They're stacked along the side of the---in the crosscut right by the track.

Q. Did they go over any of the procedures, what you do in case of fire or explosion during your annual re-training?

A. No.

Q. What about barricading?

A. No.

Q. Do they talk about the hazards associated with carbon dioxide or carbon monoxide?

A. Well, yeah. You kind of learn that when you don your --- they teach you what it's for, you know, they tell you that.

Q. What about your --- well, you said that they go over the escapeways and everything. But what about conducting escapeway drills?

A. The section foreman was the one in charge of that.

Q. And explain that.

A.	You're supposed to do it once every six weeks or whatever. And you walk your men out, a couple of your men, and you follow your intake escapeway to the outside, off your section.

Q.	And what section was that that you traveled out?

A.	What section was it? It would have just been the mains.

Q.	And you traveled both the primary and secondary?

A.	Yeah, yeah.

Q.	What about fire drills?

A.	Fire drills? In what way do you mean?

Q.	Do you conduct them or ---?

A.	Yeah, we simulate. The section boss does that, too, and he records it in his book, that you simulated a fire on a piece of equipment, teach your men how to fight fire.

Q.	What about first-aid training? Do they go over first-aid training?

A.	I 'm not understanding what you're saying there.

Q.	Do they cover first-aid in your annual re-training?

A.	Some. Some of it.

Q.	What about explosives?

A.	No.

Q.	Do you use explosives in the mine?

A.	No.

Q.	Do you know of any magazines or anything that are underground?

A.	No.

Q.	What about covering the roof control plan and the ventilation plan?

A.	The section bosses do that on the section.

Q.	Do you also do it as part of your annual re-training?

A.	Yeah, there's talks about it.

Q.	Did they go over any of the seal construction?

A.	No.

Q.	None of that. Do you think the training was good?

A.	Yeah. I mean, it teaches you what you need to know, I guess.

Q.	Do you think there's anything they need to add or cover?

A.	After this happened, since this has happened, I would say that all mines should learn --- teach their men how to barricade theirselves properly, to do whatever is possible to protect themselves from carbon monoxide.

BY MR. CONAWAY:

Q.	Just one thing. Owen, did you get the feeling --- you know, you had the initial, what you felt was an explosion. Did you have the feeling that there may be, you know, fires burning or --- I mean, just what was your impression, or did you --- did you have any idea what was taking place while you was there underground?

A.	I knew we had a methane explosion. But how big it was and what damage it done, no, I didn't know.

Q.   And you didn't know if it maybe was smoldering or burning or going, you didn't know that?

A.   Didn't know that.

Q.   Really no indication?

A.   Right.

Q.   Okay. So it's really just a big unknown then?

A.   Right.

Q.   You know what you felt, but the rest of it you weren't sure?

A.   Right.

Q.   Okay.

A.   I mean, you know you had the explosion, but you don't know what's burning or not.

Q.   Got you.

MR. O'DONNELL:

    Hank, do you have any clarifying questions?

ATTORNEY MOORE:

    No, I don't have any questions for him.

MR. KITTS:

    I have one clarification question.

BY MR. KITTS:

Q.   When you first called outside immediately after the explosion, which phone was that?

A.   It would have been the one where we come down along the track from --- the first one we come to, Sam, from our mantrip, the first phone that I come to along the track there.

Q.   So it was outby One Left switch?

A.   Yeah, it was outby One Left switch.

MR. KITTS:

    Okay. Thanks. I wasn't clear on that.

A.   Okay.

MR. O'DONNELL:

    Owen, we're going to take a quick five-minute break, and then we have a closing statement and we'll be finished.

A.   Okay.

MR. O'DONNELL:

    Is that okay with you?

144

A.   That's fine.

MR. O'DONNELL:
      Thank you.

SHORT BREAK TAKEN

MR. O'DONNELL:
      Back on the record.

BY MR. O'DONNELL:
Q.   Owen, I just have a couple more questions to ask. You mentioned 15 that there was a pallet of Omega block somewhere. Could you describe where they were, and if you can, mark it on our map for us?
A.   You want it on the big one?
Q.   That's fine.
A.   Here's the switch. I'm going to say they're either sitting here or here. Now, I might be wrong, but they was -- I do remember seeing them inby, so I want to say they're here or might even been here. don't think there's nothing there, but I can't remember.
Q.   So you're saying that they were in the --- between the Number Five and Number Six entry on the Four Main, 46 or 47 crosscut; is that right?
A.   Right.
Q.   And were they still on the pallet?
A.   No. They just stacked them there loosely, stacked on top of each other, laying there.
Q.   Now, you said you noticed them. Did you know that they were there before the accident or did you notice them after the accident?
A.   They was there before.
Q.   They were there before. So you ---?
A.   They'd been there for several days.
Q.   So you say you knew of them. But that day, did you observe them at all?
A.   No.
Q.   So you didn't see them at all that day, but you knew they were there?
A.   Right.
Q.   And they weren't used?
A.   Right. They was ---.
Q.   Okay.
A.   Blocks just stacked up there.
Q.   Okay. Good. What about when you went in the mine, did you have to energize anything? Did you ---?
A.   We did not, no. We was heading right straight for the section all the way.

Q. Do you know if the belts were running?

A. That's what I say, I can't remember, but I don't think they was. I don't think.

Q. Okay.

A. Because sometimes I look across to see if it is running. But I don't think it was.

Q. Who turns the belts on once you get into the section?

A. Well, you can either start them up from outside or ---?

Q. Yes.

A. The beltman would start it.

Q. Okay. Is he outside?

A. No. Your beltman is sometimes, just like I said, inside.

Q. Okay. Do you know who it was that day?

A. It would have been Terry Helms.

Q. Okay. All right. Here's another one. Have you received any kind of specialized training or extra training in examinations of the workplace?

A. Went to that mine academy school. I don't know, it's been a couple months ago. The federal mine inspectors went over how we're supposed to do everything the right way and everything.

Q. Do you recall when the training was? How long were you there?

A. Two days.

Q. Two days.

A. It was --- I think I took mine in August sometime, I think that's when I went.

Q. And do all the foremen get sent to the school?

A. They was sending them all, fire bosses and all the foremen, yes, which is a good thing from the company.

Q. Owen, what do you think --- just your opinion, what do you think caused it?

A. I would say possibly a gas well, you know, where they're drilling. And you mine close to gas wells. Everybody knows coal mines does that. Maybe there was a leak come up through the bottom, down through the top even. I got two ideas. Either lightning hit the steel pipe, run down and ignited it or you had a roof fall in there. And there's sandstone in those mines, and a piece of rock could have fell and hit a roofbolt plate. And there's a large screen that they bolt up in there to protect the walkers through the intakes, and that wire could have had a roof fall. You know, the wire screen could have hooked on a rock or on a roofbolt or something and possibly done it. That's my only ideas.

Q. I figured I'd ask you. Why not; right?

A. Yeah.

ATTORNEY CONAWAY:

We don't have any questions, Owen. We appreciate you coming here today and giving us your testimony. And we can only hope that through that that we'll be able to prevent something like this from happening again.

146

A.   Me, too.

BY MR. MOORE:

Q.   Owen, you were asked earlier about what you did when you came out of the mine. And was there --- when you came out of the mine, did you meet with a state inspector or federal inspector to talk about what you all had done in the mine?

A.   Federal inspectors took us into Jeff Toler's office immediately and said, sit down there. They said, we ain't here to lecture you. We want to know what or where you all made it to and what you done exactly in the mines, how far you made it in and what exactly you done with the ventilation.

MR. O'DONNELL:

Owen, on behalf of MSHA, I want to thank you for appearing and answering the questions today. Your cooperation is very important to the investigation as we work to determine the cause of the accident. And we ask you ot to discuss your testimony with any person who may have already been interviewed or who may be interviewed in the future. This will ensure that we obtain everyone's independent recollection of the events surrounding the accident. After questioning other witnesses, we may call you if 14 we have any other follow-up questions that we feel that we may need to ask. If at any time you have additional information regarding the accident that you'd like to provide us, please contact us at the contact information that we gave you, that number provided to you. The Mine Act provides certain protections to miners who provide information to MSHA, and as a result, are treated adversely. If at any time you believe that you've been treated unfairly because of your cooperation in this investigation, you should immediately notify MSHA. If you wish, you may now go back over any answer that you have given during this interview. And you may also make any statement that you would like to make at this 15 time. Again, I want to thank you for being here, Owen. Take care.

A.   You, too.

ATTORNEY MOORE:

Before you get off the record, Owen, you have a right to get a copy of the transcript that the court reporter prepares. Do you want a copy?

A.   Yes, I'd like to have that.

ATTORNEY CRAWFORD:

Submit a written request to MSHA, and we'll do that --- to the address that's stated on the card.

A.   Okay.

MR. O'DONNELL:

Okay. Thank you again.

A.   There is one statement I would like to make.

MR. O'DONNELL:

Go ahead. Back on the record.

A.   That I would like to see in all the mines in the whole United States or whatever, that they got extra apparatuses on the sections for the men and close enough thereafter all the way to your outside so a man could at least crawl and get to a new one, if he had to, just in case 23 something like this ever happens again, within every 500 or 1,000 feet of each other, have new ones or good ones sitting there. That's my only request.

MR. O'DONNELL:

It's a good one, too. Thank you.

SWORN STATEMENT

CONCLUDED AT 1:36 P.M.

Resource for Owen Jones Transcript: WV Office of Miners' Health Safety & Training
1615 Washington St. East, Charleston, WV 25311-2126

Viper Mine Rescue Unit Member Cannot Shake Memory of Sago

More than a month after the January 2, 2006 explosion at Sago No. 1 Mine in Tallmansville, West Virginia, a rescue unit member talks about recovering the 12 dead miners. Viper Mine located in Central Illinois responded with a rescue unit following the deadly explosion. Viper Mine is owned by the same company as Sago Mine.

Brett Bushong, 26, E.M.T. and trained volunteer fire fighter was one of the responders. More than a month later memories of the dead miners is difficult to shake. His impression of the miners, huddled together, some sitting up, one miner with his hands together in prayer, giving the appearance they are on break and they would resume work shortly.

Rigor Mortis had set in by the time the miners were found. They felt cold to the touch. Terry Hellms, the fireboss, died from impact of the explosion and sole survivor, Randal McCloy, was within moments, if not hours, of dying when found.

Notes written by these miners to family members were found by this unit. They did not read the notes but kept them private out of respect for the dead miners and their families.

The Viper Rescue Unit was not a part of the miscommunication which played an additional tragic role in this mine disaster where family members believed for more than three hours 12 of the miners were alive when officials knew the truth.

Bushong reported all the miners died at peace.

<u>Aracoma, Alma No. 1 Mine accident, Logan, West Virginia</u>

Fire In The Hole

"Every Mine Law Has Been Written With the Blood of Miners"
Nick Rahall, January 21, 2006, at the site of the Alma No. 1 Mine

Author's note: January 19, 2006, Logan County, West Virginia Melville, Aracoma, Alma No. 1 Mine. We have not even begun to deal with the Sago mine disaster which occurred this January 2 resulting in the death of 12 of our miners; barely 18 days have passed and already another mine disaster in the West Virginia coalfields. The latest disaster resulted in the death of two miners in Logan County. Graves of Sago miners are still mounds of fresh dirt, the flowers have not even had time to wilt. Those families are just beginning the grieving process, but this scene is playing out again, this time in Logan County. Ones left behind in Logan County will now share the endless days and nights of suffering and longing with those left behind at Sago. Coal mine communities are families and we are all hurting.

I am surrounded by coal mine communities one hour plus from both of these mine sites. To my north is Sago, to my south is Melville in Logan County.

Massey Energy's Aracoma Alma No. 1 Mine
Bandmill Hollow

"I am a roof-bolter for Alma mine. I could hear poppin' and crackin' sounds, you could see flames everywhere, the smoke was thick and black and men were yelling. Yes, I was scared. I believe we were all scared. If it had not been for my boss pulling me back and away, I don't know what would have happened to me. Now, all I can do is sit. I keep thinking could I have done more to save those 2 men? Could I have yelled louder? What else could I have done to save those men? We are a family but I can't go back there to work. I can't go back in the mines. When we reached the portal, we took off our hats, bowed our heads and prayed." That is what Joe Rose, a young miner at Alma No. 1 mine told a reporter for a Charleston, West Virginia, television station. The interview aired late Saturday night. On the same day the bodies were recovered, some 44 hours after the fire broke out on the beltline in Alma No. 1 mine.

In the same report, Joey's wife, who is five months pregnant, told the reporter she does not want her husband to return to mining.

At 5:36 p.m. on Thursday evening, January 19, 2006, an alarm sounded in the Aracoma Alma No. 1 mine. The carbon monoxide monitor located approximately 10,000 feet from the entrance of the mine set the alarm off signaling trouble. The conveyor belt that

150

carries coal to the outside had caught on fire. Twenty-one miners were inside. The terrain was rough, but nineteen escaped.

Authorities reported the fire started where a side conveyor belt meets the main line that brings the coal to the outside. Haskell Shepherd, a repairman on the overnight shift stated there had been problems before but nothing as serious as this, but like he said, everything is bound to tear up now and then. But another detrimental fact in this case, the belt carrying the coal to the outside also doubled as the fresh air-intake. This simply means the Alma No. 1 mine used its conveyor belt to draw fresh air to the miners at the working face. The face is the area where coal is being mined. In case a fire occurs like the one here, the fire on the belt is carried directly to where the miners are working along with dangerous gases. In emergencies this could hamper or debilitate miners from exiting the area. The plus side seems to be on the coal operator's side. Massey Energy had received special approval in August 2000 to operate outside normal mine safety standards through a "petition for modification." Only one entry and return required. This means a coal company using the longwall method of mining may quickly develop sections and extract coal. The Alma No. 1 mine operated a longwall machine in the mines where the fire broke out.

On this particular cold, dark, rainy Thursday evening, an alarm signaled "trouble ahead." It is reported one of the miners called on the mine phone and told control center they needed help. One crew of miners who were working in a different section made it out safely. Another crew of 12 were told to move toward the exit. The crew boarded the mantrip and started out when they ran into trouble and had to disembark. They dropped to their knees, put on their self-rescuers and formed a human chain crawling towards the outside. Ten of the miners in the second crew made it out safely, but two were lost, somehow they had gotten left behind. The other ten miners did not know two miners were left behind because the visibility was so poor. It was reported when the 10 miners reached safety, two attempted to re-enter the mine to search for the two miners but the intensity of the heat and the smoke turned them back. One of the miners who escaped the fire to the outside, a young man, told a CNN reporter the smoke was so thick and black you could not see with your miner's light.

Rescue efforts began but it was 11 p.m. Thursday night before the first team could enter the mine because of the intensity of the fire, smoke and dangerous gases. Five and one-half hours had already passed. Alma No. 1 mine is described as a very large mine encompassing 6 or 7 miles through the sections of mined out coal.

Governor Manchin immediately left for the site of the mine disaster. Family and friends of the two missing miners were huddled together in the Bright Star Freewill Baptist Church. That is where the governor went to be with the family members to watch, wait and pray. At least 20 rescue teams were on the scene from four different states.

By 10:30 Friday morning the fire remained a major factor slowing down any rescue efforts. The fire had spread. Workers had to switch gears from rescue workers to firefighters trying to contain the fire. The fire appeared contained in the afternoon of January 20, and rescue efforts again turned to locating the missing miners. Some had ideas of where the miners were located, but the black smoke was still thick. It filled the areas they were trying to search; visibility was low.

Jesse Cole, who works for MSHA as district manager, was coordinating rescue efforts with Doug Conaway, director of the state office of Miner's Health, Training and Safety, told the waiting public, fresh search teams have entered the mine to set curtains which would help direct the airflow.

On Friday afternoon an ounce of good news overshadowed the dark, dreaded feelings people were beginning to experience. Officials reported air, coming out of the six inch hole which had been drilled near the site of the fire, had carbon monoxide concentration below 1,000 parts per million. Jesse Cole said 1,200 parts per million is considered the "imminent harm" level. By Friday night around 9 p.m. carbon monoxide had dropped to less than 800 parts per million.

Two women widowed on January 2, 2006, by the Sago Mine disaster drove to Melville to the Bright Star Freewill Baptist Church to comfort and pray with the waiting families on Friday evening.

A media frenzy was once again in operational mode in a small coal mining community in West Virginia. According to Governor Manchin, the media was much more respectful, for the most part, to the families of the missing miners this time.

Still no miners had been located by midnight Friday night, marking more than 30 hours. Finally, at least rescue teams were able to devote their time to searching for the miners, but 24 hours had been lost to intense fire and dangerous levels of carbon monoxide. The six inch hole drilled down to where they thought the miners were located brought no response from the miners tapping on the drill nor when a camera and microphone were dropped down. Water was poured down the hole and a foam used to help extinguish fires.

Authorities refused to release names of the missing miners for a period of time but in the small community where the mine is located it didn't take long to figure out who was not accounted for.

At least 50 rescue workers were on the scene by late Friday night, but early Saturday morning safety expert Jesse Cole reported the fire had erupted again and this time they realized the seam of coal was burning. The closeness of the space was keeping rescuers from entering key locations that needed searched. Intense heat and heavy smoke kept the teams from advancing beyond the burning conveyor belt. More problems arose hampering rescue efforts; the fire weaken the walls of the mine and roof cave ins became a hazard.

Hopes were beginning to fade.

The bittersweet history of coal mining looms large in Logan County. Alma No. 1 mine is on the outskirts of historic Blair Mountain. Blair Mountain is the site of the historic battle between miners attempting to unionize under the leadership of John L. Lewis in 1921 and coal operators with help from mine guards, many known as Baldwin-Felts Agents. A young, 28 year old, Bill Blizzard led the march of the miners to Blair Mountain. Later, he was tried for treason. John L. Lewis assumed the leadership role of United Mine Workers in 1919. Massey Energy's Alma No. 1 mine is non-union.

According to documentation by MSHA, this mine was cited for more than 90 violations in 2005, and more than 100 in 2004.

Close to 40 hours into the rescue efforts on Saturday morning there was still no word on the missing miners. It was a typical January day from where I worked, a little over an hour away from Melville. I imagined the dark cloud hanging over the Bright Star Freewill Baptist Church at this troubled time. People outside the portals prayed for the return of the two men.

Governor Manchin remained on the scene for the duration. Senator Jay Rockefeller and House of Delegate member, Nick Joe Rahall joined the Governor. Senator Robert C. Byrd stayed in Washington to prepare for the congressional hearings scheduled to began on Monday, January 23, 2006, regarding the Sago Mine Disaster.

It is a well known fact in these cases that time is the enemy. The spreading flames would suck up all the good air.

A Governor, looking strained and down-hearted, spoke to the media and the general public at 12:50 p.m. on Saturday. A heavy burden lay on his shoulders. The families were given updates well ahead of the media and the public, a lesson learned at Sago. The Governor began by requesting prayers for the two miners and their families. He said the families were holding strong. He thanked the public for the outpouring of love and support through food and other acts of kindness. He then officially released the names of the miners so prayers could be directed specifically towards these two men: Don Israel Bragg, 33 years old; wife, Delorice; 2 children, Billy and Ricky. The family makes their home in Accoville. Don has 15 years of mining experience, 5 years at the Alma No. 1 mine. Bragg was called "Rizzle" by friends and family.

Ellery "Elvis" Hatfield, 47 years old; wife, Freda G.; 4 children. The family makes their home at Simon. Elvis has 12 years of mining experience, 5 years at the Alma No. 1 mine. * Freda told the governor Elvis had told her so much about the mine she felt as if she knew everything about it. They were planning a trip for Freda into the mines in the near future.

The two deceased miners were close friends. They started in this mine together. Their bodies were found close together directly behind the fire.

The governor was asked if Massey Energy officials were on hand. He responded, "no" not while he was there. Later, news reports revealed Don Blankenship, CEO of Massey was present in the church when the bad news came.

The two miners were found about 4:50 p.m. after the fire had cooled down enough for rescue teams to search immediately behind the area on fire. They had been in heavy smoke.

4:57 p.m. Saturday, January 21, 2006
The tragic scene witnessed again with family members coming out of the church in tears. They were hopeful even after 48 hours. Some thought they could find a place to hide away from the fire the size of a football field.

Manchin hugs Linda Curry of Chapmansville
Photo: Courtesy of Logan Banner

Press conference January 21, 2006 5:07 p.m.

Gov. Joe Manchin

For over 45 hours we have been together with these families. We did not have the outcome we were hoping for, two brave miners have perished. We are supporting these families. That is the role we want to play at this time.

During the last three weeks I have spent over 85 hours in churches. The suffering and pain is more than any person should have to endure. This has got to stop. We are going to change. We have the investigation going on at Sago; 12 miners at Sago and now here; 14 families whose lives have changed forever. If I have the power to change things, I want to change things to make sure no family ever has to go through this again.
Monday, I will introduce two pieces of legislation.
1 – Rapid response
2 – Electronic tracking – we have technology, and we are going to use it.
3 – Oxygen reserves – mandate oxygen reserves in the mines at various locations

Tuesday, I will go to Washington D.C., and I will be with my representatives. We are going to work to make changes in West Virginia.
I can't tell you the pain we have. I can't express the sorrow I have for the Bragg family and Hatfield family. This is what makes West Virginia different. We are hurting bad as much as anyone can hurt, but if we stick together, we can make it through. We are in total support mode.
These two men who perished in this mine, I feel a part of, and the 12 miners at Sago, they will not have died in vain. Their families can look back and say my dad helped make this change. We are going to commit and make this change as quickly as humanly possible in West Virginia.
All the tough jobs we take on in West Virginia to make America strong, I make this commitment to you, that I will see that this does not happen again.
I want to thank you all for the prayers; we felt them. The families felt those prayers. Your support is truly appreciated.
Thank you and God bless each and every one of you. Our prayers and love are with the families.

It was extraordinary to be in the Bright Star Freewill Baptist Church when the news came. There was so much crying. They were torn apart. I was torn apart. After about an hour, there was a coming together. Their healing is spiritual; the legend, the danger, the saga of working in a coal mine.

What is on my mind at this time is that we had two of these accidents in such a short period of time. There is something here called "coal" and no one has paid much attention to this until now. The delegates who met in Sago yesterday are committed to making changes. We can make coal safe. I think there is going to be an enormous growth in coal mining. We can not solve the oil problems so we have to rely on coal. There has to be changes.

You can talk easily to someone on the moon, but you cannot talk to a miner 1,000 feet away to help a miner by drilling a hole down to where he is located.

Coal mining is going to be changed forever. We will do that through federal laws. We are dependent on coal.

I talked with a mother here who was sobbing because her son is going to work in the coalmine. We don't want her to feel that way. That is not all going to be easy.

These people here are human beings and when you see them go through what these people have gone through, you are never the same.

House of Delegate Member Nick Rahall

Our thoughts and prayers are with the families. Forty-eight hours have passed.

Thanks to the rescue teams for putting their lives on the line to save others. Doug Conaway and Jesse Cole, two organizations have worked closely together.

We can not continue to allow these tragedies to continue. We must give MSHA what they need to do their jobs.

Every Mine Law is Written with the Blood of Coal Miners.

Families and friends of the dead miners are pouring out of Bright Star Freewill Baptist Church. They now must go prepare to bury their dead and begin the long painful process of grieving.

Ellery "Elvis" Hatfield's funeral was Friday, afternoon, January 27, 2006 at the Long Branch Freewill Baptist church at 2 p.m. Rev. Lonnie Blankenship and Pastor James Vance of Bright Star Freewill Baptist Church of Melville officiating.

When Don Bragg was laid to rest on Sunday, January 29, 2006, a caravan of more than twenty coal trucks covered in black ribbons and wreaths lined up along US 119 as the funeral procession went by as a tribute to Don Bragg and his family.

Bragg is one of 14 West Virginia coal miners killed in mining accidents during the month of January 2006. His funeral was held at the Man High School field house to accommodate the overflow crowd. Signs were held with messages such as "W. Va. Loves Our Coal Miners."

<u>Two Boone County Miners Die in West Virginia Mines Bringing Death Toll to 16 During the First Month of 2006</u>

Two more West Virginia miners died in separate mining accidents in Boone County, West Virginia. Long Branch Energy's Number 18 Tunnel miner was the scene of a death before noon on Wednesday. A wall support broke loose killing the underground miner. Killed was Edmund Vance, 46, a miner with 28 years experience. "He was everyone's best friend," Mrs. Vance said.

Massey Energy's Black Castle Surface mine was the scene of the second death when a bulldozer operator hit a natural gas mine which sparked a fire. Killed was Paul Moss, a 58-year-old miner at the Elk Run's Black Castle strip mine in Drawdy. Paul had 15 years mining experience.

Every mine law is written with the blood of coal miners.

West Virginia Lawmakers pass mine safety legislation:

On January 26, 2006, three weeks following the explosion at Sago mine resulting in 12 deaths of West Virginia miners Governor Joe Manchin signed new safety law for miners on Thursday, January 26, 2006. Law passed unanimously.

Mandated:
- ➤ Emergency communicators
- ➤ Tracking devices
- ➤ Extra air supplies stored underground
- ➤ Hot line set up

March 04, 2006
Article in The Charleston Gazette: Mine safety

Resolve fading?

IT HAS been two months since the Sago explosion caused the deaths of 12 underground miners, and a month since subsequent coal deaths.

Gov. Joe Manchin became a national hero by sitting with grieving families, then rushing back to Charleston and to Washington to push for mine safety improvements. Lawmakers responded. West Virginia now requires additional oxygen supplies, wireless communications and miner tracking devices in deep mines. Airtight survival chambers were added as an option.

But already, the sense of urgency seems to be fading.

Manchin has given mine owners more time to install the rescue gear and allowed them to delay submitting plans for how they will install wireless communications and miner tracking systems. The governor will appoint a labor-industry task force to work out concerns about the technology. That report is due in 90 days, and some time after that, Acting Mine Safety Director James M. Dean is to start requiring the devices. Months will pass before improvements are in place. Courtesy of the Charleston Gazette

Updates

<u>West Virginia Health and Safety Director resigns post:</u>
Director Doug Conaway announced last week that he plans to leave that post and take a job in the private sector after more than 20 years in mine safety enforcement. Conaway agreed to stay on until Manchin picked a successor.

<u>Sago Mine scheduled to re-open:</u>
The Mine Safety and Health Administration has finished its underground investigation at the Sago Mine, clearing the way for owner ICG to begin operations. International Coal Group announces two months after the Sago mine explosion occurred the mine is scheduled to reopen sometime during the week of March 13, 2006. The section where the explosion was thought to occur will remain off limits. The mine will re-open beginning with two shifts. It has not been determined the cause of the explosion.

<u>Sago Survivor, Randal McCloy, making progress:</u>
Anna McCloy, wife of Sago mine survivor Randal McCloy, spoke with the media during the first week of March 2006, two months following the explosion where 12 miners died. Anna reports Randal is making progress. He remains in a rehabilitation center where he is receiving treatment. Doctors say his recovery is remarkable. He can move with assistance, eat and breathe on his own. "It's like a resurrection basically. He's a new person, a different person" Anna tells reporters. When questioned whether or not Randal remembers the accident, Anna says that they do not know and she does not press him to talk about it. If he wants to talk, I listen but I do not initiate it. She is worried he will become depressed which could slow down his recovery. Her job now is to get him home to his two children.

<u>W. Va. Governor calls for "mine safety stand down" in wake of two more miners' deaths:</u>
Governor Joe Manchin's response to the latest accidents was swift and decisive. Manchin called for the coal industry to cease production and go into a mine safety stand down. Coal production is put on pause until a safety check can be performed before each shift – mine operators are required to review mine conditions, go over safety checklists and designated escapes routes.

<u>Public Hearings on Sago rescheduled from March to May:</u>
Sago Mine disaster hearing to start May 2, 2006

W. Va. Governor announced public hearings on Sago Mine disaster will begin May 2, 2006 instead of on the original date of March 14. Miners' family members requested a delay.

"It's a complex investigation and, as the miners' families have said, it's more important to determine the facts carefully and thoroughly than to act before all the facts are in," said Davitt McAteer, Manchin's special adviser on mine safety.

West Virginia Wesleyan College in Buckhannon will be the location of the hearings. J. Davitt McAteer will moderate the panel which will include federal investigators, labor and coal industry officials.

Hawks Nest Tunnel Tragedy

Another Tragedy in the Coalfields of West Virginia
Fayette County, West Virginia 1930-31 (Great Depression Era)

Author's note: Arthur Stull of Mount Nebo, Nicholas County, West Virginia, was one of the tunnel workers who lived many years after completion of Hawks Nest Tunnel. He suffered all those remaining years from respiratory complications, according to his daughter, Phyllis Stull Armes. She told me, "Every breath he drew was labored." Arthur had a portion of his lung removed and died from respiratory complications. He received no compensation for this illness from which he suffered until his death. This story is dedicated to Arthur Stull and the other tunnel workers who died as a result of working on the tunnel at Hawks Nest.

Many of the migrant workers were buried in my town of Summersville, West Virginia.

Chilling Facts

- Characterized as one of the nation's worst industrial disasters.
- Hawks Nest Tunnel began in June 1930, completed December 1931, moving forward at 250 to 300 feet per week.
- Major portion of excavation completed in just 18 months – two year contract.
- 3.8 miles of drilling through 99.44% pure silica, 32-36 feet in diameter.
- Black migrants from the South made up the largest percent of workforce.
- A few locals (whites) were employed mainly working as foremen and drillers.
- Local blacks could not tolerate the horrible treatment by the contractor.
- Living conditions dreadful - Segregated camps were overcrowded.
- Shootings, stabbings were common.
- Workers were rousted out of camp at the beginning of shifts, often beaten by company hired bullies.
- Hawks Nest Tunnel workers were specifically excluded when West Virginia finally made silicosis compensable under Workmen's Compensation
- Untold number of workers buried in Summersville, Nicholas County, West Virginia (my hometown) in unmarked graves .

Significant Facts:

*Purpose of tunnel – to divert water of the New River through Gauley Mountain over a drop of 162 feet.

*Hydroelectric power provided to Alloy beginning January 1937.

*Maximum power generated - 103 megawatts.

*More than 200 lawsuits had been filed by spring of 1933 against Rinehart & Dennis Company. All the suits charged that men were either dead or dying because they had worked in the tunnel.

*The first lawsuits, tried in the spring of 1933 were settled out of court after a disagreement. The lawyers representing 300 men, compromised upon payment of a total sum of $130,000. As the lawyers had undertaken to try the cases upon a 50 percent contingent basis, they pocketed one-half of the total after paying court costs of $1,000. This left a very small sum to be divided among a large number of men.

*Mrs. Jones, mother of three sons who died in the tunnel, Shirley 17, Owen 21, Cecil 23 and her husband, became suspicious when she saw the amount of sediment left in tub when she washed their clothes. Before, Shirley, her youngest son, died of the disease, he told his mother to have him opened up to see that the tunnel work killed him, file a suit and use the money to buy herself a little house

*The defense called on medical witnesses, Dr. Henry K. Pancoast, an expert roenologist and respected pioneer in silicosis research. He interpreted two of the plaintiff's chest x-rays for the jury. In his expert opinion, the shadows in Johnson's lungs indicated advanced tuberculosis.

Author's Note: As I drove around the twists and turns of Gauley Mountain late in the afternoon on February 23, 2005, a fog hung lightly in the air. I twisted and turned my jeep around the hairpin curves slowly, winding up the steep mountain towards Hawks Nest, site of the Hawks Nest Tunnel tragedy, a tragedy characterized as one of the nation's worst industrial disasters. This tragedy occurred in the early 30s but has remained shrouded in secrecy to this day.

My thoughts were of Jack Pitckett, subject of Albert Maltz's simple, but tragic story about the black tunnel worker he nearly ran over in the tunnel underneath the railroad in Gauley Bridge and ended up giving a ride to Weston. On that rainy, foggy evening on the trip from Gauley Bridge, West Virginia, to Weston – a distance of 100 miles over mountain roads Maltz described as curvy as snakes on the run, up one mountain five miles and down the other side fives miles – Jack Pitckett became to Maltz and the rest of the world "Man on the Road."

As I travel up Gauley Mountain, I retell Maltz's story to myself, visualizing Maltz on the driver's side of the old car, swerving around the curves, giving it the gas going up the steep terrain, then on and off the brakes on the downside on the old Weston-Gauley Turnpike Road. I see Jack Pitckett sitting on the passenger's side described by Maltz as a big burly man about 35, not fleshy but big-boned with wide nostrils and big horse teeth, chipped on the ends and stained with tobacco. He carried a brown paper poke which he laid in his lap after climbing into the front seat of the vehicle.

Maltz could easily describe his old car, the dangerous road, the view of the coal camp houses with dim oil lights barely visible through the rain, the burning coal slag piles, but words could not describe Jack Pitckett. When asked a question, Pitckett would utter a word or two and sink back down into a recess within himself. His eyes held a vacant

160

stare. For almost four hours the two sat together in silence. Once along the way, Pitckett made noise – he was seized with a coughing fit that shook him from head to toe and lasted for what seemed like an eternity, shaking his body and trying to hack something up. He was not successful. Maltz described the sounds made by this fit of coughing as a scraping sound as though cold metal were being rubbed on the bone of his ribs.

Maltz was curious. What was troubling this man to the depths of his soul and what was his ailment? He wanted to get it out.

When they arrived at Weston, Maltz invited his passenger in for a cup of coffee. Besides feeling sorry for him, he wanted to make one last stab at finding out what was inside this tortured shell of a man.   The coffee came and Maltz offered Pitckett a sandwich from the diner. Pitckett smiled for the first time and took him up on the offer. In his story, Maltz says that the smile was like a corpse beginning to stir. When the feast of coffee and a sandwich were nearly over, Pitckett looked at Maltz and asked, "Will you do me a favor?" Maltz was wondering what was in store next for him. Maltz replied, "Yes, if I can".

Pitckett slowly unbuttoned his clean, blue work shirt and there carefully pinned to his long handle underwear with a large safety pin was a letter neatly folded. He asked Maltz to rewrite the letter to his woman.

Letter written by Jack Pitckett to his wife.

My dere wife –

I am awritin this yere leta to tell you somethin I did not tell you afore I left from home. There is a cause to wy I am not able to get me any job at the mines. I told you hit was from work abein slack. But this haint so. Hit comes from the time the mine was shut down an I worked in the tunel nere Gauley Bridge where the govinment is turnin the river inside the mountain. The mine supers say they wont hire any men war worked in that tunel. Hit all comes frum that rock thet we all had to drill. Thet rock was silica and hit was most all of it glass. The powder from this glass has got into the lungs of all the men war worked in thet tunel thru their breathin and this has given to all of us a sickness. The doctors wirt it down for me. Hit is siliosis. Hit makes the lungs to git all scab like and then it stops the breahin.

Bein as our hom is a good peece from town you aint heerd about Tom Prescott and Hansy MCCulloh having died two days back. But wen I' heerd this I went to see the doctor.

The doctor says I hev got me thet sickness like Tom Prescott and thet is the reeson wy I am coughin sometime. My lungs is agittin scab like. There is in all ova a hondred men war have this death sickness from the tunel. It is a turible plague becus the doctor says this wud not be so if the company had gave us masks to ware put a right fan sistem in the tunel.

So I am agoin away becus the doctor says I will be dead in about fore months.

I figger on gettin some work maybe in other parts. I will send you all my money till I can't work no mohr. I did not want I should be a burdin upon you all at hum. So thet is wy I hev gone away. I think wen you doan here frum me no mohr you orter go to your grandmaws up in the mountens at Kilney Run. You kin live there an she will take keer of you an the young one.

I hope you will be well an keep the young one out of the mines. Doan let him work there. Doan think hard on me for agoin away and doan feel bad. But wen the young one is agrowed up you tell him wat the company has done to me.

I reckon after a bit you shud try to git you anotha man. You are a young woman yit.

Your loving husband,
Jack Pitckett.

162

Maltz finished recopying the letter, handed it to Pitckett who folded it neatly, pinned it carefully to his underwear with a large safety pin, said, "thank you." He disappeared into the rainy night.

This story had played out in my mind by the time I pulled into the Hawks Nest Tunnel State Park overview. I got out of my Jeep with my camera and began walking the path to the edge of the cliff, halfway, I noticed a plaque placed there by the National Park Association in 1987, acknowledgement some 50 years after the date of this terrible disaster.

According to historical records, the story of unsafe working conditions in the tunnel broke on May 30, 1931, when the Fayette Tribune, the local paper, had a splash on the terrible conditions in the tunnel. However, a court "gag order" put an abrupt halt to any follow up on the story.

In the summer of 1934 the Daily Worker (The *Daily Worker* was a newspaper published in New York City by the Communist Party) established a relief fund for 91 people dying in the abandoned village of Vanetta – a camp for workers.

Map of Vanetta

Publicity to raise funds for the sick tunnel workers stated the community was 14 miles away from the relief office – the people would get up at 4 in the morning and drudge through the deep snow to get to the office in Gauley Bridge. The funds were needed to move the people out of Vanetta and closer to the office. The message stated it, "inadvisable socially to keep a community of dying persons intact." In December 1935 the People's Press, a radical Chicago weekly, broke the Hawks Nest Tunnel story with headlines: 476 DEAD 1500 DOOMED IN W. VA. TUNNEL CATASTROPHE. Six months after the story broke Albert Maltz's story "Man on a Road" was published in the New Masses.

People around here have been trying to forget the Hawks Nest Tunnel tragedy ever since it happened, especially the people in Gauley Bridge, site of the tunnel. The small, picturesque, river town of Gauley Bridge, where the Gauley and the New River meet to form the Kanawha River, was labeled "Town of the Living Dead." The passage of time has almost lifted that burden.

The story of Hawks Nest Tunnel tragedy cannot be forgotten in spite of the gory details. It is part of our national, state and local history. Time can ease a broken heart and heal a bruised spirit but the cold, hard, historical facts surrounding this tragedy remain - lives were lost needlessly, families destroyed and social injustices occurred on a major scale. This simple story from the mountains of West Virginia depicts the desperate era of the Depression years where men were willing to risk their lives to earn enough money to feed their families. Unfortunately, the history behind this story continues to play out in West Virginia - workers up against big corporations doing business from outside the state. The workforce at the Hawks Nest Tunnel was mostly African-American migrants who hopped rail cars to get to jobs in the mountains of West Virginia. These workers bore a hole 3.7 miles long through Gauley Mountain which consisted of 99.4 percent pure silica - and an untold number suffocated to death as a result of deplorable working conditions.

I began researching the Hawks Nest tunnel story last summer when contacted by a legal firm in Houston, Texas, supposedly working on an environmental case. They needed the case where Dr. Henry K. Pancoast, an expert roentologist and pioneer in silicosis research, testified as an expert witness for the defendants, (Rinehart and Dennis) . The court case records were housed at the Fayette County Court House in Fayetteville, West Virginia. The paralegal representing the firm promised me compensation for finding the specific case, travel and any other expenses incurred. The paralegal told me, "You will be helping many, many people by finding this information and sending it to me here at the firm." I took vacation time from work for two days and went to the Fayette County Courthouse - about a 20 minute drive from Summersville. When I told the women in the office my request, they said, "Oh yeah, we had that call a week ago." They went on to say that they did not have the time to do extensive research. That surprised me. I thought it would be short and sweet. I figured on a couple of hours. They led me to a back office, pulled out the oversized, heavy ledger and showed me where to begin. There were hundreds of names of claims against Rinehart and Dennis. I was told between 300 - 500 claims. Of course the ledger did not list witnesses.

I wrote down a name and the civil action suit # and attempted to locate it in one of the many file cabinets in an adjoining room. When I was lucky enough to find one of the suits, I carefully unwound the thin legal paper, which was yellowed and fragile with time. Each case was rolled up and secured with a piece of twine or ribbon and tied into a bow. I skimmed the document for the name of Henry K. Pancoast. I spent two days there and copied up to $27.00 worth of documents without finding the name of Pancoast. I realized this research could take more time than I had to give. I faxed a portion of a suit to Houston. I received nothing for my work, nothing for travel or copying expenses incurred. I stowed away my copies of the documents. It did not enter my mind I would be using these documents for my own story a few months later.

Up in the fall I picked up my research again on the project after receiving a call from Charlotte, publisher of our local paper, suggesting we collaborate on a story about Hawks Nest Tunnel. I was excited about the suggestion. Later, Charlotte became too busy to continue working on the story. I was already hooked on this haunting neighborhood tale so I continued alone.

I began with local sources. First, I called Helen, daughter of Handley White, the Summersville undertaker who had been awarded the bid to bury the tunnel workers at $50.00 per body with a promise of plenty of business. Helen told me, "The workers were buried on my mother, Martha White's, farm in a field here in Summersville, right down from where you live." She also said, "Another burial site is downtown behind the Summersville Presbyterian church on property now owned by Farrell and Sarah Johnson."

I visited both burial sites within the next couple of days. The graves were unmarked on the farm but when I asked about the downtown site, the Johnson daughter told me, "Oh, yes, they are buried right there on the hillside behind the house. I used to go there and play with my dolls when I was little. The graves are marked with little round stones."

During the early 90s, when Route 19 made its way through the Martha White farm, a number of the dead were dug up and buried in various places including down by Gauley River.

In addition to local sources for information I was able to do extensive research through documents contained by the Gauley Bridge Historical Society on Hawks Nest Tunnel.

Personal memories told to me of Hawks Nest Tunnel tragedy:

Nancy Taylor, Gauley Bridge resident, with a close connection to Hawks Nest Tunnel:

The house I live in now in Gauley Bridge has been in the family for many years. The house is along the road where the tunnels workers passed by on their way to work daily. Members of my family became friends with one of the tunnel workers who said he was a famous jazz musician from the south. The black tunnel worker would stop by the house and play music on the piano my family owned, and in return he would get a good meal. That is why I still have that little red piano in my house today.

My mother dated one of the tunnel workers and he had a car. One time he actually drove my mother back into the tunnel. They were not supposed to be in there.

Kathy Eakle of Summersville talks about her grandmother and Hawks Nest Tunnel:

"My grandmother, Della O'Dell, moved into a house across from the Martha White farm in 1931. She had a six month old baby boy. She would tell us they could hear the wagons coming late at night pulling the dead to a resting place here in Nicholas County."

Owen Sims, a life-long resident of Summersville and Nicholas County told me, "I used to know the location of many of the graves on the White farm. When I was rabbit hunting, I would see the ground hoved up in some places and sunken in other places on the second knoll, along the fence line. These were graves of the tunnel workers."

According to reports, workers began dying as soon as 2 months after construction began on the tunnel. It was not possible to get an accurate account because of the nature of the disease, and the black migrant workers began wondering back home and died after returning there.

The deaths were painful. It was reported when the oldest Jones boy, Cecil, died after struggling so hard for his breath that he kicked the wooden slats out of the baseboard of his bed. His widow, Dora Jones, filed a suit against Rinehart and Dennis. A portion of this case is included. This was used as the test case. Dora sued for $10,000. Cecil's lungs were analyzed. A doctor by the name of Dr. Emory Hayhurst appeared as an expert witness on behalf of the plaintiff during the case. The local doctor, Dr. Harless, consulted with Hayhurst on the analysis of the lung tissue. He described the progressive nature of the disease as follows:

"...the (silica) dust is not irritative immediately, so that the lungs and respiratory passageways do not tend to throw it out as it comes in, which is true of most other dusts. Once in, it begins to undergo a very slow dissolving, and when it gets in a dissolved state it is poisonous, and as result of that poisoning...scar tissue begins to form around the particles of dust, even one particle...and that scar tissue is what we see in the x-rays as these nodules...

The silicotic patient is very much more susceptible to pneumonia, particularly in the first two-thirds of the disease. After that he is more susceptible to tuberculosis... Those scar tissues and the slow poison in there invite tuberculosis...

Silicosis by itself will cause death if the exposure is excessive and the process is rapid. It does that through, to put it in simple terms, plain suffocation.

The first case that came to trial in Fayetteville was that of Raymond Johnson. This proved to be the longest case recorded in Fayette County. The case lasted five weeks and ended in a hung jury. After the workers began filing their suits against Rinehart and Dennis, four doctors were brought in to examine the workers. Doctors came from Cincinnati, Mayo Clinic, Cleveland Clinic and Baltimore.

During Johnson's trial it was alleged the Department of Mines inspector was refused admittance to the work site until an order from the State Attorney General Office was obtained giving his department jurisdiction over the project. It was later revealed a system of signals was worked out to inform the foreman when inspectors were on site.

One of the troubling aspects of this case was the burial of tunnel workers. Why were they not returned home or kinfolk notified of the deaths? When I spoke with Handley White's daughter again I brought this up and she explained to me, "The reason family members could not be notified, no one knew who the family members were or where they lived. These were migrant workers coming to Gauley Bridge because word had spread that a big job was going on near Gauley Bridge, West Virginia, and workers were needed."

Construction of Hawks Nest Tunnel
Depression Era Project

In 1929 the stock market crashed and important, powerful, wealthy men, reduced to peasants by unstable economics, leaped to their deaths from windows in skyscrapers in places like New York City. It was the Depression Era, a dreary time for the State of the Union. President FDR had his hands full with people starving to death, banks failing, joblessness and even extreme weather conditions including blizzards, tornadoes, floods, droughts, and dirt storms. Both the "Dust Bowl" and the CCC were born out of the bitter Depression Era. Migrant labor became popular. Men, desperate for any job they could find, traveled as hobos from town to town on railcars.

Lieber Cutlip's memories of Hawk's nest Tunnel:

"I was friends with Tux White. He was one of Handley White's sons.

I owned a flatbed truck Tux asked me to help him out once-N-awhile, hawling dead tunnel workers up here to the farm to bury."

But not all important, powerful, wealthy men felt the urge to meet an untimely fate. No, a group of businessmen opted for a back office somewhere in New York City developing plans for one of the greatest engineering feats of the times. In fact as early as July 31, 1928, a deed was executed between National Water and Power Company and New – Kanawha Power Plant – called Hawks Nest Dam.

Their plans involved harnessing the powers of Gauley River, directing the waters through a tunnel converting the water into electricity. This engineering marvel was slated for the remote, isolated Appalachian mountains in West Virginia. This generated electricity would provide the power needed to begin what was later to become known as the "Chemical Valley of the World." The world of plastics was about to immerge and the invested partners were to become extremely wealthy and powerful.

The Hawks Nest tunnel, located in Fayette County, West Virginia, was part of a project to supply hydroelectric power to the Electro Metallurgical Company, a subsidiary of the Union Carbide Corporation. The excavation work was contracted to the firm of Dennis and Rinehart of Charlottesville, Virginia, which received much of the blame for failing to take proper precautions after it was found that workers were blasting through silica rock.

After he was elected to the U.S. Senate in 1934, Rush Holt brought the plight of the Hawks Nest workers into the national limelight. Holt: "Congress has just started to investigate the building of Hawks Nest Tunnel, known as the village of death. I personally believe that two thousand men are doomed to die as a result of ruthless destruction of life by American industry."

In 1936, West Virginia Congressman Jennings Randolph sat on a Senate subcommittee investigating the catastrophe. The subcommittee's report lambasted conditions at Hawks Nest but failed to take further action. Despite the controversy surrounding the project, the tunnel was completed in 1935 and has performed its intended purpose ever since. Workmen's Compensation was specifically denied the Hawks Nest Tunnel disaster workers, but the tragedy resulted in the designation of silicosis as an occupational disease with compensation.

<u>Date and Description of Project:</u> 1930-1932

Rinehart and Dennis Company, Charlottesville, Virginia, was given a timeline of two years to complete the underground tunnel about 32-36 feet in diameter and close to four miles in length.

<u>Location of Tunnel:</u>
Beginning at a point on the north side of New River near the village of Hawks Nest and extending under the mountain to a point on the same side of said river near Gauley Junction, in Fayette County, West Virginia.

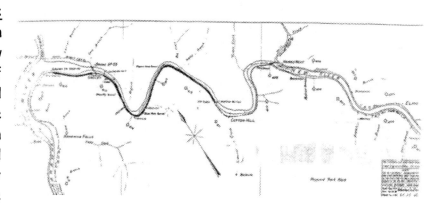

<u>Owner of Project:</u> UNION CARBIDE CORPORATION, a corporation organized under the laws of the State of New York, and having its office and principal place of business at 270 Park Avenue, New York, New York 10017.

Some of the documents and references mention Electro Metallurgical Company and New-Kanawha Power Company, Union Carbide Corporation is the owner of the project and the successor to Electro Metallurgical Company and New-Kanawha Power Company.

<u>Purpose of Project:</u>

HAWKS NEST DEVELOPMENT: The flow of the New River is diverted, by means of the dam and intake, through the tunnel and penstock system to the turbines in the power house and through the said turbines back into New River. The flow is utilized for the production of hydroelectric power. The capacity of Hawks Nest is 102,000 K.W. in deed executed January 18, 1929 between National Water & Power Company, a corporation, State of Delaware, and New-Kanawha Power Company, a corporation, State of West Virginia. (an excerpt from testimony found in Health Conditions of Public Utility Workers, page 3 – Statement of Philippa Allen: "This tunnel is part of a huge water-power project which began in the latter part of 1929 under the direction of the New Kanawha Power Co., a subsidiary of the Union Carbide & Carbon Co. That company was licensed by the State of West Virginia Power Commission to develop power for public sale and ostensibly it was to do that; but, in reality, it was formed to sell all the power to the Electro-Metallurgical Co., a subsidiary of the Union Carbide & Carbon Co., which was by an act of the State legislature allowed to buy up the New Kanawha Power Co. in 1933."   July 31, 1928, a deed was executed between National Water and Power Company and New –Kanawha Power Plant – called Hawks Nest Dam)

<u>Hawks Nest Development</u>

Dam and Pool. Constructed: The dam crosses New River at a distance of 3400 feet downstream from MacDougall Station on the Chesapeake and Ohio Railway and is founded on solid rock. The normal elevation of the natural water surface of the dam site before construction was approximately 764 feet above sea level. The dam is 948 feet long, including main spillway section, trash spillway, and abutment structures. The main spillway section is of mass concrete, ogee gravity type, up to elevation 795. Above elevation 795 the main spillway section is occupied by 14 steel crest gates of the stony type, with their supporting piers and overhead operating bridge of reinforced concrete. The gates are 25 feet high and 50 feet in clear length between piers. They are raised for the passage of excess flow and lowered to maintain the level of the pool by means of two traveling gantry cranes which are operated by electric power, either transmitted to the dam from the power house or generated by an auxiliary 150 K.V.A. gasoline engine driven generator installed in the west abutment of the dam. The gantry cranes may be operated by remote controls from power house switchboard to raise or lower gates. When the gates are in closed position their tops are at elevation 820, or approximately 56 feet above original normal river level.

Copy of official transcripts of court case materials – copied from official records of the Fayette County Circuit Clerk's Office, Fayette County Courthouse, Fayetteville, West Virginia – March 19, 2003 by B. L. Dotson-Lewis

STATE OF WEST VIRGINIA
COUNTY OF FAYETTE, TO WIT:

IN THE CIRCUIT COURT THEREOF.

Dora Jones, as administratrix of the estate of Cecil L. Jones by way of amendment to the declaration filed in the Circuit Clerk's office of Fayette County, West Virginia, at August rules 1932, says that she is the widow of the said Cecil L. Jones; that he is the same person who instituted an action of trespass on the case in the Circuit Court of said County against Rinehart & Dennis Company, incorporated, and E. J. Perkins, on July 18, 1932, to recover damages caused by the wrongful acts, neglect and default of the said defendants and that pending said action the said Cecil L. Jones died on September 24, 1932, from the injuries caused by the wrongful acts, neglect and default of the said defendants; that the death of the said Cecil L. Jones died on September 24, 1932, from the injuries caused by the wrongful acts, neglect and default of the said defendants; that the death of the said Cecil L. Jones being suggested the said cause of action was revived in the name of said Dora Jones, as administratrix of the said Cecil L. Jones, deceased, by order entered in said action on the 11 day of October, 1932.

The said defendant, Rinehart & Dennis Company, in order to facilitate the building of said tunnel divided the work into three parts, namely, Project No. 1, Project No. 2 and Project No. 3, and began work on each of said projects on or about the _____ day of April, 1930, and has been continuously engaged in the promotion of said work from the said last mentioned date to the present time.

Said tunnel was driven through silica rock for the greater part of its length. This rock, which is composed of approximately 99.4% pure silica, was shot from the headings and inner surface of said tunnel by the use of explosives placed in holes from four to seven feet deep drilled in said rock by means of steel drills operated by compressed air and manipulated by the employees of the said Rinehart & Dennis Company. The drilling of these holes, the use of explosives, the use of electric shovel, and the use of gasoline motors produced great quantities of silica rock dust which remained in said tunnel suspended in the air.

Under the specific directions, orders and instructions of the defendant company given by and through its officers and authorized agents, the drills used in drilling the silica rock in Project No. 1 in said tunnel were operated without the use of water to keep down the dust, which manner of operation together with the dust and fumes produced from the combustion of the explosives, the use of electric shovel and gasoline motors caused the tunnel at all times to be filled with blinding clouds of silica rock dust, suspended in the air therein, all of which was known to both of said defendants.

Plaintiff says that the defendant, E. J. Perkins, was on the 18th day of July, 1932, and for many years immediately prior thereto had been Vice-President and General Manager of the said Rinehart & Dennis Company, and was in active charge, management, supervision, direction and control of the construction of said tunnel for the said defendant company from the beginning of the work to the present time; that he directed how the work was done, what appliances, tools and machinery were used, the place and under what conditions the employees labored.

Plaintiff further alleges that the defendants knew that said silica rock dust is composed of particles of silica, which, when inhaled from day to day, after a few months, causes the disease of acute silicosis, and knew that said disease was very dangerous and fatal to human life, and knew that said tunnel was being driven through silica rock and that the method by which this was being accomplished produced great quantities of silica rock dust and knew that this was suspended in the air in said tunnel at all times and knew that this made and rendered the place where the employees of the said defendant company, including plaintiff's intestate, were required to work, unsafe and dangerous.

Plaintiff further avers that the crystalline particles of silica in said tunnel did through the process of inhaling enter the alveoli and air sacs of the lungs of plaintiff's intestate, producing no traumatic effect, but there gradually passed from a crystalline form into a state of silica sol, poisonous to cell life, thus setting up a pathological process in his lungs which resulted in an inflammatory fibrosis which after lapse of time caused extensive and fibrous nodules to appear with general distribution, resulting in the impairment of his breathing area and the lessening of the elasticity of his lung tissue, which condition gradually grew worse and after many months resulted in the physical disability of plaintiff's intestate herein described.

Plaintiff further says that Cecil L. Jones entered the services of Rinehart & Dennis Company in November, 1930, to work as a steel "nipper" in Project No. 1 in said tunnel; that his duties were to carry steel drills to and from the heading in said Project No. 1; that he worked continuously from the day of his said employment to December, 1931; that the conditions in Project No. 1 of said tunnel hereinafter described existed continuously throughout the period of his employment.

Plaintiff alleges that it was the duty of the defendants to use due, reasonable and ordinary care to provide a safe and suitable place for the said Cecil L. Jones to work in said tunnel. Yet the said defendants not regarding their said duty in this behalf, but wholly neglecting so to do, did on or about the _____ day of November, 1930, direct the said Cecil L. Jones to carry steel drills for the defendant company to and from the heading of said tunnel in Project No. 1, where the air was so laden and filled with the particles of silica produced by the drilling of the holes in the silica rock, by the combustion of explosives, the use of electric shovel and gasoline motors as to make the place where he was required to work an unsafe, unsuitable and dangerous place, and a place where he gradually inhaled from day to day the particles of silica which caused him to develop the disease of acute silicosis. The said defendants with full knowledge of the unsafe and dangerous condition in Project No. 1 of said tunnel, wilfully, wantonly, and in utter disregard of the resulting consequences to the said Cecil L. Jones, and with the deliberate intention to produce injury to him, did send him as an employee of the defendant company into the said tunnel to perform labor for said defendant company as hereinbefore set forth, and as a direct result of the wrongful, wilful, wanton, deliberate and intentional acts and conduct of the said defendants, the said Cecil L. Jones was caused to inhale particles of silica, fumes and gases and thereby gradually contracted a disease known as silicosis from which he died on September 24, 1932.

Plaintiff avers that by reason of the matters and things in this count mentioned, she as administratrix of the estate of the said Cecil L. Jones, deceased, has sustained damages to the extent of $10,000.00.

Summary of Wages Paid by Rinehart and Dennis Company
(Hawks Nest Tunnel)

Hourly Wages

Class of Workman	March 13, 1930 to Aug. 12, 1931	Aug. 13, 1931 to Feb. 17, 1932	Feb. 18, 1932 to June 8, 1932
Blacksmiths	65 cents	60 cents	55 cents
Carpenters	50	45	45
Carpenter Foreman	60	60	60
Carpenter Helpers	35	30	25
Car Repairmen	50	45	45
Concrete Finishers	35	30	25
Crusher Feeders	35	30	25
Crusher Foreman		50 – 70	no reductions
Drillers	35	30	25
Drill Foreman (Outside)		65 – 70	no reductions
Drill Mechanics		35 – 50	no reductions
Dump Foremen	50	50	50
Electricians		40 – 50	no reductions
Hoisting Engineers	65	60	55
Laborers	30	25	22-1/2
Labor Foremen		40 – 65	no reductions
Mechanics		35 – 70	no reductions
Motor & Dinky Skinners	50	45	40
Pump Skinners			
Steel Erectors	60	60	60
Steel Sharpeners	60	55	50
Steel Workers		40 – 60	no reductions
Steel Workers Foremen	65	65	65
Track Foremen		50 – 60	no reductions
Truck Drivers	30 – 35	25	25
Tunnel Drill Foremen	75	65	65
Tunnel Muck Foremen	60	50	50

ORIGINAL NOTES TO ACCOMPANY
LIST OF DECEASED PERSONS FOR WHOM WHITE AND CRAVENS OR H. C. WHITE WERE UNDERTAKERS

In order to present the truth concerning the much publicized colored cemetery in Summersville this list of deceased persons has been prepared. On this list are the names, cause of death, places of burial, etc, for all Rinehart and Dennis deceased employees and camp followers or drifters for whom H. C. White or White and Cravens were undertakers. The information concerning each person on this tabulated list of names is the same as on the other lists except that the names of the camp followers and women who died have been added. The information was obtained principally from the files of the Bureau of Vial Statistics of the West Virginia Health Department and supplemented by the records of the undertakers and the Coal Valley Hospital.

Under the heading of "Cemetery" it has been recorded which of the two cemeteries in Summersville these people are buried. The Lewis Cemetery is the old burying place of the few negroes who have ever died in Summersville. The nine buried here used all available grave space. The Colored cemetery is the one laid out by the undertaker on the undivided estate of his mother about one mile out of Summersville. In this cemetery are the graves of thirty six of the persons on this list and nine Fayette County paupers.

Following is a summary of the number of names appearing on this list and their places of burial.

	White	Colored	Total
No. of Rinehart and Dennis Employees on List	5	56	61
No. not employed by Rinehart and Dennis		5 (including) (3 women)	5
Total number on list.	5	61	66
Of the 5 white persons:			
No. whose bodies were shipped to other states			3
No. buried in cemeteries in West Virginia			1
No. on whose death certificate place of burial is not recorded			1
Total			5
Of the 60 colored persons:			
No. buried in Colored Cemetery in Summersville		36 (including 2 women)	
No. buried in Lewis Cemetery in Summersville		9	
No. buried in other cemeteries in West Va.		6 (including one woman)	
No. whose bodies were shipped to other states		10	
Total		61	

Deceased

(C – Colored) (W – White) (C.V.H. – Coal Valley Hospital)

Name	Race	age	Date of death	Last day at work	Cause of death	Physician	Place of death	Place of burial/cemetery
Abraham, Eugene	C	21	7/28/31	6/12/31	Pneumonia, Lobar	Wilkerson	Montgomery, C.V.H.	Summersville/ Colored
Alexander, James	C	32	9/2/31	9/1/31	Killed by rock fall in tunnel-skull fractured	Mitchell	Camp No. 2	Logan, W.Va.
Allison, Robert	C	39	9/20/31	9/4/31	Broncho-Pneumonia	Wilkerson	Montgomery, C.V.H.	Summersville/ Lewis
Andrews, Sidney	C	22	1/27/31	1/24/31	Pneumonia, lobar both lower lobes	Wilkerson	Montgomery, C.V.H.	Summersville/ Lewis
Bales, Alonzo	C	about 24	2/4/31		Pneumonia, Lobar right lower	Wilkerson	Montgomery, C.V.H.	Summmersville/ Lewis
Berratt, Nathan (or Barrett)	C	45	7/18/31	7/17/31	Drowned while swimming in New River	Mitchell	Camp No. 2	Summersville/ Colored
Bostic (Mooney), Willie	C	16	6/30/31	6/22/31	Pneumonia, Lobar	Harless	Gauley Bridge	Vanetta
Brown, James	C	26	5/25/31	5/25/31	Accidental drowning no doctor	No doctor called	Camp No. 3	Summersville/ Colored
Brown, Walter Burley	W	21	3/18/31	3/18/31	Pneumonia, Lobar	Brugh	Montgomery, C.V.H.	Syrie, Va.
Browning, Fred	C	30	4/24/31	3/4/31	Pneumonia, Lobar right lower	Wilkerson	Montgomery, C.V.H.	Summersville/ Colored
Chambers, Bennie	C	23	2/2/31	1/3/31	Pneumonia, Lobar right lower.	Wilkerson	Montgomery, C.V.H.	Summersville/ Lewis
Clark, Nelson	C	30	4/20/32	3/15/32	Tuberculosis with Silicosis as contributory cause.	No physician Signed cert..	Vanetta	Summersville/ Colored
Cooper, Mack	C	35	2/19/31	2/12/31	Pneumonia, Lobar	Wilkerson	Montgomery, C.V.H.	Summersville/ Lewis
Daugherty, George	C	35	6/15/31	6/10/31	Fractured pelvis. Compound with ruptured bladder.	Stallard	Montgomery, C.V.H.	Summersville/ Colored
Devine, Henry	C	61	10/17/31	3/14/31	Pneumonia		Montgomery, C.V.H.	Summersville/ Colored
Dixon, James	C	46	12/31/31	12/4/31	Killed with axe in fight at Camp No. 2	Stallard	Montgomery, C.V.H.	Summersville/ Colored
Elders, Sylvia	C	35	12/31/31		Struck by falling tree	Mitchell	Camp No. 2	Summersville/ Colored
Euill, Gaston	C	36	11/6/32	11/5/32	Gunshot wounds	No physician Signed certificate.	Gauley Bridge	Amerst, Va.
Evans, H. C.	C	26	7/22/31	6/16/31	Pneumonia – found dead in bed.	Mitchell	Gauley Bridge	Summersville/ Colored
Flack, Dewey	C	21	5/20/31	5/6/31	Pneumonia, Lobar right lower lobe.	Wilkerson	Montgomery, C.V.H.	Summersville/ Colored
Green, Clemon	C	28	6/23/31	3/28/31	Pneumonia, left lower	Wilkerson	Montgomery, C.V.H.	Summersville/ Colored
Harvey, Calvin	C	38	5/16/31	5/11/31	Pneumonia, right lower and middle lobe	Wilkerson	Montgomery, C.V.H.	Summersville/ Colored
Hicks, James	C	42	5/14/31	5/14/31	Killed by rock fall in tunnel – skull crushed	Mitchell	Camp No. 1	Union S.C.

Hockens/Hawkins) Richard	C		1/9/32	6/4/31	Pneumonia			Montgomery	Summersville/ Colored
Hunt, Thomas	C	45	11/21/31	9/14/31	Pneumonia, Lobar	Wilkerson	Montgomery, C.V.H.	Summersville/ Colored
Inabinet, S. Walter	W	27	9/17/31	9/17/31	Rock fall at intake portal-skull crushed	Mitchell	Camp No. 3	St. Matthews, S.C.
Jackson, Whirley	C	24	7/18/32	7/9/32	Gunshot wounds	Mitchell	Hawks Nest	Not noted
Jackson, William	C	40	6/29/32	1/9/32	Contusion cord and Hemorrhage.	Stalllard	Montgomery, C.V.H.	Summersville
Johnson, Luther	C		12/18/33	12/14/33				Summersville/ Colored
Jones, Lindsey	C	36	6/23/31	6/16/31	Pneumonia, Lobar, right upper lobe.	Wilkerson	Montgomery, C.V.H.	Vanetta
Lane, Henry	C	26	9/20/31	9/20/31	Fall of rock in tunnel	Mitchell	Camp No. 2	Knoxville, Tenn
Littlejohn, Mary	C	40	4/23/32		Killed by knife wounds at Camp No. 1	Mitchell	Camp No. 1	Summersville
McCalton, John	C	30	7/21/32	5/17/31	Pulmonary, Tuberculosis	Mitchell	Camp No. 1	Summersville/ Colored
McCrorey, George	C	31	4/13/32	4/4/32	Pneumonia, Lobar	Harless	Gauley Bridge	Chester, S.C.
McKeever, Grover	C		7/30/31	5/7/31	Tuberculosis, Acute and Pneumonia		Montgomery, C.V.H.	Summersville/ Colored
McKission, James	C	30	6/13/31	6/11/31	Pneumonia, Lobar right upper middle Lobe	Wilkerson	Montgomery, C.V.H.	Summersville/ Colored
Miller, J. H.	C		5/8/31	5/1/31	Pneumonia	Wilkerson	Montgomery, C.V.H.	Summersville/ Colored
Mitchell, Fred	C	40	12/12/33	12/12/33	Crushed by Dinkey	Stallard	Montgomery, C.V.H.	Rock Hill, S.C.
Monagon, John	C	about 35	2/1/31	9/29/30	Pneumonia, Lobar right upper lobe	Wilkerson	Montgomery, C.V.H.	Summersville/ Lewis
Mooney, Willie	(This man also used the name of Willie Bostic and is so listed herewith)							
Moore, James	C	47	9/20/31	9/20/31	Fall of rock in Tunnel – head crushed	Mitchell	Camp No. 2	Summersville/ Colored
Murphy, Robert	C	46	9/23/31	9/23/31	Electrocuted	Mitchell	Camp No. 1	Camden, S.C.
Murphy, Sam	C	24	2/27/31	2/10/32	Broncho-Pneumonia	Wilkerson	Montgomery, S.C.	Summersville
Nelson, Alex.	C	44	8/30/33	8/30/33	Died suddenly at work, apparently from heart condition	J. E. Coleman	Gauley Bridge	Summersville
Patterson, Charlie	C	about 25	2/3/31	1/30/31	Pneumonia, Lobar left lower lobe	Wilkerson	Montgomery, C.V.H.	Summersville
Powell, Will	C	36	5/13/31	5/13/31	Killed by shaft of rock crusher	Mitchell	Camp No. 1	Mt. Holly, S.C.
Reed, W. M.	C	55	6/17/31	6/15/31	Endo-Carditis Chronic.	Mitchell	Camp No. 2	Summersville
Robinson, Will		36	5/13/31	9/10/32		No doctor in attendance	Fayetteville	Bayes Cemetery .Fayetteville
Sandusky, Albert		49	5/4/32	12/9/31	Lobar Pneumonia	G.C. Lawrence	Vanetta	Vanetta
Scott, Joe	C	45	5/1/31	5/1/31	Gas fumes in Tunnel	Mitchell	Camp No. 2	Knoxville, Tenn

Shephard, Howard	W	21	5/16/31	5/16/31	Crushed by motor	Stallard	Montgomery, C.V.H.	Summersville
Sherrod, John	C		6/27/31		Pneumonia, Lobar		Montgomery, C.V.H.	Summersville
Singleton, Roosevelt	C	31	5/14/31	5/2/31	Pneumonia, Lobar, right lower lobe	Wilkerson	Montgomery, C.V.H.	Summersville
Slaughter, Hudson		25	12/13/32	2/26/31	Pulmonary Tuberculosis Renal Tuberculosis.	M.F. Pain	Fayetteville	Pierce's Cemetery. Fayetteville.
Sloan, Mat	C	31	4/30/31	4/29/31		Mitchell	Gauley Bridge	Summersville
Smith, Frank	C	45	8/9/33	7/25/33	Hypertonsial & Arteria seleric Cardia Renal Disease-Starvation, acute Malnutrition	Wilkerson	Montgomery, C.V.H.	Summersville
Smith, H. L.	W	60	10/26/34	10/4/34	Fractured skull	Laird	Montgomery, C.V.H.	Mt. Holly, N.C.
Smith, John	C	28	4/2/31	2/13/31	Pneumonia, Lobar	Wilkerson	Montgomery, C.V.H.	Hot Springs,Fla.
Smoke, Emanuel	C	50	12/4/31	11/26/31	Pneumonia with Harnisorphy operation.	Bruch	Montgomery, C.V.H.	Summersville
Stokes, Tillie	C	40	7/13/32	7/13/32	Run over by cars in Tunnel – leg amputated	Stallard	Montgomery, C.V.H.	Summersville
Strong, John	C	37	3/4/33	5/21/32	Silicosis	no physician signed cert.	Gauley Bridge	Summersville
Thompson, Enoch	C		7/31/31	7/14/31	Pneumonia, Lobar, left lower lobe	Wilkerson	Montgomery, C.V.H.	Summersville
Ward, John	C	26	10/19/31	10/18/31	Crushed pelvis, struck by shovel	Mitchell	Montgomery, C.V.H.	Kings Mt.,N.C.
Ward, Sam		38	2/15/33	3/30/32	Acute Silicosis-with pulmonary Tuberculosis as contributory cause.	Harless	Gauley Bridge	Vanetta
Watkins, Sam		38	2/5/33	4/17/32	Acute Silicosis with pulmonary Tuberculosis as contributory cause.	Harless	Gauley Bridge	Vanetta
Watts, N. A.	C	42	9/28/31	9/24/31	Influenza – Penumonia as contributory cause	Mitchell	Montgomery, C.V.H.	Not recorded
White, James			11/24/30	11/4/30	Lobar Pneumonia	Wilkerson	Montgomery, C.V.H.	Diamond
Williams, Joe	C	30	2/21/31	2/11/31	Pneumonia, lobar	Wilkerson	Montgomery, C.V.H.	Summersville
Williams, Willie	C		7/30/31	5/8/31	Pneumonia lobar	Wilkerson	Montgomery, C.V.H.	Summersville
Wilson, James		32	10/17/34	11/8/33	Silicosis	Lunken	Bachman	Sumerlee
Woodard, Calvin	C		3/2/32	12/22/31	Tuberculosis	Wilkerson	Montgomery, C.V.H.	Summersville
Woodard, Will	C	40	1/27/31	8/20/30	Pneumonia, Lobar left lower	Wilkerson	Montgomery, C.V.H.	Summersville
Woods, Frank	C	23	6/9/31	5/27/31	Broncho-Pneumonia	Wilkerson	Montgomery, C.V.H.	Summersville

Death Certificates

Name	Cemetery Certificate number	Name	Cemetery Certificate number
Abraham, Eugene	10143	Evans, H. C.	8777
Allison, Robert	13077	Flack, Dewey	8804
Andrews, Sidney	238	Green, Clemon	8809
Bales, Alonzo	251	Harvey, Calvin	8803
Berrat, Nathan	8776	Hicks, James	6223
Bostic, Mooney, Willie	7528	Hunt, Thomas	16105
Brown, James	6225	Inabit, S. Walter	1516
Brown, Walter Burley	3230	Jackson, Whirley	8775
Browning, Fred	8801	Jackson, William	4766
Chambers, Bennie	249	Jones, Lindsey	8808
Clark, Nelson	7461	Lane, Henry	11565
Cooper, Mack	1741	McCalton, John	11721
Daugherty, George	8307	McCrorey, George	4761
Dixon, James	16100	McKission, James	8806
Elders, Sylvia	16103	Mitchell, Fred	16662
Euill, Gasto	14431	Monagon, John	248
		Moore, James	11582

Remarks to accompany List of Colored Employees of Rinehart & Dennis Company who died in West Virginia, April 1, 1930 – December 31, 1935.

This list was compiled from the information on file in the Bureau of Vital Statistics of the West Virginia health Department and supplemented by the records of the Coal Valley Hospital of Montgomery and the reports to the State Compensation Commission. The name of each colored man appearing on the payroll of Rinehart & Dennis Company was individually checked in the death lists of the Bureau of Vital Statistics for the six year period since construction started.

This list is complete in that all available records have been examined and the information contained therein has been recorded here. There is no knowledge or record of the death, in West Virginia, of any employee or former employee who is not included in this list.

There are nine men included in this list for whom no death certificates have been filed but in each of these cases the undertaker's records are complete and show the place of burial. It is probable that some of these itinerant negroes were known by more than one name, and this would account for some omissions in the records.

General Notes to Accompany list of "Colored Employees of Rinehart and Dennis Company who died in West Virginia, April 1, 1930 – December 31, 1935"

Abraham, Eugene – There is no death certificate on file for anyone bearing this name or for anyone with a name which could be reasonably taken for this man. The records of the Coal Valley Hospital, however, show that he "ran a typical lobar pneumonia course and expired on July 27, 1931."

Adams, Infred - On this man's death certificate are the following notes:
Trade or Profession – "Laborer in Tunnel"
Industry or Business – "Rinehart & Dennis, Hawks nest, W.Va."
Where did injury occur? "Camp #1 Rinehart & Dennis, Hawks Nest."
Manner of Injury – "Rock fall in Tunnel."
Was disease or injury in any way related to occupation of deceased? – "Due to occupation."

Alexander, James – No remarks.

Allison, Robert – On the death certificate it is noted that an X-Ray was taken to confirm the diagnosis of broncho pneumonia White's records show that he died of "typhoid and acute bronchitis."

Andrews, Sidney – Dr. Wilkerson, who attended this man in the hospital, made the following note on the death certificate: "Living in construction camp – very unsatisfactory living conditions."

Bales, Alonzo – No remarks.

Berret, (or Barrett), Nathan – On the death certificate this man's name is spelled 'Barrot" but on Rinehart and Dennis Company's payroll it is spelled "Barrett."

Brown, Parker – The death certificate for this man is not signed by a physician and on the certificate there is noted, "No physician in attendance." Also the word "silicosis" is written in a different hand, this handwriting being similar to that on other irregular silicosis certificates.

Browning, Fred – Answering the questions on the death certificate asking if the occupation of the deceased was in any way related to his death, Dr. Wilkerson wrote "yes – crowded living quarters."

Caldwell, Henry – Certificate No. 1054, the one accepted by the Bureau as it stated a cause of death (silicosis) was filed December 30, 1933. This certificate is not signed by a physician and seems to have been written by the Registrar, Mrs. J. C. Dunbar. Another certificate number 15050, marked "Duplicate see 15054", was filed Jan. 10, 1934 by Mrs. J. H. Barr, Registrar in Montgomery. On certificate No. 15050 the man's age is given "about 40", while on the other as "30."

Chambers, Benny – On the death certificate for this man, Dr. Wilkerson wrote "Unsatisfactory living conditions in construction camp."

Chatfield, Fred – The following information is contained on the death certificate for this man:
Trade, Profession – "Laborer"
Industry or Business – "Tunnel Construction"
What test confirmed diagnosis? "Autopsy findings"
Was there an autopsy" "Yes"
Was disease or injury in any way related to occupation of deceased? "Yes" If so specify. "inhalation of silica dust".

Clark, Nelson – The death certificate for this man, in the files of the Bureau of Vital Statistics, is not signed by a physician. Except for the medical statement, the certificate is written in the unmistakable hand of H. C. White. Under Principal Cause of Death there is written "Pulmonary Tuberculosis" and under Contributory Cause "Silicosis." These words are written in what appears to be the same hand and ink as those appearing on John Strong's certificate indicating that at the time of filing and recording of the certificate, the cause of death was "unknown or unclassified."

Jones, Cecil L. – attributed to Silicosis.

Jones, Owen – Death certificate in order.

Jones, Shirley – Death certificate in order. It states:
Trade – "Steel drill nipper."
Industry – "Tunnel work."
Employed by – "Rinehart and Dennis."
Confirmed diagnosis by "Autopsy."

Shepherd, Howard – No remarks

Skinner, C. M. – No remarks

Smith H. L. – No remarks

Street, Lewis Walter – Death certificate states:
Trade – "Laborer"
Disease contracted – "In tunnel work at Gauley Bridge, W. Va."

Yarber, George – Death certificate notes "Tunnel Work."

List of Rinehart and Dennis Company Foremen
Who Are Known To Be Dead

Name	Occupation
Andrew, Oscar	Heading Foreman
Andrews, Clive	Muck Foreman
East, W. E.	Shovel Runner
Gont, W. H.	Day Talker
Inabinet, S. W.	Steel Erecting Foreman
Lynch, Frank	Shovel Runner
Matter, D. H.	Drill Foreman
Pitts, M. A.	Heading Foreman
Skinner, C. M.	Shop Foreman
Smith, H. L.	Carpenter Foreman
Waugh, C. C.	Tunnel Superintendent
Watts, W. A.	Muck Foreman

The 124-ft.-tall steel water tank at Dow Chemical Co.'s South Charleston Technology Park — the plant's last reminder of predecessor company Union Carbide — is coming down after standing 48 years. Contract demolition crews from Bierlein Co. removed the top half of the 125,000-gallon container on Thursday and worked on the other half Friday. Dow opted to put in a water line to serve the plant because maintenance for the tank was getting too costly, said plant maintenance director Dan Wilcox.

Afterword:

Carbide's long history with the community ended in 1981, when the Alloy plant and associated properties were purchased by Elkem, a multinational corporation based in Oslo, Norway, which maintains facilities in all corners of the globe.

Author's note: I had occasion to visit the H. C. White Funeral Home in Summersville, West Virginia, on Tuesday evening, May 30, 2006 to attend the wake of a friend's father who had passed away on Saturday. I entered into conversation with H. C. White, undertaker, and son of Handley White; the undertaker awarded the contract to bury the dead tunnel workers in Summersville. Handley maintained a funeral parlor in both Galley Bridge and Summersville at the time.

I told Mr. White my second book included the story of the Hawks Nest tunnel tragedy. H. C. told me sometime back, a man came here working on the story of the Hawks Nest tragedy. The story was slated for publication in a well-known national magazine. This man heard the tunnel workers were buried somewhere around town. The magazine employee was taken to my mother's farm, the Martha White Farm, where most of the tunnel workers were buried in a designated burial spot; however, the writer photographed the cornfield and labeled it as the tunnel workers' burial ground. H. C. said that the story was printed and widely circulated nationally saying the tunnel workers were buried in shallow, mass graves in a cornfield with cornstalks as their grave markers in Summersville, West Virginia.

White said this was not the case. The workers were buried in a meadow adjacent to the cornfield and that each worker was placed in a handmade wooden box about 5' down in individual graves. He went on to tell me when US 19 came through, many of the workers had to be moved. When the highway department began digging up the graves, he was summoned to the site. He said a big pile of lumber, still good, was left from the original coffins. He said the boards used to make the coffins were thick and wide and of a good grade.   He went on to tell me all that was left of the workers, of course, were skeletal remains which were placed in boxes about 3' long and buried again, this time down over the bank across Hughes Bridge by Gauley River.

White also told me in regards to the controversial matter as to why the bodies were not shipped back to family members, three or four bodies were shipped back, but no one claimed the body when it arrived at its destination.

182

Part 2 – Stories of Strength and Survival

Eula Hall and Mud Creek Clinic
Dr. Donald Rasmussen and Miners for Democracy
Ralph Baber's story of WWII

Author's note:
The 4th International Rural Network conference
Southwest Virginia Higher Education Center
Abingdon, Virginia - Friday, June 24, 2005

Yesterday was wonderful in an odd sort of way. I traveled to Whitesburg, Kentucky, on one of the mobile workshop planned by the Rural Network Conference Program Committee to visit the coalfields of Eastern Kentucky. Now, it seems odd that I would purposely want to see more coalfields and everything associated with Eastern Kentucky coalfields since I live in the West Virginia coalfields.

As you might expect, the trip there was so beautiful, the meadows green, the lay of the land perfect, not boring but exactly perfect to the keep eyes interested with the soft roll of the land, round bales of hay, dilapidated barns, and vegetable gardens flourishing.

One beautiful place I remember driving by was Norton before we finally left Virginia and crossed over into Kentucky. The trip took approximately one hour and forty-five minutes one way. You could hear lots of oohs and aahs from the bus load of foreign visitors as we crossed the high mountains and wound down into the narrow hollow to Whitesburg, Kentucky.

Our first stop was Appalshop located on Madison Avenue. The building was as I expected – brown wood, cedar siding. A house trailer sat behind Appalshop across a little creek. An old railroad bridge with a pedestrian foot bridge in the middle was used to cross the creek. I took this photo of the bridge. We were excited to get there. Arriving meant we were off those winding, treacherous mountain roads unfamiliar to many of the guests.

We had a warm reception at Appalshop with Herbie Smith, Laura and a couple of other workers as greeters. After refreshments everyone was ushered into the auditorium/stage area. Herbie Smith gave us a brief history of Appelshop. Lex Sexton and James Caudill were onstage with Herbie for the program. James Caudill was the first performer. He talked about the Old Time Regular Baptist Religion – a little about the religion and lots about the music and its history. He has just returned from Yale University – Yale University is studying Caudill and others involved in old time line singing.

Lex Sexton, retired coal miner and banjo picker, talked about his life – his work in the coal mines and more importantly, his music. He told us the story of how he got his first banjo - "I wanted to play the banjo so badly I would borrow a banjo anytime I got a chance and practice." This was when I was a young boy, probably nine or ten years old. Then one day a boy at school who owned a banjo announced he wanted to sell it.   The cost, $1.00. I asked my grandpa for $1.00. My grandpa said, "No, he would not give me a dollar without earning it." Grandpa told me if I would cut a big field of cornstalks down, pile them up and burn them, he would pay me $1.00. I worked on that field of cornstalks every free moment I had, after school, on weekends, I cut down corn stalks. Finally, the job was completed and my grandpa gave me a $1.00.

Herbie Smith, left, Lex Sexton, right. Photograph by B. L. Dotson-Lewis July 2005

I took off running as fast as I could go to the boy's house to buy that banjo. The banjo was covered with a groundhog hide with the tail left on. (Groundhog hides were used in early days to make banjos.) Later, someone asked me why the tail was left on the hide and I told them, "It was there to wipe the sweat off your brow caused by playing the banjo."

Lex played lots of tunes and sang a few songs. I thought he was wonderful. He was funny but turned sad when he talked about his youngest son getting killed in an automobile accident – he drove a UPS truck. He had two sons and both were musicians. He told a funny story about his youngest son. He said that his youngest son came up to him one day and said, "Daddy, I'm quittin' you. I'm forming a gospel group and going to work for the Lord." Lex said, "Well, I hate to see you go, but I guess there is nothing I can do about it and I have been trying to think of a reason to get rid of you anyway." (He laughed and told us it was a joke.) He also said that the gospel group his son formed was outstanding.

Lex's granddaughter, Staci, took the stage. She is about 20 and a struggling banjo student. She feels compelled to carry on the music traditions of her father and grandfather. She is trapped between two cultures, her own and her grandfather's. She feels the secret to knowing her father, who is deceased, is through his music. She told us, "My father never talked to me. When I was little he would carry me around and sing, but he never talked, so I know so little about him." Staci has worked off and on at various jobs and finally is on her own now.   She is enrolled at Berea College to begin classes this fall.

We got back on the bus for a tour to a coal mine, coal mine processing plant and a ride through abandoned coal camps. The coal mine was not far out of Whitesburg. When we stopped on the dirt road and got out, Herbie gave us a few instructions, most importantly, "Do not go down to the mine." Guess the photojournalist from Bangladesh didn't understand because when Herbie turned around to answer questions, the photojournalist was off, up over the briar patch, across the fence and to the entrance to the mine in a flash, snapping photos right and left. The crowd told Herbie and he took off after the photographer. Herbie caught up with the photographer just in time to stop him from going inside the mine. About this time the miners emerged. The shift was over. The photographer was so disappointed that he did not get to go inside the mine and take photos.

Everyone was able pick up a lump or two of coal to take home when we stopped at the coal processing plant. I did not need to get a lump of coal; we have a big coal pile behind the maintenance building at work since some of our schools are still heated by coal operated furnaces.

Herbie stood at the front of the bus beside the bus driver and talked about what it was like growing up in the coalfields. He grew up at Seco, right next to Neon. He told our group he had heard in early days you could not walk down the streets of Neon because it was so crowded during the coal boom. That is hard to imagine because now it is a deserted, shabby little town. He explained to the visitors the different extraction methods for removing coal, environmental problems, etc.

Afternoon sessions began when we returned from the coal mine. Three women were on stage. A woman by the name of Eula Hall was seated in the middle. All three women had extraordinary stories of service; one, is responsible for a radio program on diabetes on PBS. One is responsible for starting a free health clinic for the homeless in Hazard but Eula's story hit home and to me represents the perfect example of the theme of the conference I was attending, "The Power of Place."

Eula Hall and the Mud Creek Clinic

Eula was great- so unimposing but her looks were deceiving. Her appearance was motherly, kind, looking a little like a Pentecostal lady, her grayed hair piled high on her head, her kind face bore no makeup but when she began speaking, telling her story, you forgot about her country appearance; she was dynamite with a mountain twang. We, the audience, were completely spellbound by the power of this unassuming mountain woman.

Eula Hall born in 1927, grew up on Joe Boner Holler off Greasy Creek, Pike County, Kentucky. Eula was born in a land of bittersweet contrast of bountiful coal resources and record breaking numbers of people living in poverty. This rich man/poor man scenario is a common theme in the coalfields of eastern Kentucky.

Besides Greasy Creek, Pike County can also boast of Civil War cemeteries and records from the early days of cotton growing and shipped to New Orleans and the final

186

home of Ole Randl McCoy, arch enemy of the famous "Devil" Anse Hatfield of Hatfield-McCoy Feud. Randl lived out his days walking aimlessly about Pikeville.

Places like Greasy Creek, only 16 miles out of Pikeville, the county seat of Pike County, have always been notorious for violence in the coalfields in early days, and as recently as 1985, when Administrative Law Judge Donald R. Holley handed down a decision involving United Mine Workers District 30, Local 1834 and Samyoed Energy. This case was based on coal strike incidents occurring on July 19, 1983, and other dates where Samyoed Energy was reopening a coal mine in the area and refused to employ union miners. Picketing occurred with miners blocking the entrances and exits of the mine. Threats were made to bust open the heads of the company's employees if the coal company failed to hire former Greasy Creek Union employees.

Eula Hall was born in the coalfields of eastern Kentucky and grew up shouldering a heavy burden by sheer geography, if nothing else. The daughter of a sharecropper family, Eula's family grew corn and sold eggs to buy flour and beans. Living in poverty and doing without was a way of life, but accepting the suffering and dying due to the lack of health care as a way of life, was one thing Eula did not buy into, even at an early age. At the young age of nine Eula began dreaming of a way to bring health care to her community. She saw so much suffering and death in the early days as family members stood by helplessly. She even witnessed her own mother nearly bleeding to death.

Many times community members traveled to homes to wait out the long days and nights with friends and relatives while men, women and children went to an early grave because there were no doctors in the community and transportation to hospitals was simply not available. TB, whooping cough, dysentery and coal miners with black lung were common illnesses throughout the mountains. Eula told us, " Many a time nothing else could be done except sit and watch them die while you prayed." She would pray her family would not die. She would pray that health care would become a reality for her family and community some day. Frivolity of youthful living was short lived in the southern Appalachian coalfields. Eula, very bright, completed eight years of education in five years. She had to drop out because of hardships.

At the age of 16 she said goodbye to Greasy Creek in Pike County and moved to the adjoining county of Floyd working as a hired girl for whomever needed her or her family could arrange. She received room and board for her work. This made the load lighter at home with one less mouth to feed. She told us one of the hardest jobs was ironing shirts for the well to do people. If one wrinkle was in the shirt she had to wash, dry and iron it again. She married at the age of 17. Eula had five children. Her first husband died. She told us, "He was a mean man." Eula settled on Mud Creek in the community of Grethel.

Eula learned to drive a car, and people began calling on her to drive them to the doctor and hospital. Not many people in the area knew how to drive automobiles or owned automobiles. It soon became apparent health care was a luxury for people with money since the sick were turned away so many times after she had driven them to the doctor's offices or hospitals. She traveled up the winding, steep, narrow roads to places it seemed only accessible to horses pulling sleds. She would bring people out to the doctor or hospital, and in the winter time it was especially difficult on those slick, winding, narrow, dirt roads.

It hurt and angered Eula Hall that sick people were turned away for lack of money or because they did not have health insurance. Often she drove expectant mothers to two or three medical facilities only to be turned away and when the baby was about to come, she would take the woman to the nearest health facility and tell the health care professionals to do whatever they wanted, but she was not going to have that baby delivered in her car.

Eula continued to bear the burden of no health care for Mud Creek in Grethel, Kentucky, as the years passed. Through love, anger and determination, she continued to focus on her dream conceived when she was only nine years old. She would say to herself and anyone else that would listen, "If there was anything in the world I can do to bring health care to the poor people in this community, I will do it. Anything in the world." She became a community activist focusing on issues pertaining to wellness such as school lunch programs, etc. She would say over and over again "If I can ever do anything to change this health care business which eliminates health care to the poor, I will do it no matter what it takes."

Activists came and went in eastern Kentucky, riding high on the popular War on Poverty Congressional Bill passed in 1964 and set in full motion by LBJ following Kennedy's assassination on November 22, 1963. Yes, activists came and went in eastern Kentucky but Eula stayed in place, steadfast and as forceful as one of the coal trains rolling up and down those hollows. The farthest move she made was 16 miles from Greasy Creek to Grethel, Kentucky.

The drama of the late 60s and early 70s was just the ticket for a forward thinking woman like Eula Hall to began an earnest approach to break ground for a clinic in Grethel. Her pitch to politicians and other possible donors for the community based clinic was the isolation and remoteness of the area making it necessary for sick people to travel many miles to get treatment. Public transportation in the area was none or next to nothing. The area was behind times. Mountain folk were lucky to have electricity in many parts of that region by the mid 60s, much less public transportation.

It was 1973 when Eula's dream of a primary health care clinic began to actually take form. With a meager donation of $1,400 and commitment of two local doctors, Mud Creek Clinic was born. The first clinic opened in Tinker Fork, about five miles out of Grethel. In no time the facility became too small to handle the great need. Eula's home was larger and more centrally located, so Eula and her family moved into a small two bedroom trailer and her home became the clinic by converting the three bedrooms into six exam rooms to accommodate doctors and their patients. The rest of the house was converted into offices and a waiting room.

Eula did not dream small; her vision encompassed the community as a whole. She was concerned about safe water and environmental issues and jumped on the band wagon to protest the strip mining of coal - a method used to peel the layers of hillsides off until the precious coal can be extracted, often setting the stage for flooding the coal camps below for and causing other environmental ruins. Our government failed to implement regulations to reclaim the naked areas. In the early 70's environmentalists and concerned citizens like Eula began pushing for legislation to address the unclaimed surfaces.

Eula, with many other concerned citizens, was hot on the trail of strip miner operators. They protested the loss of jobs and benefits when non-union mines took over and failed to sign contracts with the UMWA. One such strike was in neighboring Harlan County where she helped organize women to block the road at the Brookside mine strike during 1973-74.

During this presentation the question was asked of Eula why there were no medical facilities in the coalfields. Did the coal operators supply any health benefits?

Eula replied, "In the 70s the United Mine Workers of America built at least eight top notch hospitals located in Kentucky, Virginia and West Virginia. They were staffed with the best trained doctors and interns you could get. Miners received a UMWA health card which entitled them to treatment at any of these hospitals, but the problem was getting to these hospitals from the out of way places. Transportation was a major problem. Then, a few years after the realization of these medical facilities, corruption was uncovered in the UMWA and all out war broke out. The UMWA could no longer fund the hospitals, the well-trained professionals left and the Presbyterian Church under a non-profit organizing agency was able to save a few of the clinics."

Federal dollars came in 1977 when Mud Creek Clinic merged with Big Sandy Health Care, Inc. The merger was out of necessity. Mud Creek Clinic was no longer able to meet the needs of the people - the need was so great. Ten people staffed the clinic by 1982, and the clinic was in dire need of a pharmacy so medication could be dispensed on site.

An arsonist burned the clinic to the ground in June of that year. Many community members thought that would end Mud Creek Clinic, but Eula had weathered too many storms to let this arsonist get the best of her. She did say it was the hardest thing she had endured except for a death in her immediate family. The burning of this clinic represented a death in her family. Medical needs of the people were not on hold because the Mud Creek Clinic lay in a pile of ashes. Eula and one of the doctors pulled out a picnic table and made it into a makeshift clinic to meet the needs of the day. A two-bedroom trailer, second hand, puttied and patched, was converted into a clinic and the medical needs were met continuously. Three months later word was received from the Appalachian Regional Commission pledging funds for a new clinic. "One of the happiest days in my life," Eula recalls but of course matching funds were required in the amount of $80,000, a sum the people in Mud Creek would not sneeze at. For many, the only place holding such a huge amount like $80,000 was Ft. Knox but Eula was elated by the vote of confidence from the ARC and began her fundraising campaign.

Eula called a community meeting and hundreds turned out. More than 400 people pledged their support right on the spot, giving what they could. Raffles were organized offering quilts for sale, chicken-n-dumpling dinners and a radiothon. The immediate need for matching funds gave birth to the now famous Eula Hall Roadblocks. She took a gallon bucket with a handle, placed signs on each side of the railroad tracks, "Please help raise money for the Mud Creek Clinic." Eula would straddle the yellow line giving drivers an opportunity to drop money in the bucket as they drove by. The initial fundraising events raised more than $40,000 above the needed $80,000 matching, which paid for X-ray equipment for the new clinic.

Eula was finally able to secure the assistance of the combined efforts of community members and politicians. Eula told us the secret to handling politicians is by making them look bad and if you hold on long enough and they can't beat you, they will join you. ARC and the unyielding force of Eula resulted in a beautiful 5,200 square-foot-facility gracing Mud Creek today A model of a rural primary care clinic which proudly serves more than 7,000 patients a year. Payment is based on a sliding scale with 20 percent as minimum. Patients pay for health care services based on what they can afford but no one is turned away. The facility has an adjacent 1,800 square foot building complete with pharmacy, a dental clinic, clothing room and food pantry that serves more than 100 families per month with food items. The building also houses the Mud Creek Water Department providing potable water for a community that 30 years ago averaged 90 percent contaminated wells.

Eula tells us the health care professionals are so dedicated. They do not try to shove a few pills toward the patient hoping they will just go away. They follow through with needed tests and treatment. Doctors and other health care professionals are there to serve the underserved. Prescription drug costs are a concern for all of us, but especially for those living below poverty level. It has been discovered many of the patients at the clinic were trying to stretch their medications by taking the prescribed dose only every other day instead of every day, or one-half prescribed dosage instead of the full dosage. That was one of the important factor in establishing a pharmacy at the clinic so that medication can be dispensed and monitored closely to make sure the patients understands and are taking the proper dosage regardless of costs.

The way Eula sees it, "If the patient can't pay the $12.00 charge for medicine this month, then perhaps next month." She maintains a slush fund to makeup the difference and when that gets low she gets out her bucket, places signs at each end of the railroad tracks and straddles the yellow line so drivers can help raise money for the Mud Creek Clinic. A pop machine inside helps to keep the slush fund going as well with proceeds being divided between the pharmacy and the clinic.

After the clinic began operating smoothly, staffed with doctors, nurses, an obstetrician, dentists and psychologist caring for patients suffering from diabetes to hypertension to cancer, Eula, acting as social director since 1982, devotes more of her time assisting with black lung compensation claims and other disability claims. She attends hearings and acts as an advocate for the client. She told me, "I have driven many a miner to Beckley, West Virginia for examination by Dr. Donald Rasmussen." However, a well stocked pharmacy and equally well staffed clinic did not guarantee the clinic of any additional near fateful events, in 2002 Mud Creek Clinic was flooded inside and out. I talked with Eula by phone today getting details on the flood. She told me, "Everything in the clinic was flooded and had to be removed, scrubbed up or replaced." I asked her what caused the flood. She said, "It was a flash flood, coming on us before we could turn around. I think it was caused by so much strip mining." But then, there are people who have ideas and commitments that are indestructible so Eula and the clinic survived the big flood of 2002.

Now 78 years old, Eula doesn't even entertain thoughts of retiring. She is too busy continuing to wage the war on poverty in a section of the country where 60 percent of those living and working in Kentucky's Appalachia live below poverty level. According to studies, it is an established fact poverty and health related problems go hand-in-hand and even though $400 million dollars has been designated to alleviate poverty in many minority groups, the poor in Appalachia were left out in the cold. So apparently it is left up to people like Eula Hall to single handedly stamp out poverty one community at a time. A study shows one out of six children grow up in poverty. The poor children have always gotten to Eula's soft side. The poverty rate in Floyd County, Kentucky, home of the Mud Creek Clinic, is an average of 30 percent below poverty level. In the U.S. alone, the land of billionaires, more than 34 million people wake up every morning to face another day living in poverty.

Eula, armed with a 8th grade education, understands more about poverty and the importance of elimination of poverty, than many of the experts who are dedicated to studying only the economic factors involved. She knows living in poverty represents more than the hollow-eyed starved looking child in dirty clothes, or the old man bent over with work and worry. Overcoming poverty means more than giving people sufficient material goods for a life of dignity. It means giving the poor a voice in making decisions which directly affect them. It means giving them a place in society with their culture. It means a healthy body. Jobs are essential in defeating poverty, but for the working poor who earn minimum wages, they cannot keep a family out of poverty because of the increase in the cost of living and the continuous slashing of social programs to supplement their needs. It means having potable water, a warm coat and a voice in our government. Eula Hall understands all of this.

Someone in our group asked Eula if she had come into harm's way during her campaign for community development which often stepped on toes of those in power.

She told us that she had been threatened, shot at, had the windows broken out of her car. "One night two men were coming into my home to cause me harm." Eula said, "I picked up one of my daughter's high heel shoes, and, as the first man came through the door, I busted his head open with that high heel shoe. He turned around and left with blood running down his face."

These days Eula is receiving lots of recognition:

The Transportation Cabinet has named the entire length of Kentucky Route 979 in Floyd County the "Eula Hall Highway."
Eula Hall received an honorary degree of doctor of human letters from Berea College in May of 2005 along with the Archbishop Desmond Tutu of South Africa.

2003-2004 Annual David S. Shuller Spirit of AMER award was presented to Eula Hall on February 12, 2004 at Mud Creek, Grethel, Kentucky. Inscribed: "To Eula Hall, a woman who nurtures healing and community in Mud Creek and witnesses for AMERC students the powerful gift of a life lived for others."

I gave Eula a hug, presented her with one of my books and told her how much I admired her.

On August 1, 2005, I called Eula at the Mud Creek Clinic to talk about her story. She wanted me to add this poem.

A lady wrote this and put it on a plaque and framed it for Eula.
Eula: This woman came in to the clinic. She was very sick and her medicine was so expensive she could not afford to buy it. She didn't know what she was going to do. I told her if there was a cent of money to be found, we were going to get her medicine, and I gathered up some money and bought her medicine. I started working to get her a card to purchase her medicine. She is better now. She is not well, but she is going so good.

One day she came in carrying this poem – it was framed in a little plaque.
She said, "I brought you something" and she handed me the poem.

Eula said, "Did you write this yourself or copy it from someone? Because if someone else wrote it the poem would not mean anything but if you wrote it yourself, it means something."

She said, "I wrote it. This is from my heart."

Angel of Mercy

The world has become a dog eat dog situation
but now and then we see one of God's creations.
I am glad I found this one who saved me,
For I was dying but I was saved by this lady

They say she has become heroine to those in need,
this I can testify to, and I am just one of her good deeds

She has made it her mission to help everyone she can,
and the selfless way she does it, is like is all planned.

I don't know why we were so fortunate to have her,
but I thank God for her and wish there were others

for this world right now is in trouble,
and needs a lot more for those unfortunate, sick, disabled, or just poor

My thanks and prayers go to her Eula Hall for you have helped so many cross that brick wall

You have done more to help people than anyone I know
You should immortalized, because Eula, we all love you so.

To Eula Hall, God's Helper on Earth

Miners for Democracy - Oral History Interview with Dr. Donald Rasmussen

Author's note: My oral history interview with Dr. Donald Rasmussen, except for Miners for Democracy, is found in my first book titled, Appalachia: Spirit Triumphant.   The book was published before this interview was finished.

Miners for Democracy was formed as a fusion of the Black Lung Association and the remains of the people who worked for Yablonski who had strong support around southwest Pennsylvania and adjacent Ohio and northern West Virginia.   He had support through the Union, at least in most all the districts. After Yablonski's death in January, 1970, his sons, Chip and Ken and people like Mike Trbovich, along with a group of others close to Yablonski, including Arnold Miller, President of the Black Lung Association, joined in this close alliance, Miners for Democracy. The idea was to get moving on having the Justice and Labor Department look into that election of December, 1969.

Eventually, that election was found to be fraudulent.

At any rate we had meetings. Mostly we would meet in St. Claireville, Ohio, a central location and easy to get to. We would plan various strategies.

Our feelings were that Yablonski had enough support to have won that election. On the other hand, a lot of people were not Yablonski supporters, but when he was murdered that changed their idea about Tony Boyle. A lot of good union people were fearful of ousting Boyle. They thought this would harm the United Mine Workers and they were always loyal to the UMWA.

Miners for Democracy held a convention in Wheeling to select a slate for running for office.   Personally, I felt the non-miners should not participate in that. I felt that should not be their business but everyone, who attended the convention, got involved, except me. I did not attend. They selected Arnold Miller to be President and Mike Trbovich to be Vice-President.

They traveled around and spoke at rallies all over the country. I don't know if they got way out west or not but they campaigned. It looked like they had good strong support. One of the provisions made when they threw out the original 1969 election was that they would have observers at all the polling places to make sure they was no fraud. They had the election and the Miller slate won.

Arnold was one of the movers and shakers in the strategies in the Black Lung Association in West Virginia lobbying for changes in the West Virginia law and the federal Act.

He wasn't one of the actual initial organizers but shortly after that he was elected President of the Black Lung Association. He worked night and day getting things organized.

Arnold was one of the movers - when Yablonski ran for President, Arnold was one of his chief guys. I knew him then. We traveled together a lot. Yes, he was a personal friend. As I had done for Yablonski, I campaigned with the Miller people at various rallies. When they held the election, there was a good solid win for the Miller team. There is no longer a need for Miners for Democracy. After Miller went in, there were still people loyal to Boyle. There was tension and friction there.

Today the Union is just solid. There is no vestige of any split shape or form. The current leadership I think doesn't want to revisit the old subject.

Cecil Roberts is an absolutely great guy and dynamic leader. I have spent quite a bit of time with Cecil Roberts. I have introduced him at Black Lung conferences.

I have seen him several times. They give strong support to each other. In fact Cecil came down to a regional meeting at Twins Park and gave me a certificate as an Honorary Member of the United Mine Workers. I think Cecil Roberts is probably the best United Mine Workers President since John L. Lewis, even though Arnold Miller was a good friend.

After Miller was elected I didn't feel comfortable being involved in Union politics. I stayed out. I could see some of the strain on Arnold. Another personal friend was Levi Daniel, absolutely strong supporter of Arnold's. He told me a lot of things Arnold was concerned about.

Arnold had a lot of problems. He suddenly felt he was not educated enough to run the Union. He relied on some of the college people who were non miners and they tended to isolate Arnold from the coal miners.

Arnold had excellent rapport with the miners and they tended to feel he was the one who should have been running the Union. They felt Arnold was smart enough to do the job because he had the right instincts and his own personal history of coal mining. That is story you would have been glad to get, Arnold Miller's story. He was in the Normandy Invasion and got shot in the face. He was left to die by his captain who took off running and left him behind to die. His buddy came back and got him. He had multiple scars where he was shot.

Arnold worked in the mines 30 years or so and got involved in the black lung movement. Arnold and I traveled together. He came to my house. He stayed at my house. He was a good guy but he had some problems. He was not an exceptionally good United Mine Workers President but he certainly kept his promise of letting all the districts have their own elections. He totally democratized the districts. Up until that time most of the districts were controlled by Tony Boyle. Arnold certainly got democracy restored to that the Union. The local union meetings were always democratic meetings with some of the guys serving as the local officers – they were good guys. It was good to see they were accountable to their membership.

There were some interesting experiences when the district officers were appointed. Often conflict there. District officers, before Arnold Miller owed their loyalty to Tony Boyle and the District leader he had appointed.

Right now I believe the Union is running very smoothly. As far as the policy aspects, I believe it is clinging by its fingernails. If it goes under, it will be a terrible tragedy.

Health and safety were Cecil Robert's main concern. That was his main concern for the membership. As a matter of fact, what Cecil Roberts did was, develop and encourage the Black Lung Association and the United Miners Workers to get together because they had been on opposite sides. Cecil brought the Black Lung Association, the National Coal Miners' Clinics and the UMWA together. Representatives from each organization came together here in Beckley. He wanted his district officers to be aware of the black lung problems, the issues; both the medical and legal aspects. He was very active in the black lung movement. He was just a strong union guy. I guess all his people (family from years back were union people from Cabin Creek). He would have been someone you would find interesting to talk to. He spent time in jail for being out on the picket line.

Oral history interviewed continued -Dr. Donald Rasmussen at his clinic on July 11, 2003

Tell me about black lung – compare earlier years to today for me?

At present, perhaps 8% of miners applying for black lung benefits meet the medical requirements for disability. However, only about half receive benefits because of the coal companies being able to have the patient re-examined one or more times, have his records reviewed by numerous experts, etc.

The problem of overwhelming number of reports existed until the regulations were put together at the end of the Clinton Administration and finally upheld by the courts.

The results of claims for Black Lung compensation depends an awfully lot on the legal representative. If you don't have representation that is very experienced in this area, you are taking a very big chance. It is a like a morass. You have to be very careful about it.

Tell me about the advocacy program at Washington & Lee University. How did that start?

I am not exactly sure how Washington & Lee University came to be doing this. I guess they had to have some type of clinic in their law school. I am not sure if it was for underprivileged or not, but they got interested in the black lung business. They connected up with New River Health Clinic. They actually work through the clinic and John Cline who lives in Piney View -- he is doing black lung cases. He finished law school. He was the one who got it all organized. They have done a good job taking on lost cases where the evidence is not that strong but the miners have had impairment and were able to prove what it was for. They have done a good job.

Mary Natkin, is one of the professors at Washington and Lee University. They have been down here at this clinic to look at various things. We had a conference and they came down here. Occasionally, they will send down medical records to be reviewed. They do a very good job.

Do you have any closing comments at the close of this most interesting oral history interview?

It has been fascinating looking back over things. I am proud of getting the Federal Coal Miners Health and Safety Act passed. Had it not been for Ken Hechler at least, it would not have passed with the dust control clause. Had it not been for the

Congressman from San Francisco, Phillip Burton, the compensation clause would not have passed. Burton told them he would not support the Bill unless that was included because so many had been left behind by the workers compensation the statutes of limitation had expired. Because of that, many of these people got benefits which were a God send.

The part I am really proud of is the dust control clause. That has and can prevent lung disease. It sure has done a good job in controlling dust. The problem now is, the small mine operations do not have as much economically as the big coal operator. The small mines have to cut all corners to survive.

I am also glad for having participated in the Yablonski and Miller campaigns because the Union did need changes.

I would like to ask you one more question – in doing research I read about an organization called, "Physicians for Miners" – will you tell me something about that group?

In the fall of 1968 coal miners held meetings and invited Dr. I. E. Buff to speak. Dr. Buff had, for several months been publicly talking about Black Lung, later a group of miners asked me to participate. After the explosion in Mannington, Hawey Wells, a Pathologist, who had worked with me in the Public Health Service, joined us. Dr. Wells probably thought up the title "Physicians Committee for Miners' Health and Safety."

We were supposed to represent a larger body of physicians, however, we three were the total membership. My wife at the time was supposed to be the press secretary – she was working with a number of people including Brit Hume, now of Fox News. Dr. Buff, however, used to ignore the news releases by her and Brit Hume. He would phone in his own, often frustrating us.

The three of us went to many, many rallies throughout the state and once in Pennsylvania. Dr. Buff was the big entertainer bringing props, black and white helmets, etc. Wells was also a performer – crushing dried lung tissue, etc. I was last and tried to be objective, but was mostly boring.

Anyway the group worked together until the Yablonski Campaign started – Wells and I endorsed Yablonski – Buff did not – that was the end of the committee.

End of interview.

Oral History Interview with Ralph Baber, Silver Star, Bronze Star, Purple Heart recipient

WWII Decorated Soldier lives in West Virginia coalfields - INVASION OF LUZON
Craigsville, Nicholas County, West Virginia
May 29, 2004

Author's note: I discovered this WWII hero hidden away in the small mountain community of Craigsville, Nicholas County, West Virginia. I wish more people could meet this gallant soldier in person. It is an honor to listen and record his stories of battles fought on the front line.   My hope is to give this mountain soldier a voice to tell his personal story of courage, selflessness, the art of survival and band of brotherhood.

Introduction – President's Roosevelt's Address to Congress on December 8, 1941

I have selected as the introduction to this compelling military story, President Roosevelt's Address to Congress requesting Declaration of a State of War following the attack on Pearl Harbor on December 7, 1941.   Roosevelt's passionate speech stirred feelings of patriotism throughout our Nation and 18 year old boys like Ralph Baber were ready and willing to lay down their lives to preserve the freedom of this country.

PRESIDENT ROOSEVELT'S ADDRESS TO CONGRESS
(Declaration of a State of War between the United States and Japan, December 8, 1941)
Yesterday, 7 December 1941-a date which will live in infamy-the United States of America was suddenly and deliberately attacked by naval and air forces of the Empire of Japan.
The United States was at peace with that nation and, at the solicitation of Japan, was still in conversation with its Government and its Emperor looking toward the maintenance of peace in the Pacific. Indeed, one hour after Japanese air squadrons had commenced bombing in Oahu, the Japanese Ambassador to the United States and his colleague delivered to the Secretary of State a formal reply to a recent American message. While this reply stated that it seemed useless to continue the existing diplomatic negotiations, it contained no threat or hint of war or armed attack.
It will be recorded that the distance of Hawaii from Japan makes it obvious that the attack was deliberately planned many days or even weeks ago. During the intervening time the Japanese Government had deliberately sought to deceive the United States by false statements and expressions of hope for continued peace.
The attack yesterday on the Hawaiian Islands has caused severe damage to American naval and military forces. Very many American lives were lost. In addition,

American ships have been reported torpedoed on the high seas between San Francisco and Honolulu.

Yesterday the Japanese Government also launched an attack against Malaya.

Last night Japanese forces attacked Hong Kong.

Last night Japanese forces attacked Guam.

Last night Japanese forces attacked the Philippine Islands.

Last night Japanese forces attacked Wake Island.

This morning the Japanese attacked Midway Island.

Japan has, therefore, undertaken a surprise offensive extending throughout the Pacific area. The facts of yesterday speak for themselves. The people of the United States have already formed their opinions and well understand the implications to the very life and safety of our nation.

As Commander in Chief of the Army and Navy I have directed that all measures be taken for our defense.

Always will we remember the character of the onslaught against us.

No matter how long it may take us to overcome this premeditated invasion, the American people in their righteous might will win through to absolute victory.

I believe I interpret the will of the Congress and of the people when I assert that we will not only defend ourselves to the uttermost but will make very certain that this form of treachery shall never endanger us again.

Hostilities exist. There is no blinking at the fact that our people, our territory, and our interests are in grave danger.

With confidence in our armed forces-with the unbounded determination of our people-we will gain the inevitable triumph-so help us God.

I ask that the Congress declare that since the unprovoked and dastardly attack by Japan on Sunday, 7 December, a state of war has existed between the United States and the Japanese Empire.   (Source: Pamphlet No. 4, PILLARS OF PEACE; Documents Pertaining To American Interest In Establishing A Lasting World Peace: January 1941-February 1946. Published by the Book Department, Army Information School, Carlisle Barracks, Pa., May 1943)

First interview - Baber's home in Craigsville, West Virginia., May 29, 2004, 1:00 P.M. Mary, Ralph's wife, always sat close to her husband during these interviews, offering comfort and words of support as he relived the brutality of the Invasion of Luzon.

When did you come home from World War II?

I made it home the 31st of December 1945.

I have a little black book with everywhere I went written down in it.

When did you go to the Service?

July 24, 1943. We lived out in the country, here at Craigsville, and I had to get my own ride to Summersville and then on to Clarksburg for my physical examination when I got my call. I had never been to Clarksburg before.

What did you do when you got to Clarksburg after you had your physical examination?

That night for fun we threw bags of water out the window of the hotel down toward people on the street. We were able to go back home for a few days when we finished in Clarksburg and then we were sent to Ft. Hayes, Ohio. They sent everyone from this area to Ft. Hayes. From there, they loaded us all on trains and sent us to Camp Barkley, Texas. Camp Barkley is near Dallas, Texas, and Abilene where the old gun fighters use to hang out.

Where other members of your family in any wars?

No one else in my family. I think one of my uncles on my mother's side fought in the Civil War.

Did he fight for the Union or Confederate?

I don't know which side he fought for, but he is buried down the road here at Calvin, Nicholas County.

What happened while you were at Camp Barkley?

Basic training. Also the camp is the site of a German Prisoner of War Camp. That is where we went for training. That was about the most miserable place I had ever seen. It was hot.

What did you do before you went in the Service?

Before I went in the Army I drove a coal truck for Russell Catlett. I worked for his wife. They had two coal mines. He took care of one and she took care of the other. I worked for both of them hauling house coal. Most of the coal from their mines went to Meadow River Lumber Company to use in the mills' boilers.

What was it like working for a woman running a coal mine?

I would get that old truck loaded up and she would say, "Now hurry." One time she said, "You drive too fast." It was a 1941 or 42 Chevrolet truck. She thought I was having too many flat tires. It was not my fault. She said that she was going to have to let me go because I was having too many flat tires. I said that was O.K. I was going to quit anyway. It was a short time after that I got drafted.

Like I was telling you, they took us to Camp Barkley for training. They sent me to school to teach me how to drive a truck. I still have our class schedules when we were going to training at Camp Barkley. I don't know whether they taught me anything or not but that is what they sent me to school for – to learn to drive a truck. I have a paper we had in our classes and a roster of all the people that were there. Some of the trainees were in a group to learn how to drive different things. Some were sent to mechanic's school.

How long were you in basic training?

Well, let me look in my little black book – we were in Basic Training for 8 weeks. When we got through our basic training we got to come home for two weeks. We traveled by train as far as Gauley Bridge and then on home by bus. When we got into Gauley Bridge it was late at night and no buses running. (Gauley Bridge, located about 30 miles out of Charleston, West Virginia, was the nearest bus and train terminals to the rural areas in Fayette and Nicholas Counties).

There was a taxi driver seated over there across the road from the bus station. I told him, "I need to get to Craigsville in Nicholas County but I have no money on me, but I'm sure my mother will pay you."

When we got to my house I asked how much he wanted and it was $5.00. That was $5.00. He parked right over here across the road from the house. My Mother had to scrounge up $5.00. I took it to the taxi driver. It was daylight when we got to my home here in Craigsville. It was forty-five miles from Gauley Bridge to Craigsville.

When I started back to Texas I rode the bus to Gauley Bridge and I had a little bit of time to kill. I had all my belongings in my duffle bag; my extra clothes and some things they had given me from home like a camera and extra clothes. I was dumb enough to set the bag down outside the little restaurant where passengers waited for their bus. I went inside and sat down at the counter on a little round stool. I sat down by a deputy sheriff. We talked a little bit over a cup of coffee. When I went outside to pick up my bag of stuff it was gone. Some S.O.B. stole it. I yelled at the deputy sheriff. He said, "I will try to find who took your stuff, but there is not much chance."

So, I was stranded with nothing. I went back to Charleston on a Greyhound bus and caught the train at Charleston to Abilene, Texas and me with nothing. To add insult to injury, I had to pay for everything they had given me that had been stolen, including clothes and underwear. Everything. That was November 27, 1943, when I got back to Abilene.

Later on December 30, 1943, they sent us out again. I wound up in Camp Reynolds, Pennsylvania. It would have been a lot easier to go to Pennsylvania from where I was here in West Virginia but they didn't do things like that. I spent my 19th birthday in Texas. Not much of a celebration.

What town was Camp Reynolds close to in Pennsylvania?

Close to Sharon, Pennsylvania, close to Youngstown, Ohio. That is where they sent us to Chenango Personnel Replacement Depot where they gathered everyone in and started shipping them in different directions. I was there until February 10, 1944.

I got to come home a couple of times while I was there. I had a sister who lived near Morgantown, West Virginia. I would call her and she came to meet me when I could get a pass. We would meet there and she would bring me home - I would get to stay one night and then report back to base.

Where there other soldiers in the camp from this area?

From this area were several fellows from Richwood, West Virginia, that went in at the same time as I did. I can not remember if any of them went to Texas. After we went to Camp Reynolds and were ready to ship out I took the flu that sidelined me for a week or so. When they got ready to ship me out, the soldiers from this area had already gone. So I went to Camp Stoneman, California, close to Pittsburgh, California. I went by train. I was from February to March 8 getting to my destination.

What happened after you arrived at Camp Stoneman?

What happened when we got there? We were up the Sacramento River (I believe that is the name of the river - I looked it up on the map one time). We were getting ready to go overseas from Camp Stoneman, they used paddle wheel boats and I heard later the Delta Queen was hauling soldiers from Camp Stoneman to San Francisco to go overseas. It was supposed to have been the Delta Queen. While we were at Camp Stoneman we received an overnight pass to go to San Francisco. The Sgt. in charge called us all together and gave us a pep talk and a couple of threats. He told us to go to San Francisco and be back by a certain time.

The Sgt. said, "You had better be back and if you are not, you had better give your heart to God because you ass is going to belong to me."

What did you do in town that last night before shipping off to war?

I can't remember. We didn't have any money. I had a dollar and some of the others didn't have any more than I did. We didn't tarry long until we were back on the bus and back to camp.

Now, before we got shipped overseas they called us in one by one and interviewed us. We knew we were getting ready to go overseas but they asked, "Do you want to go overseas?" Everyone said, "Yeah, I want to go." It didn't matter because we were on our way.

Ralph Baber interview continues: July 24, 2004, 11:00 AM - my office, Summersville, Nicholas County, West Virginia. Mary came with Ralph.

New Caledonia, Auckland, New Zealand, out of Aitape Harbor; next stop, Luzon

Did you mind going overseas?

No. They put us on a ship called U.S. Army transport shanks. Same thing as Liberty ships - they made one everyday. One came off the assembly line everyday. We were on our way to New Caledonia Island in the South Pacific -- the Camp was Tewes - French owned Island. That was another replacement depot where they would gather you in and ship you out. We moved while we were there from New Caledonia to another camp. Left there on April 12, 1944.

April 12, 1944 - That move put us in Auckland, New Zealand. That was a good place just like being home. The people were a lot like Americans - friendly good people, nice looking country. They raised lots of sheep and some of us gained weight eating three meals a day of sheep and ice cream but we worked hard.

April 16, 1944 - July 15, 1944 - Three months, that was my stay in Auckland, New Zealand. The seasons are reversed from here. We went out on maneuvers while we were there.

I took the flu again. New Zealand was an ally of the U.S. They fought right along the U.S. what they could. Thousands of U.S. soldiers were there training. Now that is where they put me into another job. They taught me to drive a truck in Texas and they thought that was what I going to do when I got to New Zealand but I joined the 118th Medical Battalion. It was attached to the 172nd Infantry Regiment. We had to go through quite a bit of first aid there. I had some first aid before I went in the Army. I went into E Company the 2nd Battalion of the 172nd Regiment 43d Infantry Division 2nd Platoon that was where I was assigned. That was part of the company I would stay with from then on.

I didn't know at the time what I was going to have to do. When the bullets started whizzing, when soldiers got hit, I had to take care of them. I was a combat medic.

July 15, 1944 - The 43d Division arrived from New Zealand and immediately took their place in the defensive line. The terrain consisted of jungle covered plains rising with rugged mountain ranges. In this country between Aitape and Wewak, several thousand Japanese troops were faced with the decision of starving their defenses or attempting a counter-attack against the American beachhead in an effort to secure food and facilities for evacuation from New Guinea. They chose to attack.

The 103d and 172nd regiments were immediately assigned to man the main line of resistance bordering the beachhead while elements of the 169th moved to the Driniumor River ten miles to the East, where elements of the 32nd Infantry Division, 112th Regimental Combat Team and the 124th Infantry were against the mounting Jap offensive.

July 1944 (mid month) - The main attack was attempted. Elements of the 169th and 124th infantry were ordered to attack East into the jungle to search out and destroy the disorganized enemy forces. That was the last time the Japanese attempted a major offensive in New Guinea. Patrols were dispatched southerly and easterly for approximately 35 miles to detect enemy movement. Skirmishes with the enemy were frequent, and in November 1944 thirty seven- prisoners of war were captured. On the same day of this capture, well into the night, we heard voices coming toward our position. The voices were saying "Subjects of the King:, Subjects of the King." It turned out to be thirty-four members of the British Indian Army who had been captured by the Japanese in Malaya in January and February 1942.

After doing what we could for them, they were sent on for more medical help. That was a really happy group of soldiers even though they were in terrible shape.

<u>December 26, 1944</u> - The water-borne 43d (Winged Victory) Division pulled out of Aitape Harbor by way of Luzon Island. The ships were loaded and ready.

On that rainy morning men of the 43d Infantry Division marched to the beach at Aitape loaded with bazookas, machine guns, mortars, grenades, and packs. Loading was quick. Two days later, after all ships and personnel had taken part in a practice landing, the ships sailed. The Sixth Army convoy raced northward. The convoy seemed to stretch from horizon to horizon. The 43d Infantry Division and its attached troops with combat were loaded on eight APs, three APs, four AKAs, sixteen LSTs, ten LSMs and two LSDs. The men were as calm as the ocean and even the propaganda broadcasts of Japan's famed Tokyo Rose couldn't excite them, though she said, "I am broadcasting to you Munda Butchers. The Japanese Army knows that you are headed for Luzon and that you are going to land at Lingayen Gulf." Then she would tell what to expect when they arrived. It sounded as if the American invaders could expect the might of the entire Japanese Army. The men listened, shrugged their shoulders and continued reading their books and playing cards.

Other movements during this time were to the Russell Island, Solomon Island then back to New Zealand to begin the long trip to New Guinea. Luzon and on to Japan.

Who knew that so much and so many things would happen when we left our homes and families. One thing that helped us was the circle of family and friends we developed away from home. That was a necessity for one simple reason- under our circumstances your life or your buddy's life could and would depend on someone else.

As a noncombatant medic, I wasn't suppose to have a gun, but I had one. I was a noncombatant. They gave me a Red Cross arm band to wear instead of giving me a gun. I took the Red Cross arm band off and hid it. That arm band was just like holding up a red flag in front of a bull. That made a good target. Officers did not wear their stars or stripes. Anything advertising who you were was not safe to wear.

<u>January 9, 1945 9:30 A.M.</u> - Next stop for me, Luzon, Philippines. That was the day the Invasion was scheduled. (If you don't know how soldiers disembarked for an invasion, I can show you, I think). You see we were out in Lingayen Gulf. Hundreds of ships were in that gulf which brought us into Luzon.

The group I was with rode from New Guinea up to Luzon on an LST (a flat bottom boat that hauls tanks and stuff like that). The only exciting thing that happened on that almost 2000 mile trip to Luzon was a Kamikaze attack which I got to watch.

Then came the morning of January 9, 1945. The roar of the Naval guns sounded like the roll of a thousand bass drums when they hit the shoreline - a sight no one who saw it will ever forget. When the big ships finally got in position, the LST had a ramp and two doors opened up straight into the water. Twenty-five or thirty of us were stationed on each one of those amphibious tanks. You would think you were going right down in the water but they floated - it was two or three miles off the shore when we dropped out of there one by one. We lined up by the hundreds. They looked like row boats they hauled soldiers in. They had a certain position to get in line which made an inverted V shape. Line after line of those things with us poor old dumb people in them.

Were you scared?

We were a little scared when we came out of there and dropped down in the ocean (I couldn't swim). When they lined us up, there was a certain time when we hit the beach. It was 9:30 AM, January 9, 1945, when we hit the beach.

I was in the 1st row when we hit the beach of the Invasion of Luzon.

That was a Philippine Island controlled by the Japanese. It was a big island. The capital was there, Manila -- there were thousands of Japanese. The amphibious tanks attached to the ships took us right up on the beach. When we landed, they were shooting up over our heads and letting the shells come down. We had a company commander who had a handlebar mustache. We called him, "Handlebars" - he jumped in a shell hole and me right after him. He had a 30 caliber carbine. He jumped in that shell hole. The next thing I knew he was sticking his head up and shooting. He did that two or three times. I can remember him hollering. He would shoot and yell, "Take that you little yellow S.O.B." - like they could hear him. I don't know what happened to him. He disappeared like a lot of others. We had a lot of commanders come and go.

Well, we just landed, but several of the fellows in the same company had been over for three years. They didn't have furloughs or anything. Not many left of that group. One of them was Sgt. Sombric. He had been through the whole thing. I snagged on to him. I was going to stay with him.

When we landed at Lingayen Gulf we turned left and started up a hill towards Rosario. I was with this Sgt. and we were standing looking at something, about that time a machine gun opened up and shot his shirt pocket off. We got out of there fast. It just shot the pocket off and made a little red stripe on his chest. That was all that happened to him. We were on our way inland. A lot of the Japanese troops defending that place left out about two days before we came. They had gone to the mountains. It took us quite a while to get them rooted out. Then we turned toward Manila.

Up in the areas next to Rosario is where our Commander got killed. One of the first shells they shot killed our battalion commander, Col. John Carrington. I think he was an Irishman and he smoked a pipe all the time.

Did you think that was reasonable?

I don't think we knew any better. When you take a bunch of boys from the hills they don't know any better. What it boils down to is territory; they have got it and we want it. There were more hills and caves than in West Virginia. The trouble was that they were all full of Japs and guns. It took us about five weeks to complete our mission; 7,831 enemy killed. U.S. 593 killed, 1,644 wounded.

About that time or a week or two later they had to stop for a little bit to get new recruits. Our Division was short 3,805 men-enlisted men and 215 officers. We got about 1,600 replacements – some came out of the hospitals - about 500 came out of the hospitals. That is how you could tell how many men were killed or wounded by the number of replacements needed. I guess over in Europe, a bitter territory - lots of men lost.

We dug a foxhole every night. The company I was with, I remember at one place, we had all dug our foxholes and we realized there was a concrete road down below. We could hear a noise. It was Japs. They used horses to pull their artillery pieces. We were sitting up there waiting on them when they got up next to us just like they said, "All hell broke loose." They could switch their artillery around.

What we did not know at the time was that word had come down from the top that these strong points must be overrun at all cost. The Division had overrun 125 heavy artillery positions and engaged enemy tanks for the first time. Some of the artillery pieces were as large as 300MM.

We were relieved by the 33d Division and moved to Santa Barbara. The First Corps Commander, Major General Innis P. Swift, told the Division after the campaign, "I am proud of you and I am proud of your Division Commander." When this division landed at Lingayen Gulf, it had to fight the whole accursed Jap force and don't let anyone tell you differently. The rest of the troops in the Corps did not see a Jap for three weeks.

Eleven days after we made the beachhead. We found out a war correspondent from the New York Times was with us and had written a article headlined, "The Lost Battalion." I wrote back home to my sister who lived with my Mom in Craigsville, West Virginia. I told her to get that newspaper article and she did.

The war correspondent was George E. Jones. The news item was sent by wireless to the New York Times. He was with my group. (Ralph read me a sentence from the article written by George E. Jones, then he provided me a copy). It was a story about Ralph Baber's Battalion, "LOST BATTALION BEATS LUZON FOE" Japanese Fail to Shake hold on Hills to North Through Grim Days, Terrible Nights - GROUP ALMOST ISOLATED

Ralph continues telling his story to me: We didn't have helicopters to pick up people who needed medical attention. We used Water Buffalo and sleds and Filipino people to carry people. There was more than one medic in the entire company, we had three medics. We carried what medical supplies we had in a bag. We would appropriate what we could. After that, I did some traveling.

Ralph asked me, "Do you know about the Baatan Death March?"
I answered, "No."

That Baatan Death March happened in 1942, two years before we made our invasion. The Japanese captured 12,000 Americans. They started marching the prisoners toward the northern part of Luzon to a POW camp. The POWs had nothing to eat, no water and if they fell down they were left to die or the Japanese guards would walk up to the fallen soldier and shoot him or stab him to death where he lay. As many as 5,000 of them were killed or died along the way. The name of the prison camp was Cabanatuan. I read where the ones left were rescued. I don't think they were in very good condition.

August 12, 2004 interview continues at the Nicholas County Board Office, 400 Old Main Drive, Summersville, WV

Did you get one of those Bibles, a new testament?

Yes, we all had one of those.

Did they have church services for the soldiers?

We had outdoor church. Some would attend church every chance they got. It was outdoor church or if we were lucky we had a movie. We would sit on a log and watch a movie.

This war was justified – they jumped on us. They started invading countries before they got to us. We had the Canbanatuan Prison Camp and the Baatan Death march to put to rest. Sgt. Sombric was the one I stuck with.

Mary, Ralph's wife, took a picture of Ralph down from the wall to show me – picture seen here. It was a picture of Ralph when he came back from overseas.

What were your commanders like? Did you like them?

My Platoon Sgt. was one of the best men I ever knew. To the best of my knowledge he made it back home. I'm sure Sgt. Sombric did too but he came back by way of being wounded.

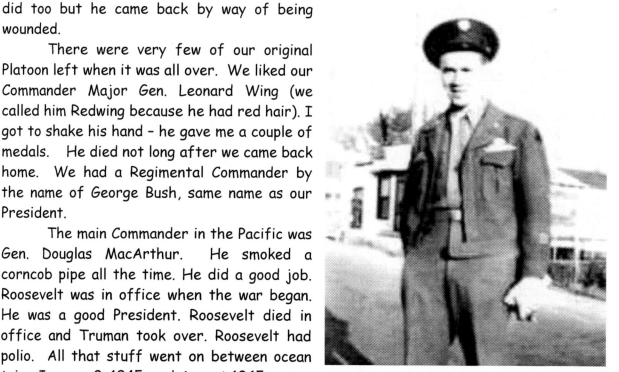

There were very few of our original Platoon left when it was all over. We liked our Commander Major Gen. Leonard Wing (we called him Redwing because he had red hair). I got to shake his hand – he gave me a couple of medals. He died not long after we came back home. We had a Regimental Commander by the name of George Bush, same name as our President.

The main Commander in the Pacific was Gen. Douglas MacArthur. He smoked a corncob pipe all the time. He did a good job. Roosevelt was in office when the war began. He was a good President. Roosevelt died in office and Truman took over. Roosevelt had polio. All that stuff went on between ocean trips January 9, 1945, and August 1945.

August 18, 2004 - interview continues. location- Ralph and Mary Baber's home, Craigsville, West Virginia (when we finished, Mary asked me to stay and sit in the swing in the backyard under a shade tree and watch the sun go down).

My military records are at the National Personnel Records Office in St. Louis. Sometime in the 70s about half the records burned. Mine were in the half that did not burn.

Who kept up with the paperwork?
We had a 1st Sgt. who did all the paperwork.

What about the different medals you were awarded – what does each one represent?
Bronze Star - goes along with the Silver Star I received. These are two certain medals automatically awarded when you do certain things during a war. In some cases the Bronze Star is awarded by itself. Silver Star is about the third highest that the Army gives out. You just do your job the way you are supposed to and you may be awarded a medal. Some medals tell where you have fought and what you did.

Tell me how many medals you were awarded:
Purple Heart
Good Conduct Medal
American Campaign
Asiatic/Pacific Campaign
WWII Victory Medal
Combat Medical Badge
Filipino Liberation Medal
Filipino Presidential Unit Citation
Bronze Star
Silver Star

Tell me about the Silver Star - what did you do to earn the Silver Star?
The war was over when I received this medal - they called a formation, several men got the same award - the General just called a formation and gave us our medals.

What I am showing you now, nobody but my wife has ever seen this - this is a copy of the Silver Star Recommendation. When you get the letter of recommendation, you supposedly get the original. No copies are made. I got mine about 1995. I ran into Bob Wise, Governor of West Virginia. I asked him if he could dig into things. He told me to call his secretary and six weeks later I had this.

Remember when you were up home and I told you about the Sergeant I liked so well? He was the second one, I saved. He got shot in the back. The first one was shot in the back. We were in a big ruckus and it got nasty. Sometimes all you could see was a little patch around you. These two guys (soldiers) got hit. We were moving back to the company but they got hit before we got back.

I was there to take care of the people who got hurt but also I would go out on patrol to see where the Japs were. I would always go with my assigned platoon and I made sure I was in the middle.

208

R-e-s-t-r-i-c-t-e-d

Headquarters 43d Infantry Division
APO #43
9th June 1945

Section II

1. By direction of the President, under the Act of Congress approved July 1918, a Silver Star Medal is awarded by the Commanding General, 43d Infantry Division to the following officer and enlisted men:

    Private First Class RALPH M. BABER, (35757414), Medical Department, United States Army. For gallantry in action against the enemy at Luzon, Philippine Islands on 21 March 1945.   During an assault for a Company objective. Private Baber, aid-man, heard a call for help from a wounded officer, and unhesitatingly responded by crawling approximately 100 yards under a concentration of heavy enemy machine gun and mortar fire to reach him. Private Baber promptly treated the stricken officer and started to carry him back to safety. In so returning, another solider in close proximity was shot from enemy fire, Private Baber, again with complete disregard for his own life, treated the casualty and started back with the two wounded men, both receiving support from him. After advancing a few yards, a Jap mortar shell fell to the rear of them wounding Private Baber. In spite of his wounds, Private Baber determinedly kept going until he reached safety with the escorted.   Private Baber's indomitable courage, determination and keen devotion to duty undoubtedly saved the lives of the two men. Home address: Mrs. Mimie V. Baber, (mother), Box #15, Craigsville, West Virginia.

R-e-s-t-r-i-c-t-e-d

(Ralph said to me, "Now, where did we leave off the last time?") **I responded with, "Day of the Invasion of Luzon, what are the details?"**

The day we made the Invasion on January 9, 1945.

How did you travel around the Island?

We didn't get to ride much, all walking. The Island of Luzon covers 41,000 sq. miles and I think we walked over at least half of it. I think from where we landed on Lingayen Gulf it was about 100 miles to Manila. After we got through the 1st phase we had to go south. There was four different areas we were in. I have written down how many killed and how many wounded. We moved to Santa Barbara for replacements. I remember one time we did get to ride. They loaded us in trucks and we went down the O'Donnell River Valley – that is where the Baatan Death March took place.

Another time we rode a truck to the O'Donnell Valley up to Sugar Loaf Hill. You have heard of Sugar Loaf Hill, haven't you?

Sugar Loaf Hill- just after we got up there, the place was bombed with napalm and the fighter planes strafed. After that little session was over, they counted 6,000 Japanese killed; small fights and big fights. The Japanese did not come back and get their men who were killed. They were left. One replacement we got was an older fellow. Older to us back then. He was maybe 35 or 40 years old but he got separated from us one day – the Japs caught him and killed him.

We finally found him. We pretty well knew where he was. The Commander told us to go get him. We went but the Japs had an ambush set up for us so we left without recovering the body. The second day we went back again and they were still waiting on us. We would put out mortar fire but they would get down in their spider holes – that is what we called the holes – spider holes. They were little round holes they dug in the ground. Just big enough for them to get down in. The Japanese would hunker down in their spider holes and cover themselves up. No one would know they were there. It was the 3rd or 4th day but we went after him until we got him.

One night two of the men in our Platoon decided that they would not dig a foxhole. The foxhole was dug about the length of the soldier so he could lay down in it. Most of them about 5 or 6 feet long. Well into the night the Japs started dropping mortar shells on us. Those two were the first to yell medic. I asked their squad leader, he was in the hole next to me, to go with me to get them, but he wouldn't go. That is where the uncomplimentary language came in.

That just shows what people are made of. I never did like that fellow after that. I don't know where he was from. When I asked him to help, he gave me some uncomplimentary language and just sat there in the dark. He finally disappeared. When I went from fox hole to fox hole I made sure our soldiers knew I was coming. During the night was when the Japanese did a lot of their work.

I will never forget, some place close to the vicinity where this last ruckus went on an old fellow, probably in his 30s - an old man to us, sat down at the base of a tree. He was looking back to where we were coming from and a Jap was in the tree. He was a sniper. He shot down at that guy sitting at the bottom of the tree. The shot went through his helmet from front to back and didn't touch his head. That is pretty close to what the old sergeant got into when we first landed on the beach at Luzon - he got his shirt picket shot off. (The guy I am talking about was a soldier with the rest of us. Anyone older than us, we called Pop.)

How did you get food?

When we got a chance to be at a camp, we would get all we could. The Filipinos would bring food in and out. Also, they would take the dead out. We would go sometimes three days without food until we captured supply dumps, we would have canned fish and hard candy. We carried two little canteens on our hips with water and we carried pills to

210

purify it. If we had to pick up dirty water, we would purify it and drink it. Occasionally they would air drop food in parachutes or just kick them packets off a plane.

I remember one time we were getting a drop. We had to mark an X on the hill where we wanted it dropped and they came over to drop us food. There was one man standing in the door of the airplane C47 transport - when we got so far back in the boondocks they couldn't find us any other way. This particular one they flew right over us and the man standing in the door. I can see him yet standing there waving at us as if it were yesterday. They went on over the top of a hill not more than 1/2 mile away. When it got over the hill there was a bunch of Japs on the other side of the hill and suddenly all were celebrating. I have never seen anything like it. I can still see that airplane going level and when the Japs finished shooting, it made a turn to the left and down it went. They got 2 of our men and an airplane.

Did you run into anyone you knew from here?

A fellow who lives up Tioga Road was there. I knew him. One day some men were marching down the road and he was in the group that passed by. I hollered at him but we didn't have time to talk. Another fellow I grew up with was there. I remember his parents died when he was little. A man and woman took in the children to raise. This man was in the medics and assigned to a hospital. I found out where he was. I hitch hiked to see him about 60 or 70 miles away. He came back home and was in the State Police and he took cancer and died, but we chased around together.

Where did the Japanese hide?

Where we fought was rough country hills 1,000 or 2,000 feet up to 5,000 feet tall and all those hills and mountains down there the Japanese dug full of caves, big caves, some would hold hundreds of people. There must have been hundreds or thousands of Japanese soldiers hiding in those caves.

I remember, one of the heaviest fortified cases. The Japanese had caves everywhere big enough to put their artillery pieces in to hide them. They would put them on tracks, like railroad tracks and roll them out and start shooting and roll them back in. They used Filipino labor to do most of their cave digging.

One particular cave we captured one evening was large. You could stand up in it and it had a little curve so you would not be in sight. We figured instead of digging fox holes we would stay in the tunnel or cave. I think every hill over there had a cave in it. One thing we didn't know when we started back in the cave. From where we were in that cave straight across from us was another cave dug and the guns were working. Our enemy knew exactly where we were. So, that night we had thought we would get some sleep, the Japanese just wheeled their guns out and started shooting at us. If my memory serves me right no one was killed but every time they shot we would bounce up and down like a rubber ball.

Now, one place they had fortified real heavy they called the Shimbuline. It run from Laguna De Bay east of Manila, north toward Ipo Dam but that is where a lot of fighting took place and it ran from 40 to 50 miles from one end to another.

February 13 - after 26 days of operations the 43d Division, with the 158th and 63d R. C. T.s attached, completed the seizure and mopped up its objectives, Rosario, Sison and Pozzorubio and adjacent mountains counting 7,831 dead Japanese. Relieved by the 33rd Infantry Division, the 43d Division moved to Santa Barbara to pick up replacements for casualties of the invasion landing.

February 25 - the Division received orders to relieve the 40th Division, heavily engaged in the hills west of Fort Stotsenberg on or before the 2nd of March. Both the 172nd Infantry and the 169th Infantry took up the attack on enemy forces composed of the remainder of an original force of 12,000 Army, Navy Air and airborne forces formerly at Clark Field.

In this area terrain was the Japanese's best ally, sharp cliffs and razor back ridges made a barrier against assault. During this action large quantities of Napalm bombs were dropped in an attempt to burn the enemy out of the crags and caves in which they took shelter. Here, also, the enemy used the 40MM anti-aircraft guns they had taken from Clark Field which caused severe casualties to our attack Infantry.

The 172nd Infantry made a 50 miles motor movement down the O'Donnell Trail to Tiaong cutting off all escape routes to the North and West. Along this same trail had marched the heroes of the infamous Bataan Death March two years before. In 10 days 1,729 enemy were killed.

March 8, 1945 - the division, less the 169th Regimental Combat Team, was ordered to concentrate in the Taytay area East of manila to relieve the 1st Cavalry Division in the Antipolo area with the mission of attacking the Southern anchor of the heavily fortified Shimbu Line. The 43d Division had been relieved by elements of the 38th Infantry. The Shimbu line ran from the Ipo Dam in the North to Laguna De Bay in the south which was made up of forces of all branches with a total of 40,000. The Japanese withdrawal from Manila had been well planned. Well stocked dumps were convenient in sheltered positions, artillery, mortars, rations and ammunition were plentiful. Civilian labor helped to turn the volcanic hills into a fortress. The zone of the 43d Infantry Division, less the 169th regiment, included a front of 20,000 yards with the 172nd Regiment assigned to the left zone and the 103rd assigned to the right zone. The 172nd regiment faced a long period of sluggish action with highly uncertain supply and evacuation facilities.

March 14 – 17, 1945 - the 172nd regiment slowly contested advances of 600 to 1,000 yards along ridge lines. Densely wooded ravines between the ridges were held by the Japs and were a constant threat to our lines of supply and evacuation. The situation in the 172nd zone was quickly approached as a stalemate. Enemy infantry fell back slowly but had whittled our rifle companies down to an average of fifty men.

March 21, 1945 - Take Ipo Dam -The next time we got marching orders – we stretched out for miles and miles. We were going to Manila Ipo Dam. That is where the big scuffle went on. I was non-combatant. I didn't shoot at people. I had a rifle I carried for self-defense. I traded up for a cowboy 6 shooter. I would have been afraid to shoot it. The gun was all pitted and rusty. I traded an old camera or something like that for it.

March 21, 1945 – I was hit by shrapnel on the night of March 21, we were on Mt. Yabang. The enemy, having awakened to the threats, of the 1st Battalion, 172nd was pushing up into Mt. Camayuman They had reorganized their strength and attacked in battalion strength against our position on the south. From the slopes of Mt. Yabang and Caumyoun approximately 150 rounds of artillery were fired from the supporting 100 3rd.

This broke up the attack and advance was resumed the next morning following heavy preparation by elements of the 82nd chemical Mortar Battalion. The reaction was felt by the balance of the 172nd Infantry positions west and north of Sugar Loaf which was overrun against light to moderate resistance. (That is what we poked at them when they attacked -- 150 mortar shells)

March 21, 1945 - Supported by extremely heavy artillery and mortar preparation assisted by Elements of the 754th Tank Battalion, 100 3rd Infantry made the final assault on Mt. Tanauan under a heavy smoke screen and killed 167 Japs during the morning. The US suffered one killed and 20 wounded. The 2nd Battalion drove through scattered resistance to secure Mt. Yabang. Along about this time in March or April we got word that we would have to go to Ipo Dam and take the dam. They were always movin' us.

April 1, 1945 Take Ipo Dam - the 43d Infantry received a new mission. We were to relieve members of the 112th infantry. We were ordered to move to the Santa Maria Bulacan area 50 miles to the north, prepared to attack and seize Ipo Dam. A strong enemy artillery position in the valley west of Sugar Loaf was held as one by one, cave positions containing prime movers and medium artillery were reduced by action of M-7's and assault parties. To break the stalemate West of Sugar Loaf one battalion of the 172 and Infantry was to swing wide through the Morong River Valley and attack north through elements of the 103rd Infantry. The mission of this Battalion was to seize Mt. Camayuman. The southern slopes of Mount Camayuam required men to crawl on hands and knees to climb the steep hillsides.

The 2nd Battalion drove through scattered resistance to secure Mount Yabang and team up with the 1st Battalion on mount Camayuman. Civilian reports and Prisoner of War testimony indicated that a strong enemy force had been by-passed in the crags south of Teresa. Initially civilian tales of 500 Japs in a cave were disregarded. Patrols searched the area with no results. Finally, a POW volunteered to guide our forces to where he said his battalion consisting of 350 officers and men were hiding. The position was attacked by the 3rd Battalion, 172nd Infantry. Virtually the entire force was destroyed in elaborate caves on Benchmark 27.

March 13 to May 1, 1945 - the 43rd Division, less the 169th Regiment had crushed the left of the Shimbu Line. Elements of the division had advanced 60 miles from Antipolo to Pagsnajan, severing Luzon and the once formidable defense north of Laguna De Bay. The Japanese, now disorganized and confused, took to the hills.

By concentrating the divisions massed strength at vital points and shifting that strength secretly and swiftly, the two combat teams were able to conduct offensive action on a division front of over fifty miles while patrols controlled the intervening expanses of mountains. Enemy dead in the operation were 2,844 with 64 taken prisoner, forty-two field pieces were captured along with hundreds of tons of ammunition and over three hundred vehicles.

We got our orders to move toward Ipo Dam. There was only one logical route and that was the Metropolitan Road, a two lane hard surface road. We had to go through Bigti Palasade's. A big pile of rock cliffs that was defended by approximately a regiment of Japanese (5000) in one cave in a fortress of caves, natural underground supply vaults with command posts and hospitals all underground. They had to be taken care of.

Approximately a regiment of infantry held the Bigti Cliffs with other forces along the road. The 112th Cavalry was relieved, and then on the night of May 6th, the 103d and the 172nd regiments attacked through the 169th outposts. Aircraft supporting the attack averaged approximately 100 planes a day most of which were used in close support of leading infantry battalion. Searchlights of the 227th AAA searchlight battalion furnished battlefield lighting to help restrict enemy night movement and to help remove our casualties.

Our Division, as a whole, saw continuous action for 175 days. Occasionally they would let a few of us come to camp for a hot meal, a few of us back at night to sleep on a bunk occasionally.   It was just about the last battle, south of Manila. I didn't know we were down there in Santa Maria, east and southeast of Manila. The end was almost here but we didn't know it.

We were ordered to the Santa Maria Bulacan, south of Manila. That was 50 miles that we had to go and prepare to attack Ipo Dam - the source of 30% water supply of Manila.   The 112th Cavalry Combat Team had been containing the enemy in the Ipo Dam area for two months. This goes into another Regiment but it was all the same Division. The 169th Regiment had effectively crashed the Shimbu line --- heavily fortified areas the Japs had there. We didn't know at the time, that was to be the last Big battle.

In Manila - some of the mountains were so steep you had to crawl up and down on your hands and knees. They had to build ladders out of bamboo.

I went up to work on the oral history interview on Sept. 21, 2004 but after a short time I returned home because Ralph became ill. He could not speak. He decided to write the rest of the story down on paper for me

---

May 12 - 13, 1945 - The enemy attacked the 2nd Battalion, 172nd Infantry, on hill 815, preceded the attack with approximately 500 rounds of artillery. One company of the 2nd Battalion suffered one killed, but counted 181 dead Japs around Hill 815 at daybreak. One more range of hills had to be seized immediately. While the 169th Regiment was to attack toward Bigti - Markings Guerilla Regiment was to come from the North toward the dam and the 103d and the 172nd regiments were to attack toward the north toward the dam. If hill 860 overlooking the Dam and dominating the Metropolitan Road were secured, any Jap attempt to dislodge the Division would not work.

<u>May 13, 1945</u> - Heavy rains turned engineered roads into pure mud holes. The 103d and 172 had been pushed behind with vehicles loaded with ammunition, rations and medical supplies hub deep along the road. Walking casualties started to the rear and non walking waited patiently where they lay. Over 1000 Filipino carriers had been secured but their efforts were feeble in carrying the materials of war to two combat regiments over country that required a three day march. Guerillas, service troops air drops were used in an effort to keep the assault troops moving. Evacuation was most critical.

Twenty hours were required to carry wounded from Battalion positions to the nearest surgical positions. We, the platoon medics, did what we could, but we were almost always short of supplies. What we usually had was bandages, sulfa powder, and, when we could get it, one quarter grain syringes of morphine. On May 15 plans were laid out for an all out coordinated attack on May 17. Maximum napalm efforts were to be coordinated for three successive days on targets along the Metropolitan Road.

<u>May 15-16</u> – During the night the enemy fired approximately 150 medium caliber rounds at the 2nd Battalion, 172nd Infantry.

<u>May 17, 1945 - At 10:30 A.M.</u> (this is the one I watched) 220 fighter bombers spread 62,660 gallons of napalm along the Metropolitan road. The 169th Infantry, under cover of this, moved to seize the Bigti Palisades. Tanks and engineers moved north to the Bigti Pass only to find it blocked by boulders blasted from the cliffs. Caves were blown open in order to use the highway. At the same time under cover of the heavy air effort, the 2nd Battalion moved Northwest from Hill 815 and seized Red Bank, dominating the Metropolitan Road West of Hill 860.

<u>May 18</u> - the 5th Air Force used 251 aircraft with nearly 68,000 gallons of napalm at the enemy North of the Metropolitan Road and for the first time in two months not one round of artillery fire was received by U.S. forces.

<u>May 19, 1945</u> - All enemy resistance had ceased in the Ipo Dam area.

<u>May 20 - June 2, 1945</u> - Mopping up continued in the countless caves and ravines that had been the Ipo defenses: 750 Japanese had been killed in the mopping up action.

<u>June 2, 1945</u> - The 43d was ordered to the South to relieve part of the 38th Division attempting to seize Mt. Oro, Mt. Ayaas and Mount Banoy The 169th Regiment, reinforced by Company C., 82nd Chemical Mortar B., and part of the 192nd Field Artillery Bn. was given the mission. The regiment attacked Mount Ayaas the following day. Other troops attacked Mount Oro.

<u>June 8, 1945</u> - The division and corps artillery laid a fifteen minute 1000 round preparation on Mt. Oro. E Company 169th Infantry overran the enemy before they could recover.

<u>June 12, 1945</u> - Patrols were unable to find any enemy within 10,000 yards of Ipo Dam. With the final victory at Ipo the Division could look back on their accomplishments.

October 25, 2004, Ralph and Mary's home, after supper. Ralph continued his story:

The Division had been in continual offensive combat for a total of one hundred and seventy days. Following is a comparison chart between our losses and losses of the enemy.

43d Infantry Division only

Area	Enemy killed in action	Prisoners
Lingayen	7,831	44
Stotsenberg	1,729	32
Antipolo	2,844	64
Ipo Dam	4,062	368
Totals	16,466	

US Losses

Area	Killed	Wounded	Missing
Lingayen	593	1,644	6
Stotsenberg	70	193	0
Antipolo	130	443	1
Ipo Dam	172	706	4
Totals	965	2,988	11

Also on Luzon were the 40th Div. 25th, 33d, 37th, 38th, 1st Cav. 121st Filipino 158th Regt. 63d Regt., 112 Regt. and 124th Regt. 6th Div.

The 43d Division then moved to a rainy season camp called Camp LaCroix near Cabanatuan. While there we received word - one more mission. On the 28th of July, 1945 we were told that the 43d Infantry was to be one of the spearheads of Gen. Walter Krueger's Sixth Army in the assault of southern Kyushu with a target date of the first of November.

That would have been one of the bloodiest campaigns was indicated later when troops of occupation found southern Kyushu to be held in great strength. However, plans were changed when the Japanese sued for surrender after two atomic bombs were dropped. The 43d was then moved to Japan to take part in the Blacklist Operation of occupation.

From Japan the Division moved HOMEWARD BOUND. I only hope that in my job as a medic for the 2nd platoon, E Co., 2nd Battalion, 172nd Regiment, 43d Division, that I did as much for them as they did for me, and that was to help see that we got back home. They were my family away from home.

June 24, 1945 - A memorial service was held at Manila Cemetery with General Walter Kreuger as the speaker:

September 20 – 29, 1945 - While engaged in the initial occupation of Japan, news was received that the 97th Division was enroute to relieve the 43d Division, which would return to the United States on return shipping. Approximately eleven thousand low score men transferred to units remaining in Japan, and a similar number high score of men were transferred into the 43d Division for return to the United States. Forty eight hours later elements of the 172nd infantry were loading aboard the U.S.S. General Pope at Yokohame Harbor.

Now General Wing was about to realize the hope and ambition of every division Commander -- that of bringing his Division home. As the ship was pulling into the dock the last round of a thirteen gun salute was fired. After a job well done the 43d Infantry "Winged Victory" Division had come home as a unit, the first United States Army Division to be inactivated from the Pacific Theater of Operations.

October 1945 - I had to go back to camp when I was in the process of getting discharged. I had to stay in longer because I got the flu. This was at Camp Atterbury.

June 23, 2004 Ralph brought to my office several items from the war he brought home in 1945. He told me about each item as he laid them out on my desk.

He handed me a beautiful Hamilton watch, made in Lancaster, Pennsylvania, 14K gold. On the back of the watch was the following inscription: To: Captain O. Matsumoto From: Mrs. Evanglista Manila, May 25, 1944 (17 jewel)

I found it in a cave - look, Captain O. Matsumoto didn't even have this beautiful watch quite a year. That same cave is where we captured the only Jap our Platoon captured while I was with it. The Japanese soldier had some shrapnel. I patched him up and sent him on back to Headquarters. It stands to reason that he was the above mentioned Captain Matsumoto.

Part 3 - King Coal expands his realm

Appalachian experiences mountaintop removal

Appalachian Experiences Mountaintop Removal

Author's note:
Written on 10/12/05 11:00 P.M.
Summersville, WV

    I live in the Appalachian coalfields; the land of milk and money, in the land of King Coal and now, the land of mountaintop removal, the controversial method of coal extraction. In my daily routine, I had not taken the opportunity to view mountaintop removal because the sites are hidden from the naked eye and the open roadways. That changed one day, around the 4th of July when I received a call from Ken Hechler and Larry Gibson inviting me to Kayford Property on Cabin Creek to take a look at mountaintop removal.

    I was excited to go to Cabin Creek and see what was there. I had heard talk, but I did not know what to expect. I asked friends what to expect. What did mountaintop removal look like? I did not know. Like most of the people here in the mountains where I live, I had neither the motive nor money to take flyovers above the region, a common practice among authors, journalists and environmentalists these days and often referred to in their writings and reports. A flyover is a flight in a plane where the pilot follows the Appalachian Mountain range giving those onboard a bird's eye view of the barren land below where mountains previously stood.   This is the results of removal of one mountaintop after another. I had not seen that.   My friend, Branscome, told me mountaintop removal in the southern West Virginia coalfields looks like a moonscape, but even that descriptive word did not prepare me for what I saw on Kayford Property up Cabin Creek.

    What I saw moved me into another world. A strange world to my eyes. A world I did not vision as Appalachia. This world had no place for me or the things I love.   In my world we look up at the green hills in the spring and summer; beautiful gold, red and orange leaves in the autumn; and, in the winter, stately oak, beech, sugar maples and pines holding out their branches as if they were protective arms serving as barriers from the cold, wintry winds and snow. I did not see that. I saw a world that did not include little wooden frame houses scattered on the creek bank up and down Cabin Creek Hollow. Many of the houses were on the creek bank at the opposite end of handcrafted, wooden bridges.   I saw a world that did not include a little garden out back with ripe tomatoes, sweet corn, half runner beans and Irish potatoes planted in neat rows with big sunflowers towering on the last row. I saw a world that did not include a woman in a blue cotton dress with a apron on, dusting the flour off her hands after putting the biscuits in the oven. I saw a world that did not include little school kids wading in the cold, clear creek water on their way back and forth to school. For the first time, I saw mountaintop removal on Kayford Property on Cabin Creek, West Virginia.

The Mountaintop removal process:

- Before mining can begin, all topsoil and vegetation must be removed.
- Since coal seams lie deep below the surface, 800 to 1,000 feet of the mountain top is removed, using dynamite, to recover the coal. It has been said that more pounds of explosives are used every 4 days in West Virginia than were used in the entire conflict in Afghanistan. In fact, three million pounds of explosives per day are used in West Virginia alone (leading the nation), with Kentucky right behind and Virginia, Pennsylvania, and Tennessee each getting a significant beating (source: Institute of Makers of Explosives/U.S. Geological Survey Minerals Yearbook). The total explosive force used in West Virginia EACH WEEK is close to that used on Hiroshima.
- Coal and debris are removed by using a piece of machinery called a dragline. A dragline can weigh anywhere from 3,000 to 5,000 tons. A dragline uses a large bucket to dig blasted rock (overburden). These buckets can carry up to 350 tons in a single load. A dragline is 22 stories high and can hold 24 compact cars in their bucket. The cost for a dragline is anywhere from $50 million to $100 million and replaces 100 miners making it necessary to operate 24 hours per day, 7 days per week – 24/7.
- The debris, known as overburden or spoil, is dumped into nearby valleys forever burying streams. These structures are unstable and likely to sink or shift.
- Trees and soil absorb water during heavy rains. Barren mountaintop removal sites do not hold back the water, allowing rainfall to quickly run down valleys, resulting in major flooding .The coal is washed and treated before shipment. The excess water left over is called coal slurry or sludge and is stored in coal impoundments. Coal impoundments are held back by debris making them very unstable.
- Slurry from the impoundments go into the rivers killing the fish and contaminating the water.

Mountaintop removal will decapitate an area larger than the state of Delaware by the end of this decade according to estimates.

On the day I met Larry Gibson on Kayford Property, we strolled among 300 graves of his family members buried there beginning pre-Civil War days. As we walked, he told me his sad story. The graves, he said, were the final resting place for coal miners, fathers, mothers, grandfathers, grandmothers, war heroes, babies, young children, teenagers and the white sheep and black sheep of the Stanley family; Larry Gibson's family. It was an emotional story. I consider it an A&E story or someday, perhaps, a History Channel story. One man up against a 22 story high machine which costs $100 million dollars – David and Goliath.

White crosses marked nearly all the graves in the cemetery, reminding us of the war heroes resting beneath the white crosses in Arlington Cemetery. However, unlike the graves in Arlington, the graves we walked among were splattered with rocks and other debris. Large cracks ran across and up and down grave after grave as a result of dynamite blasting needed to explode the mountain and expose the deep seams of coal. These blasts are so mighty they surely will wake, if not extricate, the dead.

Kayford Property, Cabin Creek, West Virginia.
View from the cemetery. Photograph by B. L. Dotson-Lewis. 2002

Oprah Winfrey's magazine O in the July 2006 issue featured a special report on the devastation caused by mountaintop removal mining in Appalachia. This articled featured stories showing the courage of the women who are standing against it to protect their families, communities, and environment.

Dragline Photograph:
West Virginia Geological and Economic Survey

According to the first book of Genesis in the Holy Bible, land is described as a gift, as a covenant of trust with God's people. Land is the foundation of the life of a people, and it is a sacred inheritance, which brings with it a new awareness of responsibility, symbolizing a deep connection between God, people and the land.

**Photo of mountaintop removal taken in Charleston, WV at the State Capitol.
Photograph by B. L. Dotson-Lewis July 2005.**

An interview with Larry Gibson on Kayford Property – in the graveyard – one of Gibson's earliest interviews regarding Kayford property and mountaintop removal.

Larry Gibson:
Thank for you for this opportunity.

This is my family cemetery. Many of the graves are cracked open from the blasting. If you look close you can see where the graves are covered. It is rock dust – dynamite dust from the site over there. If you look you will see how the grass grows here and there. This is not native grass. It grows like this because this stuff here where the water is mixed with acid kills stuff. See. Nothing will grow on this stuff. We have only cut this cemetery four times this year. It didn't need cut. There is nothing that will grow up here because of this rock dust.

The ground all around here should be black, but it is white from rock dust as a result of blasting.

You can come over here and look at these big rocks on these graves. The rocks were thrown over here by dynamite blasting.

See right here. Before this mountaintop removal started, you could sit right here and watch the horses over there in the pasture. Up in that area there was a big pasture for grazing. The top of the mountains were clear and that is where our mountaintop farms were located. My family were mountaintop farmers. My family and all their brothers had farms on these mountains. They made

**Larry Gibson.   Photography by
B. L. Dotson-Lewis July 2005**

just as much money as the farmers down in the hollows did. The soil was so rich on the tops of the mountains.

I was born in 46 when mountaintop farms were doing pretty good. My boy, my oldest boy, was born in 66. He has lived to see the time when the mountaintop farms are gone. My girl who is going to be 17 was born in 87 She will live to see the time when the mountains are going to be gone.

Cemetery on Kayford Property Mountain

Illustration by B. L. Doxon-Lewis Oct. 05

I will show you over here now and then bring you back through this way. This will give you a good view of the place.

We have a young boy buried in this part of the cemetery. He got killed in the mines when he was 14. He got killed 20 years after the Union was born in 1909. There is so much history here.

See right here. See this debris on this grave. This is fly rock flailed from three or four thousand feet across or six thousand feet across. Do you think the people who are doing this care what they are doing to this cemetery? They came in here and filled these cracks in, three or four months ago, and look now they are opened back up again. The graves are splitting open.

Three months ago if you had jumped across these ditches you would have come out in China. See right here and here. All the cracks are opening back up again. You will be walking across here and the ground will suddenly give away with you. There are underground mines here. Underground mines are honeycombed underneath this mountain.

We lost a cow back in one those mines when we were kids. We had to drop a stick of dynamite down in the hole to kill it. There is another underground mine going down through here, see the crevices here. They are deep. They filled that in too not long ago.

The machines used for mountaintop mining are big giants. I will show you. The machine works 24/7. The big giant is a shovel. They can put 28 Ford Corsica's in, three Greyhound buses, 360 upright 6 foot refrigerators in just one of them. They can hold 26 Ford Escorts.

This mountain here, turn around slow and look behind you, the mountain used to come down like this. You would go up over this mountain. You would look up at this mountain. This mountain has dropped down about 400 feet below where we are now and it used to stand up above any of those mountains. That big machine over yonder works 24/7, costs $50,000 a month electricity, cost more than a million dollars to buy, and right here, this is an improper word, but in this dirt pile is the Stanley's cemetery. My grandfather

Stanley married into the family that owned 150,000 acres in Kanawha County. That is how he got this land. You check your history. All of this as far as the eye can see. They owned it. They acquired that land through the Civil War Act. The reason I know this I hired a researcher in genealogy to work and find out for me.

This, all this destruction of the mountain in that direction, has been done since 97. It is massive. It is massive.

I asked Larry Gibson, "Do you think you are ever going to get it stopped?"

His reply. "Everyone asks me that. Yes, I do. Because of the fact of what I do, bring you here, bring other people here, PBS, most of the world. Because if I don't stop it here is where is it going to go. This is small on the scale of our universe, but if we don't stop this, and it continues to spread, it is going to destroy what universe we have. You cannot play with nature and not mess up the weather pattern. We had a tornado down in the hollow two years ago. We had never had a tornado down there before.

This is a union mine, this alone. The men make about $20.00 dollars per hour. The nonunion miners make from $9.00 to $12.00 per hour. And Larry asked me which mountaintop removal mining method was the responsible method? I replied, "I did not know."

He told me. "There is no responsible way of removing mountains."

Look right here all around the cemetery in 97 you could have stopped right here and dropped a rock 800 feet straight down in front of you. Now look.

I have a joint investigation going on with the Department of Environmental Protection and the Office of Surface Mining. In 98 I forced them to backfill the cemetery because we were losing it and we are still in danger of losing it. I find it breaking off. On one of the headstones back there is carved this saying, "Earth has no sorrow that Heaven cannot heal."

If we have to replace one of those headstones like that. I don't think we can.

It is not only wrong morally, but physically I think it is wrong. It doesn't say in the Bible to go to the valley and worship. It says to go to the mountaintop and worship.

Have you ever seen a copy of the Alabama Magazine or Mother Jones? Find a copy of that in 98 and of course U.S. News and World Report. Several magazines but we have never had anyone who decided to come in here and write a story and come out in favor of mountaintop removal.

How could they after looking at this?

How come our own government does?

Yet they come out against me.

Before you go, here is the grave of that 14 year old boy that got killed in the mines. I want you to see it.

We will go out this way which is a mile and one half down. We had 500 acres. Of course we lost it.

See, you can see more where the grass turned brown. The rain hits it but when it gets tall enough to hit the ground, it hits the acid and dies.

I inquired. "Are you in court right now concerning this?"

He replied. "We just got out of court last week. They kicked my case out of court."

When you have a coal company this big, you have very little to fight on legal grounds no matter how right you are.

I know I am dead right and that is what people have told me. I can't quit even though the courts rule against me. You see if I I don't come and my people don't come anymore, then, they win. It is about people for me. It is not about property nor money. I never got any money for this. I never got any reimbursement for this. I never got any gas money. I am not going to ask people for gas money.

Look over here to your right now. This is after all the rain we have had and you know we have had rain.

You know this thing that happened in Kentucky, the slurry spill in Martin County, is what we are looking for in the future. I'm sure you have seen the pictures on TV. It has been on the national news a hundred times. It was in Inez, Kentucky, about an hour and half west of here - 250 million gallons of slurry debris, mud and stuff that came out of the mine and went into Big Sandy. That was on October 11. This past October 11 and the coal company has taken water to those poor people but one time. Two weeks ago I went down there. They interviewed my people I lived with when I was 5 years old down there. They got sores on their legs, backs, arms and faces from using the water just to bath in. The land is not good anymore. The water is not good anymore, not worth anything but it is O.K. because it was a coal company that done it. The almighty dollar. Not only the top line but the bottom line too; nothing else means anything.

Conclusion by B. L. Dotson-Lewis

Coal is King in Appalachia where I live. That position has not changed over the many years. Politicians and elections occasionally shake up the organizational chart but King Coal continues to reign.   Unfortunately, the latest method of coal extraction, mountaintop removal, is removing more than coal from this region. It is erasing one of the oldest cultures in the United States.   This method of mining is wiping it out clean, mountain by mountain.   Not only are our lives centered around coal, but also around the mountains which cover this coal, and when mountains are removed, people are forced out of their small communities, their hamlets - the heart of sustaining this unique culture.   It is erasing the core of our existence.   Mountaintop removal forces people to go elsewhere in the mountains to live or leave altogether whether through buy out or forced out. Communities are broken up.   Families and friends are driven apart – closeness becomes distance.   When mountains are taken off to reach a seam of coal, all that disturbed dirt has to go somewhere – it fills up the hollows where people make their homes forcing relocation or unbearable living conditions if they remain.   The clear creeks are no longer clear creeks but creeks full of sludge and chemically treated runoff from coal. Grass will not grow. When many companies actually do reclamation, native grass is not sown, nor will it grow in the acidic remains. Generally, native hardwood trees are not replaced but species which grows fast and cheap to buy are planted.

The overall picture is bleak for those of us who love these mountains as they are, the way God made them.   For those of us who love and value old time traditions and the rich cultural heritage brought to us from Scotland, Ireland, Germany, England and all the other countries meshed together in the coal camps and adopted as a way of life for mountain folk, it is not looking good.   Ginseng, May Apple, Ramps are no longer flourishing on the green, rocky hillside, so steep only a mountain goat or mountain man can climb.   The hillside is non existence taking the rare vegetation with it and the mountain man has no mountain to climb.

My concern is for our culture, our history, our simple way of life here in these precious mountains. A life that is not always geared around a clock. We take time to walk out to the garden, go fishing or hunting. Stack firewood for the winter.   We still have river baptism like Jesus baptized his own disciples. The hardships are evident but the people are tough and can survive mountain life.

We are being driven out of our land just like the American Indians were driven out. I believe this is what we are facing, the eradication of the unique, laid-back, self sufficient way of life where we take pride in practicing what has been brought over from the Old country. The way of life I have chosen. The mountain man is going to be forced into the main stream of America, like it or not, if things continue in the way they are going today. We will have no mountains to hold us, shelter us from the storms of life, to gaze on in the spring, summer and fall, to hunt and fish and gather nuts and cut birch from trees to chew, dig ginseng and rancid ramps to fry with bacon and Irish potatoes and cornbread - a feast fit for a king. People will not be comfortable in the hollows sitting on the front porch playing their fiddles or telling stories in the evenings - there will be no hollows. The mountain man will be forced to conform, to give up the independence associated with .our isolation, to mesh with society, to lose our identity. The mountain man will be forced to concentrate on fitting in instead relishing our uniqueness. The mountain man will not have the luxury or surroundings to cultivate what our ancestors have passed down. All that will be lost for the price of a quick buck for the absentee landholders.

The issue of mountaintop removal should not be laid on the shoulders of the mountaineer. We are not the ones responsible for ravaging these mountain. If we did not love these mountains, we would not stay here. For many, it is the only way of making a living.   Mountaintop removal, improper reclamation or no reclamation must be laid on the shoulders of those responsible - those who choose the method of mining coal.

Part 4 – Black Lung's Legacy

Black Lung bulletin, February 1970
Cold Days Dark Nights by Jim Branscome
Highlights of 2004 National Black Lung Conference
Letter to UMWA Association President, Cecil Roberts, regarding Black Lung victim
A Christmas Wish – local newspaper article – Coal Miner, Fighting Two Battles

Striking miners outside the Highsplint mine. (Harlan County, Kentucky, 1974)
Photograph by Builder Levy

Oprah's magazine "O" features a photo and story about Marsh Fork Elementary pictured above and West Virginia women. Marsh Fork Elementary on 8801 Coal River Road, Sundial, West Virginia. Photograph by Gene Gee/Appalachian Voices. Marsh Fork Elementary School in the hills of West Virginia sets less than 300 feet from a coal silo. Every day the coal is "scrubbed" -- the mercury and titanium are literally washed off with a chemical agent.

King Coal and the coal miners' soul

Author's Note: Coal miners have owed their soul to the company store since the early 1900s when they lived in coal camp houses owned by the company, were paid in scrip instead of U.S. currency and made all their purchases at the company store. Tonight as the nation watched Primetime on ABC and Wilbur Ross, owner of Sago Mine, who sat in front of the camera, dressed in an expensive business suit, composed, dried eyed, telling the world he felt Sago Mine was safe for those miners, after receiving numerous violations, I wondered how things had changed. And when the anchorman asked what he was giving to the deceased miners' families and he said the company had established a fund and was asking the public to contribute. When questioned further it came out that he had not contributed one dime out of his own pocket but was waiting to see what the public would do, I wondered how things had changed. And as I watched photos of Wilbur Ross at a fancy wedding or party, scroll across the screen in the background and later it was reported on the show some of the miners' families did not have enough money to bury their loved one, I wondered how things had changed.

Cannelton coal in Smithers, West Virginia, is the oldest mining complex in the Kanawha Valley. Cannelton Coal opened in 1871. The world for the Cannelton miners and retirees changed drastically on August 31, 2004, when U.S. Federal Bankruptcy Judge rapped his gavel in favor of the Addington brothers, Larry, Robert and Bruce of Ashland, Kentucky, in approval of bankruptcy filing of Horizon Natural Resources, the company operating Cannelton mines.

This ruling immediately affected 270 working miners and 1,270 pensioners and their wives. This action canceled all of Horizon's obligations under the UMWA contract. These retirees and their spouses, many suffering from health problems, many work related, were left totally out in the cold – their health care, something they had been promised for the remainder of their lives, stripped away by one judge and a strong coal lobbying agency. This judge negated legislation dating back to President Harry S. Truman's pledge to John L. Lewis in 1946. These miners had sacrificed wages and other benefits for the promise of health care until death.

On the auction block in a sweet deal, Massey Energy bought Connelton complex and International Coal Group bought Sago mine. Massey changed the name from Cannelton to Mammoth Coal and reopened as a nonunion mine. ICG assumed full control of Sago Mine in November 2005, and on January 2, 2006, an explosion rocked Sago Hollow and 12 miners died. I wondered what had changed.

The Fayette County Black Lung Association hosted Dr. Donald Rasmussen, a history making black lung specialist in February of this year. Dr. Rasmussen told the group in 1969 legislation passed which would eradicate black lung. He was of the opinion he would be looking for work elsewhere in a few years. To date, 30+ years later, he is booked two or three months ahead for black lung tests. He has tested at least 45,000 miners for black lung. He told the group he is seeing symptoms of black lung disease in younger miners. Dr. Rasmussen discussed the art of filing for black lung compensation, telling the audience it takes a sharp lawyer and years of patience to win these battles. And I wondered what had changed.

black lung BULLETIN

West Virginia Black Lung Assn
NEWSLETTER #9 February 1970

West Virginia Black Lung Association
1222 Washington St. E., Charleston, W. Va. 25301

IN MEMORIAN

With regret, we want to inform the readers of the Black Lung Bulletin that we have lost one of our strongest supporters, Mr. C.P. Odum of Mensley, West Virginia. He passed away recently, a victim of Black Lung.

Mr. Odum was one of the best members of the United Mine Workers of America that we know of. He fought through out his lifetime to organize our union and make it strong and responsive to the needs of the members. But, when Mr. Odum needed help and asked for what was rightly due him, his pension and hospital benefits were denied.

No greater injustice could prevail on a member of the United Mine Workers of America. Here was a man who gave so much and received so little. He was the kind it took to build an organisation. There will be others to follow Mr. Odum; but none will contribute more to his fellow man. Our sympathy goes to Mr. Odum's family; he will be missed by all of us.

Arnold Miller

Hyden — An Editorial

In a mine accident, all the living try their damndist to place the blame on the dead. The dust explosion at the Finley Brothers' mine in Hyden, Kentucky, was no exception.

Since their mine opened 10 months before the tragedy, 38 violations were found. At times the dust level was as high as 6 times the legal limit. In all the 10 months the mine was open, The state department of mines investigated the mine twice, the Federal Bureau eight times. The Kentucky inspectors, whose director is a coal operator himself, saw violations but wrote only polite letters about them. The Federal inspectors noted violations, but the Bureau of Mines did nothing.

(More - page 3)

Death for us coal miners comes swiftly from unsafe mines or slowly as in the case of C.P. Odum, from Black Lung. This issue of the Bulletin is devoted to look at these killers

"During my recent inspection of your mine, I found conditions to be ideal..."

Bulletin: Courtesy of John Cline, Piney View, West Virginia

Pick-and-shovel work is still needed even in automated mines.
(Wolf Creek Colliery, Lovely, Kentucky, 1971) Photograph by Builder Levy

Author's note: This article by Jim Branscome, written in the early 70s, clearly shows that coal miners have struggled for decades to obtain a safe and healthy environment in which to perform their jobs.

Jim Branscome, a Berea College graduate, possessed both the intellect and compassion to lead and serve his fellow Appalachians during the late 60s, 70s and early 80s. His record for advocacy includes director of youth programs, Appalachian Regional Commission and, task force co-chairman of the 1971 White House Conference on Youth. In 1970 the President named Branscome to the National Advisory Council of Disadvantaged Children and board of directors of the National Reading Council.

In my opinion, the greatest impact on the lives of the people in Appalachia resulted from his free-lance investigative reporting, contributing stories to newspapers such as the Mountain Eagle of Whitesburg, Kentucky, The New York Times Sunday Magazine cover story on strip-mining which was credited with eventual passage of strict federal legislation mandating restoration of land, and the Washington Post.

Jim Branscome at the time of this writing was a freelance writer on staff of the Highlander Center which was doing organizing and educational work on coal mining and other Appalachian issues. (1974)

Currently, Jim Branscome serves as a member of the National Advisory Board of Directors of the Institute for Rural Journalism and Community Issues - University of Kentucky.

Cold Days, Dark Nights

By Jim Branscome

NEW MARKET, Tenn. -- "Mother" Jones, that elderly rabble-rouser who beat coal operators with brooms and became a coal-field legend in the bloody United Mine Workers organizing drives earlier in this century, promised when she got to heaven she would harass the Lord about the pitiful conditions of West Virginia coal miners. "Either Mother Jones did not make it up there or the Lord is a coal operator," a retired U.M.W. organizer said recently. The Mother Jones dilemma aside, it is still hell to be a coal miner.

On November 12, a nation at peace with the oil-rich Arabs could be at war with the Appalachian coal-miners. On that date, when the union's contract with the nation's coal and oil corporations expires--coal production in the United States is heavily owned by the major oil companies--the hell the miners have been getting may be visited upon the rest of the nation. Gasless Sundays are only inconvenient; cold days and dark nights are something else.

The coal miners' outrage is easily understandable. From 1839 to the present, more than 120,000 miners have died in United States coal mines and 1.5 million more have been maimed and disabled. The death toll averages out to more than two lives lost every single day for 135 years. Last year 132 coal miners, out of a total work force of 164,000, were killed and 11,067 were injured. So far this year 58 have been killed. Each year 3,000 miners die from black lung, a suffocating disease caused by coal dust and corporate and governmental negligence of mine conditions.

In the new contract, the reform leadership of the union's president, Arnold R. Miller, is demanding higher wages, new safety standards, sick pay, increased pensions and a number of other benefits long enjoyed by other industrial unions. Coal miners, among other union members--in steel, rubber, the auto industry--work in the most hazardous conditions and are the lowest paid.

Publicly, the Bituminous Coal Operators Association, the combine which negotiates for the industry, has promised nothing. Privately, they say they are willing to trade moderately increased wages and benefits for a guarantee against wildcat strikes, usually over safety conditions, which are as sacred to miners as their oath of obligation. Even if Mr. Miller dared to negotiate on this point, it is certain that the contract would not be ratified by the rank and file, which this year intends to look the deal over with an enthusiasm fired by the right, won last December, to approve the contract.

No matter how good the contract looks some observers are predicting that coal miners may also decide to get in a lick against Mr. Miller, who is maintaining a strange silence on the shift of the coal industry from Appalachian deep mines to Western strip miners. Coal miners who remember John L. Lewis's decision to allow mine mechanization in order to drop the miners' rolls from 535,000 to 200,000 in a decade, ushering in the new era of Appalachian poverty, see a familiar threat in the move West.

Silence on the East-to-West shift combined with Mr. Miller's refusal to do anything to get a meaningful strip-mine bill from this Congress have agitated the coal miners. They do not intend to struggle to keep from dying in the ground only to emerge and be killed on the surface by a strip-mine-induced flood or landslide. Mr. Miller, who used to call for abolition of strip mines, is headed toward a showdown with his own restless membership.

Should a coal strike come, it would be up to President Nixon to end it. He could invoke a Taft-Hartley injunction for a cooling-off period, but coal miners might not even obey their own leader's call, let alone Mr. Nixon's, for a return to work. As long as there has been a Taft-Hartley law, there has been a miner saying, "Mr. Taft and Mr. Hartley can mine the coal."

Coal supplies at utilities are already down dramatically from normal stockpiles. The Tennessee Valley Authority, the country's largest utility, has only a 26-day supply at one of its steam plants. On the East coast, only Massachusetts utilities have the normal 70-to-100-day stockpiles. Some steel mills have only a fifteen-day supply. Even if a strike should last only two to three weeks, as union spokesmen optimistically hope, for the sake of their beleaguered medical and pension fund, which draws 80 cents for each ton of coal mined, there could be selective brownouts and layoffs, particularly in the East. Unquestionably, a frenzied coal hunt this fall by utilities, which already have some coal priced at $33 a ton, three times its production cost, will force, utility bills to rise even further.

Even if a miners' strike is somehow avoided, that does not lessen the importance of this nation's collecting its corporate and moral body and repenting its sins in the coal fields. Unless that happens, coal miners may have to use coal's rising fortunes to get Mother Jones's message across themselves.

Highlights of 2004 National Black Lung Conference
Letter written in November 2004

Dear Branscome,

Slept in this morning resting up from the long trip to Carrollton, Kentucky, where I attended the annual Black Lung Association Conference held on Friday and Saturday, November 19-20, 2004. The Fayette County Chapter invited me to attend when I became a member.

I rode with Kathryn South, widow of past National Black Lung Association President, Mike South. Kathryn drove a Southern Appalachian Labor School van.

I met Kathryn at 10:00 a.m. on Friday morning in Oak Hill. She already had one passenger, Bob, when she arrived. Both he and Kathryn live in Beards Fork. We picked up Connie. He took a seat in the back. Both men were retired miners.

We headed down Route 61. A route I had never traveled before. A steady downpour of rain beat on the windshield and a heavy fog hovered around us. We sped past coal camp towns with names like Kincaid, Paige and Beards Fork and down and around Deepwell Mountain road. Coal tipples and railroad tracks were part of the landscape. I was deep in coal country.

We were entertained by Connie, the passenger in the back, and Bob, up front with Kathryn. The two miners took turns telling funny coal camp-coal mining stories back and forth across the seats of the van about the early days in the coal camps. The two miners talked about wooden tipples and women who ran boarding houses and Saturday night fights. They said both men and women fought. They talked about the old movie theaters. I felt as if I were watching a movie – looking out the window into the fog, barely seeing the dim lights in the windows of the coal camp houses and listening to the stories and laughter from the story tellers. At the same time I was unable to block out Connie's familiar hacking cough.

We had one more stop to make for passengers at Cedar Grove. Our route took us past the Horizon bankruptcy picket lines manned by UMWA members. Kathryn laid on the horn as we drove by signaling support of the UMWA.

We pulled in at a Safeway Store. Mrs. Richards arrived in a few minutes. She is 76 years old. We were a few minutes ahead of schedule so she asked Kathryn to drive up the road and pick up her son, Alvie, instead of waiting for him. The trip to Kentucky would take more than 5.5 hours.

Mrs. Richards and I shared a seat on the second row. Kathryn was driving, Bob reading directions and now Connie and Alvie were having a lively discussion on religion talking about the devil and the sins of man in old timey church language. Both sounded like preachers to me.

We finally reached our destination - General Butler State Park. We all piled out of the van and went in to check on rooms. The Black Lung Association incurred expenses for this conference for members. Everyone was checking in and getting keys to their rooms except me, I didn't have a room because I was a last minute attendee. I suggested I share a room with Mrs. Richards but Alvie spoke up and said she was his roommate.   They found a room for me near the group.

We were waiting in the lobby when others attending the conference arrived. Kathryn knew them all including Department of Labor representative James DeMarce. Kathryn introduced me. Mr. DeMarce asked what my interest was pertaining to black lung. Kathryn told him about my book. Mr. DeMarce purchased one of my books that evening.

I met LeMarse Moore, a woman coal miner who contracted black lung after only 6.5 years working in the mine. There were other miners from Birmingham, Alabama, with her – all suffering from black lung, including a member of one of the first Negro Baseball Leagues.

I attended the board meeting with Kathryn that night. A host of topics were discussed since only one national conference is held per year.

On Saturday I was up early, dressed, packed my bags and went to the lobby to wait for the others. We were leaving as soon as the meeting was over. Several people were in the stage area which was open to the lobby, a couple of steps up. They were listening to early morning gospel music which rang throughout the center. It was solo singing accompanied by piano playing. The thought crossed my mind - community members practicing for a holiday play but no, it was Alvie, singing and playing. Alvie playing the piano without benefit of any music and singing old time gospel hymns. He told us later the guitar was his instrument of choice for church singing. He and his wife sing in church. She plays the piano.

The meeting opened as scheduled with call to order, prayer and Pledge of Allegiance. The room was filled to capacity.

I really enjoyed listening to LeMarse Moore speak. She was a colorful dresser and speaker. Anita Wolfe from NIOSH gave some disturbing news; coal miners are getting black lung at a younger age– a steady increase reflected by the chart and possibility of more with an increase in non-union mines. She also reported coal miners were not participating in the free breathing test – when asked why, she said that miners are afraid coal operators will find out, another reason, the just don't want to know they have black lung.

Mr. DeMarce from the Department of Labor presented valuable information regarding black lung claims and the role of the Department of Labor. He explained the Department of Labor will pick up the tabs for Horizon former employees who lost their health care and pensions and are not covered under the Coal Act due to the bankruptcy for a short period of time. This affected the miners at Cannelton Coal.

All the speakers were excellent talking about legislative action, black lung claim strategies, names and location of new doctors who are trained to perform black lung tests, membership campaign, etc. Mr. Grant Crandall, UMWA General Counsel discussed a black lung case where evidence was purposely omitted. A hearing will be held in Pittsburg in December for a decision on this matter.

UMWA officials announced Joe Main would be leaving UMWA as Safety Director but will stay on in other roles. He told Kathryn the 60 hour work weeks were getting to him. He hoped to reduce it to 40 hours. He gave me a copy of the article Dust, Deception & Death, published in The Courier-Journal, April 1998. Kathryn told me her husband loaded up 20 oxygen tanks so he could breathe on the last trip he took to a black lung conference. He died in 2001.

I learned a great deal about black lung disease and problems associated with filing claims.

Have a wonderful holiday.
B. L. Dotson-Lewis

Mr. Cecil Roberts, President, U.M.W.A.
Fairfax, Virginia

Dear President Roberts;

I'm extremely sad tonight. I just returned from the wake of a coal miner, born June 26, 1920, died September 29, 2004. He was my friend's father. This man spent 44 years as an underground coal miner in the Appalachian coalfields. Large part of his work history was for Pittston Coal Company.

His obituary seems normal for a man of his age, but it isn't. This is why I am writing to you tonight. The scenario played out in this miner's life and his family's life is all too common here in the Appalachian coalfields.

My friend told me about her father's long struggle with the black lung compensation elusive game after she learned of my book, Appalachia: Spirit Triumphant which has numerous stories in it from coal miners. She said that her father waited until retirement before filing for black lung compensation even though he exhibited many of the symptoms long before retiring. He wanted to work as long as possible. Also, he did not want to appear to be taking advantage of the coal company he worked for, Island Creek Coal Co.

Upon retirement, the hacking cough and spitting up of black phlegm became a problem he could no longer deny. He filed for black lung compensation to help with medical expenses and in case something happened to him, his wife would receive benefits.

According to my friend the process of filing a claim for compensation for her father was unending. I don't know the full details but I believe at one point he was awarded black lung benefits but the coal company appealed and won, so, the miner had to repay what he had received. He continued to submit to numerous medical tests as required upon advice from doctors and lawyers and a hopeful family even though doctors reported early on medical tests revealed the miner suffered from black lung.

The miner and his family finally gave up. They didn't know of one more thing to do and his health was deteriorating rapidly. This miner's daughter, my friend, stood in my office holding my book of coal miners' stories and tears streamed down her face. She was crying over her father's hopeless situation.

I told her about the black lung advocacy program at the New River Breathing Center at Scarboro Loop. I put her in touch with Tony. She discussed her father's black lung claim. The family was overjoyed with Tony's sincere interest, concern and knowledge. They didn't know there were advocates out there like Tony at Scarboro Loop to help and advise families.

I spoke with my friend a few weeks ago. She informed me it had become necessary to move her father to a nursing home due to his fragile state of health and the need for constant medical attention. She also told me in order to continue the black lung compensation appeal process, the coal company required her father to submit to a full day of medical tests by one of their doctors several hours away even though he suffered from a collapsed lung, he was on a feeding tube, could not walk, unable to talk or sit up.

In the meantime, Tony at Scarboro Loop performed magic which gave hope to this miner and his family for the first time in years; Washington & Lee University took on this miner's case as one of their two cases for the year.

The large container of medical records needed to prove or disprove, this coal miner had black lung was delivered to Washington and Lee University on Thursday of last week. The miner died on Wednesday of this week.

My question is this; now, that the miner has died, is the coal company declared the winner? Can the family continue with the claim to try to obtain some type of compensation for the miner's wife to live on?

Sincerely,
B. L. Dotson-Lewis
P.O. Box 313
Summersville, West Virginia 26651

Author's note: This article appeared in our local paper, The Nicholas Chronicle before Christmas 2005.

A Christmas Wish

John Adkins, Coal Miner, Fighting 2 Battles
by Betty Dotson-Lewis (B. L. Dotson-Lewis)
Dec. 15, 2005

John has been described as "tough as nails."

John Adkins whose permanent residence is Enon, Nicholas County, has taken up temporary residence at various medical centers in the area lately.   John and his wife, Grace, are well known and well liked throughout Nicholas County.   They have lived in the vicinity for over 39 years. Grace was the proprietor of Grace's Grocery for 7 1/2 years. One of her daughters now runs the store.   Grace's Grocery is conveniently located on Rt. 39 about 3.5 miles below the town of Summersville in the community of Enon.

Since their retirement and when John is able, he and Grace spend as much time as possible with their large family and many friends. They are neighbors and close friends with Elsie and Bill McCutcheon.   Elsie tells me, "John and Bill are as close as blood brothers. They look out for each other and worry about each other. It is hard on Bill when John is hospitalized." On this latest episode, Bill told Elsie, "I guess I will not get to go see John since he is in Charleston in the hospital ninety miles away."

Enon is a small, close-knit community and most of the lives revolve around coal mining. John's life has revolved around coal mining since birth. He was raised in the Widen/Dille area. Widen, 30 miles outside Summersville, is best known as a coal camp owned and operated by J. G. Bradley. Anyone associated with Widen/Dille has a history all their own. Widen in its heyday became one of the largest non-union coal mine operation in the U.S. Following a series of attempts for unionization, violence erupted and shootings, destruction of property and bad feelings overtook the coal camp. J. G. Bradley sold out and left the area. Today, what remains is an abandoned coal camp where 75 people get their mail on a regular basis at the local post office – at one time 3,000 residents received mail there. A few stone foundations can be found which are the remains of the company store, bank and boarding houses. A few coal camp houses in rows and lots of memories. That is what is left behind.

John Adkins, raised in a coal camp began his own career as a coal miner in 1956 hand loading coal using a #4 coal shovel. He worked this job four or five years.   John's pay was $1.00 per ton. When he first began there were two men hand loading and hauling the coal out by buggy for a total of $1.10 per ton. They each received 55 cents per ton. John recalls those times - hard work and bad times. The mines were non-union. The coal was hauled out by buggy, dumped into trucks and hauled off. There was not much concern for bad top or slate falls.

It is a well know fact, coal miners share a common bond, which may be associated with the potential for hazardous working conditions. In 1968 when the Hominy Falls mine disaster occurred, John was working for Island Creek Coal Company. He was sent over to Hominy Falls to help out with rescue efforts anyway he could. John tells me the drift mouth of the mines was all you could see. The miners were trapped about a mile and a half back in the mines. John talks about how the inspector donated a live miner to each rescue worker on the job at the time the miners were found. He got the Martin boy to escort to the outside.

So, John Adkins was born and raised in the midst of battles. That has not changed. For a number of years now he has been fighting two battles. The first and most important battle is for physical well being. John has been in and out of hospitals since 1981. In this latest bout he was taken by ambulance to Summersville Memorial Hospital, later transferred to Charleston Area Medical Center Intensive Care Unit. He spent almost two weeks in the Charleston hospital. Finally, John's family requested his return to Summersville Memorial Hospital for care and treatment by his family doctor, Dr. Paul Conley. Grace tells me, "John is tickled to be back at Summersville Memorial. The medical staff are so good to John, and he knows most of those tending to his needs. His doctor, Dr. Paul Conley is taking very good care of him."

I'm not sure of all of John's medical problems but John tells me he suffers from black lung and emphysema. He went on to say he was diagnosed with black lung in the 70's at the hospital in Richwood. The state gave him 40%, the feds gave him 100% disability based on a well-known lung specialist's diagnosis. He received compensation for one year. Then, the coal company appealed his case and won. The benefits were taken away. During his early years of exposure to coal dust, respirators were not required. The equipment was difficult to wear. After many bouts with respiratory problems, John was prescribed a breathing pill to be taken daily. He is the owner of three respirators and the doctor's orders are for oxygen at night, every night.

John and Grace told me their story of the long and depressing struggle to obtain black lung compensation. They said that it was very difficult to find legal representation. When I joined the Fayette County Black Lung Association, I was able to talk to John Cline of Piney View about John Adkins. Cline is an attorney who represents black lung claimants. He agreed to take on the John Adkins case seeking black lung compensation. That is battle number two.

When I spoke with Grace last night she was feeling optimistic and told me John had a good day yesterday. She stated Mr. Cline had called last week to check on John's condition. She is hopeful John will be home for Christmas.

John Adkins finally got relief from all pain on Friday, April 7, 2006 when he went to his eternal home to suffer no more. John died at home surrounded by family. Arnold Nicholas, Grace's first cousin and a coal miner, preached John's funeral. John left instructions with Arnold twice, one time at the hospital in Charleston and again at the Summersville Memorial Hospital. Arnold was to tell John's family to get ready to come and see him. Prepare to come over.   And told Arnold to tell his family not to think about his life in the past before he was saved but to think about the man he was after he was saved. John held the family Bible in both hands on his journey.

Part 5 - Coal Camp Memories

Whatever happened to Widen Coal Camp?

Widen Coal Camp. Photograph: Courtesy of Mark Romano

Widen Coal Camp cemetery. A haunting scene. Graves are marked with numbers instead of names. No one could tell me why the markers did not have names of the deceased miners. Photograph by B. L. Dotson-Lewis

Author's note: (Widen cemetery caption continued): I was told names of the buried here are recorded in a ledger in Clay County. Some call the cemetery "The colored cemetery" or they say miners who could speak no English are buried here, but no one seems to know for sure. The graveyard was neglected for years but that has changed. Grave #23 has teddy bears recently placed there. One has a cross attached to the headstone and one has plastic flowers. I have been told it was a practice for coal operators like J. G. Bradley to contract a rail box car, send it to New York, Ellis Island and get a box load of immigrants when they got off the ships. They were brought to the coal camps to work in the mines. They could not speak English, nor had relatives to bury them if they died.

Whatever Happened to Widen Coal Camp?

By B. L. Dotson-Lewis

General Ulysses S. Grant, who having fought the bloodiest war in U.S. history, eloquently described his impression of mining after visiting one in the western states. He said, "I don't think the devil invented the mines, but it is as close to Hell as I ever hope to be."

But for thousands of settlers coming to America seeking independence and religious freedom in the Appalachian mountains, mining became their way of life.

Appalachia, an Indian term meaning "On the other side," was first settled as an agriculture region with farmers, hunters and trappers making their living off the land. When coal was discovered in the late 1800s, life in Appalachia changed forever – changed from an agriculture region to an industrial region. Farmers were lured down from their mountain farms and immigrants were met by coal agents on Ellis Island with offers of jobs mining coal.

Coal camps emerged by necessity. Coal operators were forced to provide everything miners needed in order to get workers. These coal camps were located in remote, isolated areas deep in the Appalachian mountains. They were built in clusters along the winding creeks and up hollows where the low-sulphur bituminous coal seams would be dug out and hauled away to help fuel the Industrial Revolution. Coal camp life as originally conceived span a lifetime for many people. That concept is mostly gone today, but the fascination with King Coal and the importance of the coal miner has never diminished.

This is a story of the rise and fall of a coal camp in Appalachia - one man's kingdom, J. G. Bradley and Widen Coal Camp.

Beautiful green hills surround the few remaining Jenny Lin houses in Widen coal camp. The hills look much the same today as when the white people took the popular hunting grounds from the Indians.

When the Civil War was over. Simon D. Cameron, whom Abe Lincoln had dismissed as his Secretary of War, ended up with a 93,000 acre tract of land in remote Clay County,

246

West Virginia.   One acquaintance said the Pennsylvania politician, Simon Cameron, came with a reputation so unsavory, that the only thing he would not steal was a red-hot stove.

Now, this has no reflection on his great great grandson, J. G. Bradley, the man who built Widen on the property handed down through a land grant somehow obtained during or following the Lincoln era.

In 1904 a slicked back Harvard Law School graduate, Joseph Gardner Bradley, arrived on the scene in Clay County, on family property, as a right of way agent for the Buffalo and Gauley Railroad.   Joseph Gardner Bradley, born with a silver spoon in his mouth was up for a challenge when he walked away from his upbringing in a wealthy family in New Jersey to become President of the Buffalo and Gauley Railroad and assume the role of land developer for his family's inheritance. Bradley lasted more than 50 years in the backwoods of Clay County, West Virginia.

The rise and fall of a coal camp has been compared to life and death. The remains of Widen Coal Camp is comprised of a few coal camp houses, stone foundations used to support the company store, boarding houses and bank. This is what people are holding on to from abandoned coal camps like Widen-people who were born and raised in these coal camps. The jobs and houses are gone, but the people who lived there have their memories of the high life; crowded streets, community socials, Saturday night brawls and fiddling, moonshine, knives, river baptisms, shootings and burials.   They have memories of segregation of colored and whites and a section for the immigrants. The segregation plan for workers as well as blacks and immigrants seemed so logical and idealistic from the late 1800s through the 1950s and 60s in the mountains of West Virginia in places like Widen -a pint sized city nestled in a narrow hollow.

The mines opened in Widen in 1911 and the production of coal increased annually. Initially coal was discovered at Dundon in 1898 which became the home of Bradley and wife but soon a finer seam of coal was discovered 19 miles away so the railroad was extended up Buffalo Creek and the Elk Coal and Lumber Company opened a mine and Widen coal camp was born.

This mine owned and operated by Elk Coal and Lumber Company under the direction of its wealthy owner, J. G. Bradley, became the largest non-union mine in the United States. Bradley, provided everything for his workers, wages higher than union, company houses for a small rental fee, company store for purchases of goods paid for with scrip or deducted from the miner's wages.

The company towns like Widen were unincorporated. There were no local political officials, no mayor, no city council, no ward boss to attend to the immediate interests of the miners--there was only the coal operator. A former resident of Widen recalled that the coal operator there "governed completely."   He was Mayor, Council, Big Boss, sole trustee of the school, truant officer, president of the bank; in fact he was everything.

Although sometimes referred to as a feudal ruler of Widen and its men, Bradley to many was like a patriarch. He wanted the best for his industrial family. Bradley built and maintained a top rate school system bringing in the best teachers available for grades 1 - 12. Bradley planned for their futures by making sure his workers had job security and he assured his workers jobs would be there for their sons as well. He built and maintained three churches in the town. One was for Presbyterians, one for Baptists and one for the colored. In many coal camps a community church was built and all denominations worshiped under the same roof.

Bradley staffed and maintained the YMCA in Widen which had a bowling alley, pool hall, basketball court, and a theater to provide the latest movies and news. Girls or women were not allowed in the pool hall.

The houses for the workers were identical in Widen. They were single units painted red and white. Another section of town was reserved for the bosses. They had bigger houses and in some coal camps, the Superintendent had the luxury of running water. Kanawha Street in Widen, reserved for the bosses, was sometimes referred to as "silk panty" street – On it was the Club House where you could board and get the best of food. Mr. Bradley stayed there when he came in to check on his company. Harry Taka was brought in as the chief cook. He and his wife had three children. His wife returned to Japan before December 7, 1941, with their youngest child.   During WWII Japanese elsewhere in the country were required to live in camps during the war, Mr. Taka, along with his two older children, were allowed to stay in Widen and do Mr. Bradley's work. Bradley took full responsibility for the Taka family.

Labor Problems

Several times the UMW had tried to organize Widen. In the early 30s and in 1941 there was a type of range war. Union sympathizers fired high powered rifles from the tops of surrounding hills down on the town while company men guarded the area. In one battle, Joe Groves was killed on the streets of Widen. Small uprisings continued all along, but the most severe battle began in 1952. It is described as the bitterest mine strike in modern West Virginia history. It lasted for more than a year. Bradley successfully fought off attempts by a number of miners to install the UMW as their bargaining agent. What started as a walkout by a small group of dissidents quickly snowballed into a small war that produced many episodes of killing, shooting, and dynamiting.

The small mountain town of Widen took on the appearance of an embattled fortress with Bradley as the feudal lord. One local newspaper put it this way, "While state police patrolled the highways, armed mine sentries patrolled the ridges and valleys. The bitter struggle turned brother against brother, father against son, and left scars that remain to this day."

Bradley won the battle against the UMW, but the price of victory was too costly and foreshadowed the end of his more than fifty year baron-like reign over the mining community. In 1953, after an eleven or twelve month siege, Charles Frame was killed in a drive-by shooting at Dille at what was known to be the UMW men's cook shack. This brought the strike to a head and the UMW let up its pressure. When it was over, there were not enough sympathizers to endorse John L. Lewis's UMW. Miners involved in union organization efforts were black balled. Some of the miners went to Farmington and tragically lost their lives in the mine explosion. Out migration began to Ohio and Michigan.

In 1957, faced with dwindling profits and spreading bitterness among his tightly-knit industrial family, Bradley sold out to Pittston Coal Company and left the state. The 1952-53 twelve month strike must have completely disillusioned him. After seven years under the new owners, operations ceased in 1964. Widen had supplied the economy of surrounding counties as well as the towns of Clay, Dille, Birch River, Strange Creek, and Summersville, so its demise was felt all around.

Part 6 – Stories of mountain culture and traditions

Last fiddler on the mountain, Ralph Roberts
Stories by mountain man, Earl Dotson
     Copperhead
     Shootout in the moonshine capital of the world
     Coon hunting with a cripple
     No sleep
     Agony of defeat
     Bobcat hunting
     Lost bull on Strawberry mountain

George Johnson and his sister on her porch, Myrtle, Mingo County, West Virginia 1972.
Photograph by Builder Levy

Lee Triplett, Champion Fiddler. Photograph: Courtesy of Robert Sattler

Last Fiddler on the Mountain

Ralph Roberts, Narrative/Interview

Author's note: Rural Appalachia has a history of community mindedness brought about by self-sufficiency with little help from the outside world. Barn-raising, corn and hay harvesting, apple butter stirring and fence building brought the community together for work. Following a hard day's work, the fiddling set in.

The bow, fiddle and fiddler were all essential elements of the southern Appalachian Mountains during early times. The fiddler and fiddle were revered by the community folk but the church folk held a different view of the "Devil's Box."   Fiddling was associated with idleness, liquor, and other worldly pleasures. Fiddling was said to have evolved to accompany dancing such as Flatfootin'. In early days the fiddle was often the sole musical instrument so the fiddler was creative.

My father, Earl Dotson, played the fiddle. He just took it up and practiced until he learned to play. He didn't read music or take lessons. Also, Thomas Jefferson, author of the Declaration of Independence and Davy Crockett, King of the Wild Frontier, played the fiddle.   It has been reported that Henry Ford was a fan of fiddling and even sponsored a series of contests, during the 20's in an effort to promote old fashioned values of America and dismantle the looming evils of jazz and communism.

The fiddle arrived with early settlers and more than likely spread to every part of the nation, but fiddle tunes originating in places like Scotland, Ireland and the British Isles have retained more of their originality in the Appalachian Mountains because of the isolation of the region.

Old-time fiddling techniques and old-time fiddle tunes have suffered the culture shock and evolved into standard tuning, amplification, commercialization, watered down and cleaned up versions, leaving almost nothing of the original tunes or technique. However, this evolution has been slow in making its way into the remote mountains of Appalachia. This place, where we live, is seen by many as austere and barren, in reality, the region is a Mecca of originality steeped in history including original old time fiddlers and pre-Civil War fiddle tunes.

The documentation of regional history of the southern Appalachian Mountains would be lacking without the inclusion of old time fiddling. A co-worker, Howard Campbell, made the formal introduction for me to this era of history by arranging an interview with an old time fiddler, Ralph Roberts, who is related to the famous Hammons music family.

Ralph Roberts and wife, Charlie, Photograph by B. L. Dotson-Lewis

I am Ralph Adrin Roberts, the fifth child of Grandville Coneides and Nellie Mae Roberts. I have four brothers older than me and one younger. I have two sisters. My brothers are, Lester, Cecil, Lloyd, Junior and Dale. My sisters are Bernice and Virginia.

I was born on Poplar Creek in Nicholas County on February 28, 1929, and delivered by a mid-wife Annie Roberts, as we all were. Annie lived to be 102 years old. I remember she smoked a clay pipe and never went to the doctor in her life.

We lived in a Jenny Lin house. I don't remember anything from the time I was born until I started to school. We had to walk five miles to school and five miles back home. I went to a one room school that taught eight grades. Our teacher was Ada Scott. I had the job of building a fire at school for two years and got paid $8.00 every three months. I remember in the 7th grade putting chewing gum in Lea Dodrill's hair and the teacher gave me a pair of scissors to cut it out.

In the summer we went bare foot and wore knee breeches. We got one pair of shoes per year and a pair of artics to wear over our shoes to keep them dry. Cecil cut all of our hair during those years. We had to cut wood every day for cooking and then when winter came we had to cut wood for heat. We never had homework when we were in school. We played fox and geese tag and softball at school. We had no snow days either.

All I remember is cutting wood and working all the time. Dad worked away all the time and we, the kids and mom raised big gardens and potatoes and corn patches. We raised nearly everything we ate and enough corn for horses and cornbread all year. We sold eggs for flour, coffee, salt and a few other things. Dad hunted bee trees in the woods. He would put sugar water on the ground and watch for bees. Dad would take flour and put on broom straw and mark the bees and time when the bees left till they came back to the sugar water. From that, a person would know how far away the bee tree was. The bees would circle up two or three times and then fly straight to the bee tree. We had our own grist mill and if water wasn't high enough we had to go to Birch River to grind corn. We had a big trough that ran down and turned a big wooden wheel with paddles and a big wheel turned a shaft where burrstones were, which ground the corn.

When Dad came home he would bring us peppermint and horehound candy. Dad worked in logging camps which was real hard work. They worked from daylight till dark with horses and crosscut saws to cut timber. Dad could only write his name but he could look at a tree and tell how many board feet was in a tree. When Lester, Cecil and Lloyd got big enough they went to work with Dad in the woods. Times were hard but Dad and Mom managed to save enough to buy 40 acres off Grandma Roberts' Dad. When I was 14 years old we moved to Powell's Mountain. That was a better place. I went to Summersville School. That is when I started fooling around with the fiddle. Dad's dad and a couple of Dad's brothers played music. Dad had seven brothers and two sisters. Mom had one sister, one half brother and one half sister. Cecil volunteered for the Marines, Lester was drafted in the Navy. Junior was drafted in the old Army Air Corp.

We lived on Powell's Mountain about five years and then moved on Buffalo in Braxton County. While living on Buffalo I volunteered for the Army because I was going to get drafted anyway. Dale, my brother, joined the Air Force. Cecil, Lester and Junior were all in WWII. Me and Dale was in during the Korean conflict. We were in Korea together. He was a cook. I was a combat medic.

They put you where they want you. I fought hard for nine months in Korea and won five campaign battle stars. I went in Service May 1949. Went to Japan and from there on to Persia, Korea. Started pushing Koreans back and away to Pyongyang, the North Korea Capital. Chinese pushed us all the way to Persia – then just seesaw back and forth. If anyone says there isn't Hell on earth, I'm here to tell them all war is Hell. I left Korea March 1951 and came back to the U.S.

Went to Korea on a ship – we had cornbread and navy beans every morning for breakfast – for a month. That got old, but I did without food four days and four nights while in Korea one time. Couldn't get any food during the war. It was so bad then, some of those beans and cornbread would have tasted good.

Got home for three or four days then on to North Carolina and discharged in 1952. Dale, my brother, got out in 1952. We were in Korea together but didn't see each other. When I got back, the first thing I did was find me a girlfriend and then, of course, I had to fine a job. Went to Ohio and worked in Fisher's Body plant. Got homesick for West Virginia and came home. Went to work at a saw mill. Worked about six months then Dale and I joined the Air Force in 1954. Back to Korea I went I worked in air freight this time in passenger service, routing service men all over the world. One thing I found unusual was all people used the same bathroom and they had public baths but everyone took a bath before they got in baths. They can fix rice a 100 different ways. I ate a lot of rice, vegetables and fish in Korea and Japan.

The women do nearly all the work in Japan but in Korea men work. The first time I went to Korea the people lived in mud huts with straw thatched roofs but the second time I went they was mostly replaced with high rises and brick buildings. Other countries must like for us to war with them because we rebuild their countries after war.

The Korean people wore skirts above their breasts and no underclothes.

During the war in Korea the people carried A frame on their back with all their belongings on the frame. Mostly men carried them, but some women did too. In Korea they have lots of cats. They have a few dogs but lots of cats. Stayed in Japan until 1954 came back to the States in 1958. Uncle Sam wanted me to re-enlist but I didn't want to. You are not free when you are in the service.

After I came home I began fiddling around some with the fiddle. Did odd jobs – worked in the coal mines and for the railroad – went to Ohio worked for school board for a few years. Worked in Wisconsin and New Jersey. I worked in a ketchup factory and "no" I don't eat ketchup. I also worked in soy sauce factory.

Couldn't stay away from West Virginia for very long, so I came back home and went to work at the airport tie yard in the mill division and worked seven years. They shut down and I went to work at Coastal Lumber in Gassaway. I worked 15 years all together at three different times until I retired.

I lived at home during these years. I thought about getting married during these years but was too busy drinking.

My brother Cecil had a lady friend and I really liked her a lot so I took her away from him with her consent. We got married on my 58th birthday. Now this was a new way of life for me. I quit drinking and haven't drank for eight years.

I play the fiddle, guitar, mandolin more now.

I visited the Hammons quite a lot. The Hammons family is famous now because of their old time music. Use to camp a lot with Sherman Hammons and Dad. I remember Eddin Hammons coming to grandpa's house. He would play music with Grandpa John Roberts. Grandpa use to show me some things about fiddling. He used all of a bow – a long one. Most of Hammons played in cross-tuning. Grandpa played on open A tuned in BEAE or EADE.

My wife bought me a fiddle that was found in Germany in an abounded house and this man sent it home to his brother. This man's boys had it and sold it to my wfe. It doesn't matter where you got the fiddle from; how much it cost, or how old it is, it's the tone that is important.

How I really got into this old time music was a long time ago when a young man, Jimmy Triplett, visited the Hammons and they sent him to see me.

Me and my wife go to the music festivals – Folk Festival at Glenville Jubilee at Jackson's Mill and String Band Festival at Clifftop where I met Betty Lewis.

I play for seniors at Burnsville and Gassaway twice a week.

I did a lot of drinking in my life, which I am not proud of, but it did ease the war memory for awhile.

When I was saved God pushed those memories way, way back in my mind. You don't ever forget them. Charlie (my wife) and I have a good life together. I teach music in open A tuning when they want me to for Augusta at Davis and Elkins College. They ask me to teach several years ago but I play by ear and didn't think I could teach as I can't read a note of music, but I guess I have succeeded.

Well, I guess I will keep fiddling as long as I have strength to fiddle the bow across the strings.

We always used a lot of herbs out of the woods such as snake root and mullin for sickness. We used a lot of turpentine to put on cuts, suppose to take out soreness, put scrapped raw potatoes pieces on burns.

My mother never worked in public work. Her mom died when my mom was five years old and she had one sister, Stella. Her dad remarried and she has another half sister and brother. Her step mother was real good to her. Grandpa Goff lived at Boss, West Virginia and I remember going to their house and spending the night when I was little.

We never went out anywhere hardly except to Grandpa Roberts' up the hollow from us and Grandpa Goff over the mountain at Boggs. We went to the store once a month.

We never had friends spend the night with us because we had each other.

We had 40 something acres up Poplar and Dad sold out to Ernest Tinnel. We moved to Powell's Mountain. I liked Powell's Mountain so much better than Poplar because it was so much easier going to school and to the store.

We had company every weekend and they usually spent the night. We would listen to Amos and Andy and Jam Up and Haney on the battery powdered radio. We kids would play in the woods on grapevines, climb trees and play in creeks. Mom made most of our shirts and breeches until we wore jeans. The most I remember is getting wood and working in the cornfields.

Ralph Roberts at Camp Washington Carver. Photograph by B. L. Dotson-Lewis

Ralph picked up his fiddle and bow and played for me:

Old Jimmy Johnson, Washington March, Sugar in the Gourd, Old Horse & Buggy, Cherry River Line, Arkansas Traveler, Cricket on the Hearth, Casey Jones, Cold Creek March, Wildwood Flower, Black Velvet Waltz, Soldier's Joy.

Ralph told me: Fiddle leads in old-time music, guitar leads in Bluegrass music. Charlie said that Ralph plays several songs that no one plays because his grandfather taught him the songs.

Ralph: The bow is made from horsehair so you have to have rosin, otherwise it would be slick and not make any sound.

What kind of dances did you do when you were young:

Ralph: Flatfootin'

What is the origination of the Roberts' name?

Roberts is an English name.

Are you playing the same songs your grandfather played?

Ralph: Yes.

What influence did he have on your life?

My grandfather had no education, but lots of wisdom. He said that if you never accomplish anything in this life besides getting a good fiddle and a good pair of shoes and a good bed that is enough, because if you are not in one, you will be in the other.

Did you spend a lot of time with your grandfather? What did he do? What did he look like?

Yes, he lived right above us about two miles. I was up there a lot. He fished and he hunted groundhogs. He was a big, tall, raw-boned, good-natured man. He was not afraid of nothing. You could have called him a Nature Man. He loved the woods. He loved to get out and roam the woods. He loved to hunt. He hunted groundhogs and squirrel in the fall of the year. He hunted ginseng. I still like to hunt ginseng. It sells for about $300.00 to $400.00 per pound today. When I was a kid, it was $3.00 to $4.00 per pound. May Apple went for about half a cent per pound. We dug it to sell. We would take it down to Birch River to Greg Coffman.

Was your family a close-knit family?

Yeah. Charlie added, his family are clannish - real clannish.

Do you teach people to play the fiddle the way you play?

I taught one girl my way of fiddling. I'm no regular teacher but we go to the Augusta Heritage Festival at Davis & Elkins College and I get paid. I sit in the classroom and explain how I play. Then, we jam.

Do you play everyday?

Yes, I usually pick up my fiddle and play a song or two.

What does playing the fiddle do for your?

It gives me a peaceful feeling. It takes your worries away and I play for fun.

Charlie: He is gifted. He can hear a song a few times and than play that song. He used to be able to play 62 songs and all without music.

Have you made a CD?

Yes. Me and my nephew, Ricky Roberts made a CD. He plays with me. He teaches. He does backup for Mike Morningstar.

Ralph's closing comments: I remember growing up we lived out so far. We had no vehicle. The old time fiddlers would come up to grandpa's place and they all would play, Uncle Emmett, Aunt Hazel and Uncle Cyde. They played music like I have never heard before. It was unique.

The musical Hammons family have lots of interesting stories following them. One of my favorite stories is about Eddin' Hammons. The story goes, he carried his fiddle around in a flour sack and when he got it out to play, he would have flour dusted all over his face. The story also says the Revenuers could never find his hiding place for moonshine. He would put it underneath a big rock at the front door and they would step on the rock coming into the house but never think to look underneath the rock.

Earl Dotson, middle, Lena (sister) on left, Frank (brother) right
Photo taken in Buchanan County, Virginia - Jim Fork, family farm

Stories by Mountain Man, Earl Dotson

Introduction

My father was a writer, storyteller and fiddler. He spent much of his life in the woods and on the riverbank. His sense of humor kept him young and worry free. He was one with nature. Family and friends meant everything to him as reflected in his personal stories - a characteristic of people rooted deeply in Appalachian traditions. He was called "The General" or "Chief" by everyone, including his own children.

His roots were in Buchanan County, Virginia – a place he always referred to as home. His love for new experiences, bigger and better hunting grounds and vast timber - his life trade, led him first to West Virginia and then on to Oregon and Washington State. In reality, he never left Appalachia. He simply created Appalachia everywhere he traveled, pulling out his old fiddle to play or whistling a tune. It was all about Appalachia.

Author's Note: My father grew up on a large farm in Buchanan County, Virginia. The farm was a portion of a larger tract of land my grandmother's family owned when my grandfather married into the family. The portion my father lived on was located up Jim's Fork, known for its steep, rocky, hillside farms as well as the moonshine it exported. The area was known for its valuable coal – "punch" mines lined the hollows.

When my father was growing up chores were assigned to sons and daughters at an early age and since the land was farmed without benefit of modern farming equipment, it was necessary for the entire family to help.

This is one of the stories my father has written about growing up on a farm during the early 1900s in southwest Virginia in the hills of Appalachia.

Copperhead

We lived on a large farm and kept two or more milk cows. On this particular summer evening, my parents had gone to a church gathering. My sister Rose and I were all alone at home. She was around 17 and I was seven or eight.

Rose told me to go to the field and drive the cows home so she could milk before dark. We all knew there were many rattlesnakes and copperheads in the area, especially the cow pasture. When Pa cleared the timber to make a cow pasture, he cut tree stumps as close to the ground as possible with the remains left to rot - the perfect hiding place for snakes.

I was soon able to hear the cowbells far back near the timber about a mile from the house. When I climbed the hill and got near the cows, I came close to an old stump with a fresh groundhog track on the upper side. My older brother Frank often talked about hunting and trapping groundhogs and I thought that would be a good place.

Well, I thought while I am here, I will smooth the dirt out and pack it down, and make a place to set a trap. When I stuck my left hand back in the hole something struck hard. My hand was bleeding and burning real bad.

Now, just to think how foolish a boy can be, I done the very thing I should not have done. I thought the groundhog had bitten me. So, I thought, I will carry rocks and stop up the hole and tomorrow Frank and I will come and dig him out. I carried a few rocks but my tongue began getting stiff and swollen. My hand and arm was swelling also. The two small holes in my hand where bitten, were oozing black blood out.

I tried to unbutton my shirtsleeve but I could not. I started walking toward the house but I kept staggering and falling down like a drunken man. All I could see was just a blur. I got close enough to see the house and I tried to holler out for help but I could not. My tongue was so swollen it was choking me to death. My legs gave way. I fell and could not get up. I knew I would not make it.

Rose had come hunting for me. She carried and dragged me to the yard. Rose knew it was a bad snakebite but did not know what to do, no phones, no car, no neighbors close by, no doctors within miles. The only sound I remember was my sister Rose crying and praying - my heart was pounding and fluttering like it would tear out of my body.

My fate was in the hands of Rose and the good Lord and she was constantly talking to him. I went into shock or a coma. I do not know which one.

I had always wondered what plans the good Lord had for me - why he did not just let me go away and save all the agony my family went through for the next four days. But in four days, the smell of turpentine woke me up. Rose was by my bed. She was the first to notice my eyes were open and I was looking at all the empty bottles of turpentine on the floor. She began to cry. My hand was in a pail of cold water laced with the medicine. She said that she changed the water every hour and poured in turpentine each time.

My family was all there. I could hear them talk. They talked so low, almost a whisper. They talked so kind to one another.

I heard them say, "He may be a cripple. The poison may settle in his joints or in his brain, but thank God he is alive."

I told Frank where it happened. He took his rifle and found the place. He said that he found a very large copperhead snake coiled up on the stump sticking out her ole black tongue.

She would bite no more.

Shootout in the Moonshine Capital of the World

Two men had come together and neither one would run
I stood and watched them closely as each one carried a gun.

Not a word was spoken as I was standing by
All they did was stand and look each other in the eye

Before the day was over, the lead would surely fly
And the question would be answered, who would be the first to die.

Baker had a problem, which he was quick to see.
I had pulled my German Lugar and stepped behind a tree.

His men were standing ready, but not a word was said.
They knew if either raised his gun, all three would soon be Dead.

(Poem written by Earl Dotson)

I was born in Buchanan County, Virginia in 1910 near the Kentucky, West Virginia lines. In the 1930s, you need not be in Dodge City or Tombstone, Arizona to witness a gunfight or help bury dead men who were shot and killed every week. By the time I was twenty-five I had seen about as many dead men as Wyatt Erp or Doc Holliday.

The roads were bad and most people rode horses. It was rough in mountain country but the creeks ran clear and cold, ideal for making moonshine whiskey. That was the way of life and the way of death as you will learn in this story.

The story I will tell is one of many I remember from my younger days. Everyone carried a gun including the preacher. He rode a mule and carried his gun in the saddlebag along with his Bible.

My Dad and Mother owned a 200-acre farm and being church going people never had anything to do with whiskey, making, selling or drinking. They would not let anyone make whiskey on their land. My parents made all of us go to church as long as we were at home.

I had six brothers. My parents done everything that laid in their power to keep us away from the whiskey and the bad guys. In thinking back, I believe they done a very good job as none us were never in any bad trouble.

They did almost lose one case however, as I will relate to you.

Making and selling whiskey was a competitive business as any other business in those days. Most of the moonshine went to West Virginia coal miners. The big operators wanted all the whiskey business and having money to buy off the law, they were seldom ever bothered.

The place I am referring to was known as the Moonshine Capital of The World. The Prosecuting Attorney at Grundy, Buchanan County, Virginia, called it "The Hell Hole." The little operators were the targets for the law.

Recipe for Moonshine Whiskey

For corn whiskey: Use 28 gallons of water: 12 gallons of hot boiling water - 16 gallons of cold water. This will make all the beer that you need in a 35-gallon pot. You need at least five bushel of corn. Let the corn sprout - grind it into mash. Put it in your barrels. Then let it sour. You use about two gallons of corn meal to pour into the barrel with the corn to make a cap on top of the beer. When the beer is ready to run for making whiskey, it will clear off the top of the beer.

For straight corn whiskey: You run it only one time. For double corn whiskey you run it, two times. For making double and twisted, you run it in the boiler three times.

For making sugar and corn mix - which is a better drink: you use 25 pounds of corn and let it sprout, 25 pounds of sugar with the same amount of water.

For making sugar whiskey, you use two gallons white meal, fifty pounds of sugar.

I stayed at home and worked on the farm until I was twenty-two years old. Now, I will go back to my story:

A family lived down the road that had come from East Tennessee. They had four sons. I went to school with two of the sons who were about my age. One of the boys was my favorite. He was always with me in any trouble I had. After we finished our education, which ended at the eighth grade level, he and his older brother started making moonshine whiskey.

My friend, the moonshiner, was a quiet man, wore nice clothes, and always had a nice haircut. He carried a 44 Smith and Wesson at all times. He had been in a number of shooting scrapes but never bragged about what he had done or what he would do. We shot our pistols daily at targets and went to all the pistol matches.

I had just helped Dad bury two men on this particular morning and then I walked down towards the store. I met my friend, his brother and a companion in a Model A Ford. They had a rifle with an empty shell hung in the barrel and wanted me to try to get it out. I did that and rode on the running board down the road with them. They told me the law had destroyed their moonshine still and arrested the wife of their companion.

About a mile on down we saw two cars blocking the road. We stopped. I told the boys to wait while I walked down to see what was going on. There was a bypass which was a narrow road down by the creek.

As I approached the men, I realized I knew all four. There were two men in each car. They were a bunch of professional killers. As I watched, the Chevrolet drove down the creek using the bypass road. The other car remained parked.

Just as my friend got out of his Model A, one of the killers fired through the window breaking the mirror by his companion's head. Peace Officer Baker was with the killers. He walked toward my friend who was standing beside his car at the creek. The other men stood ready to kill.

As no one had been charged nor resisted arrest, I knew these men had come to destroy the still and kill the owners. My best friend would be the first to die. I knew that as soon as Peace Officer Baker made his move toward my friend. There was no other choice for my friend but try to defend himself against the law and the killers.

I, on the other hand, was a victim of circumstances. I had a decision to make quickly. I refer you back to the poem. I had my German Lugar, which I carried as often as I wore my hat. It was loaded with nine rounds and a clip in my pocket with eight more rounds. At that distance, I knew I would not miss. Peace Officer Baker gave one hard look at me standing within 20' of three killers. He didn't like what he saw. He came over and talked with his men. I never heard what was said but I do know what George Armstrong Custer said to Chief Sitting Bull:

"We will fight another day."

The killers got in their 1927 Chevrolet and went the way they came.

My friend came over to where I stood and asked, "Why did you stay around?" I told him, "I was trying to keep a dumb friend from being shot." He said that he saw me go behind that tree with my gun in my hand.

I told him I remembered hearing Baker's brother preach one time and the scripture he mentioned I will quote:

"No Greater Love Is This, Than For a Man to Lay Down His Life For a Friend."

My friend said, "I am going home to see if any of my brothers at home or other family have been shot."

I met Officer Baker walking back. He seemed real friendly but he did say that he was going to town to get more men and guns. About that time, I heard my friend's 44 crack from the top of the hill. The bullet hit a post nearby. He called out, "Just letting you know I am still around."

I told Baker if he would wait and come back the next day with warrants, there would be no trouble. The fact they arrested the wife of my friend's companion without cause was proof they were not the law. I told him if he brought back that bunch of professional killers, someone would be shot!

The officer's reply was, "I don't believe their powder will burn."

Baker wanted me to go back in to Grundy with him. I went along thinking I could talk him into severing ties with the professional killers. When we got into town, he locked me up and told the jailer not to let me out till he came back with the prisoners. That was a long time, as you will find out and after I found out, I'm glad I was locked up.

Now, I want to point out the reason I got involved. I had no part of any moonshine still, nor was I related to any of the men. They were just my friends. But these men were not officers of the law except for the one, Peace Officer Baker, who was not required to destroy moonshine stills.

One of the hired killers had just killed a man, but not charged. Now, he had just tried to kill two of my friends. Baker and the other men had driven by the post office and saw smoke from three different moonshine stills. Since these men were traveling 25 miles after men, guns and moonshine stills, it occurred to me that these men were working under a contract to destroy the stills and kill the owners.

I knew the capability of my gun, a 9 shot automatic. The other men all had revolvers. If they missed the first shot, their chances were slim. My reputation for using a gun was well known. I knew these hired guns had no intention of letting my friend and me walk away alive.

Chapter 2

My friend told the rest of this story to me. I was retained in the Grundy jail during the following events. Based on the evidence I heard at the trial, I know he told the truth.

The companion's house was on a side road and on that afternoon two cars drove up and parked nearby. Inside one car were three men from Grundy, Virginia, including Baker. They got out of their car carrying high-powered rifles. They went up a trail and stopped in the timber opposite the house. The other killers stayed in the second car.

Two of the hired killers slipped through the brush and got past the house. Baker fired the first shot. He fired at the man who had been traveling with the brother whose wife they had arrested. Baker shot him three times in the head. He then stepped over the dead body lying in the front door.

Then, my friend shot Baker three times in the chest with his 44. Baker walked down the road with his jacket on fire and held onto the fence until he dropped dead.

The remaining hired killers on the hill started firing through the windows. Splinters were flying off the walls. By this time my friend inside the house was under the bed. He was hit in one hand. His finger was shot off. Blood was flying in his face and on his gun. The hired killers were moving in on my friend. As one of the killers tried to shoot him through the window, my friend shot him under the right arm. It came out over his left hip. He then saw another killer trying to crawl into the house through another window. He broke this killer's legs. And, all got still.

The remaining men on the hill came down, put their guns away, loaded the wounded and dead, and drove away.

My friend went in to Grundy to see a doctor. He had his hand treated. He then surrendered to the authorities. He was tried and sentenced to 17 years in prison. He was freed in 15 months. He came home and married the schoolteacher. My friend went back to making moonshine whiskey.

As for me, I was turned out of jail that night after the shootout. I went home and got ready to shovel more clay. I would sing a gospel song or two, help bury the dead, go home and get ready for the next episode.

For years I would visit the old graveyard and look at the markers on the graves. I often wondered why these men, most of them I had grown up with, had placed such a small value on their lives or the lives of others.

One day I wrote a poem and nailed it on a tree in that graveyard that read as follows:

Where men lived raw and broke the law
And Hell was nothing to shun
But we buried them neat,
Without preacher or sheet
And carved on their tombstone cruel, but sweet
These men were slow with their gun.

I admired Peace Officer Baker for his courage. He had one weakness, however, and that caused his death and the death of others. He seemed to think all problems had to be solved with a gun.

Coon Hunting with a Cripple

I lived in West Virginia at the time this story takes place. My friend, C. Z. Bryant, had been hunting in Pennsylvania and had brought a nice looking Bluetick hound back with him. He asked if I wanted to look at the young dog. He said the reason he had the dog was that he would not stay at the tree. He was a nice Vaughn bred Bluetick with medium ears and an intelligent looking head. It looked like this pup had been handpicked from the litter.

To my surprise, Mr. Bryant told me he would give me the dog with the only requirement being that he could breed to him if he turned out good. He said, "He outruns my dogs but is never there when I kill the coon."

"How old?" I asked.

Dottie - Walker hound (a Dotson dog).
Photograph: Ruby Young Dotson Collection

"One year," he said. "His sire and dame are very good," I was told. I called him Troubles.

The first time I took him out, he treed a coon. With me being over six feet and part Cherokee, and close by, I killed the coon. This went on for a while and Troubles was staying longer at the tree. But Troubles liked to run those white-tailed deer, and the longer I hunted him, the worse he got.

I had no shocking collar at that time, so I took the dog to my brother, Charley. He had an apple orchard and deer were coming in there in droves. I told him to let the dog run loose and feed him very little. I went back in a week and asked how Troubles was doing. He said that the dog had run three days and nights, had come in twice for food, but he was well content now just to lie on the porch. He would not even go near the orchard.

"If you think he will tree a coon, up the creek there are some coon tracks." After dark, we walked one-half mile and Troubles was missing. We waited for a while and I told Charley I had not come prepared to coon hunt. I just had my flashlight and my automatic shotgun to do some light turkey hunting. I would wait for the dog and my brother could go home and go to bed. I walked up the creek and found dog tracks on the dry rocks where he had been in the water. I could not make out other tracks. I topped a ridge and heard Troubles treed. I went as fast as I could go for fear he would leave. He stayed.

I laid the flashlight on the right side of the gun and pulled the trigger. The slide came back and broke the glass, bulb and all, the only light I had. I waited till my eyes got accustomed to the dark and found the dog chewing on the coon. Three hours later, I found my truck, loaded my dog, and went home.

When I got home, my other brother was there. Clark had bought a Redbone pup. Clark was never much for coon hunting. He never liked to walk. He had been hit by a car and had trouble with one leg. I asked if he wanted to go hunting on Bull Pasture River. He said that his leg would not stand much walking and he did not want to hunt the pup with a deer dog. I told him I would go to the dog if treed, and he could stay at the truck. As I said earlier, Clark was never much for walking, if not for a bad leg, his shoes hurt his feet.

The coon had not come down to the river yet. I told Clark we would walk up to an old orchard and maybe we could have a deer race if nothing else. Clark said he had a potato sack and would carry everything we caught with that dog, but he said we would have to hang on flat ground due to his bad leg.

Troubles took a cold track and went uphill out of hearing. "That's out for me," he said. Then the Redbone pup started trailing. We followed the pup. When we topped a high ridge, Troubles was treed far down the other side. We killed the coon and put it in the sack.

"How's the leg?" I asked. "Bad?" "When we cross back over it will be downhill all the way."

When we topped up, we went too far to the right and went down the wrong creek. We heard Troubles running below and treed on a steep hill. I told Clark to just rest and I would go to the tree. The coon I killed was very large and when I came back, Clark was taking a nap.

I put the coon in his sack. I never mentioned being lost. Another half mile we treed another coon on a steep hill. "Go and get that dog, I am not carrying another coon." When I got to the tree, the pup was barking treed. When I killed the coon, Clark was almost there. There was another coon for the sack. I never said anything about carrying anything as he had agreed to carry all.

When we finally came to the road, we were about four to six miles from the truck. Troubles was not there. One half mile up the road, the dog came over the hill. Due to a high bank, we got him caught.

"The best thing that happens to a coon hunter is when the coon gets away," said my brother.

We stopped at a gas station. A game warden was there. I asked the owner if they had any scales. "Did you catch a big one?"

I said, "The biggest one I have caught in the area."

"My partner and I caught one that weighed forty pounds," he said.

Our coon weighed twenty-one and one-half pounds. I asked Clark if he wanted to take Troubles and the potato sack and find a forty pound one. He said, "No, but I want you to stop at the first beer joint and see if they have anything that might help my crippled leg."

Troubles never ran another deer and made a coon dog that any man would be proud to own.

Rita - Walker hound (a Dotson dog)
Photograph: Ruby Young Dotson Collection

No Sleep

It has been over thirty years but I still remember very clearly, when my Plott pup quit barking in the middle of the night. I told my wife that he had barked himself to death and maybe we could get some sleep. The next morning I went out before daylight to feed the pup. He was tied to the woodhouse where he slept. The two weeks I had kept him he had not slept, neither had I. When I put the food in the pan, a very large coon came out and ate with the pup.

Well, I scratched my head, blinked my eyes, and leaned against the building. I concluded that losing sleep and coon hunting had taken its toll. The best thing I could do was get a ride to Weston State Hospital. That is where they keep the feeble minded in that area. Now, I will try to explain what I think happened and the reader can be the judge.

In 1952, I moved from Buchanan County, Virginia, to Nicholas County, West Virginia. I lived on a farm on a country road. This was a coon hunter's paradise with lots of wilderness, small rivers, creeks, mountains, and plenty of food such as wild grapes, cherries, most all kinds, and plenty of big fat coons.

My neighbor, Johnny Groves, and I both had two coon dogs; each ran loose on the farm. Johnny worked in the coal mines in Richwood, West Virginia. He asked me if I wanted a nice looking Plot pup. A man that he worked with was going to move and could not take the pup. I said, "Bring him over."

He was four to five months old, had a very loud mouth, and barked day and night. The evening after I saw the coon, I went and told Johnny what had happened. He said that

 when he got the pup, the man gave him a large pet coon that the pup was raised with but he had given the coon to James Moore, who lived about two miles up the road.

He called James; the coon had left the night before. Now the question is, did he hear the pup barking? Did he recognize the pup's voice? How far can a coon hear anything? How did the coon get by four coon dogs undetected?

Appalachia Crosses the Great Divide

Author's note: When my father headed west he took those things he treasured most: His family, his hunting dogs, guns, fiddle and bow and an old typewriter. He also took with him a chunk of Appalachia in the form of stories, traditions and customs of the mountains. He loaded everything in his truck and headed across the Great Divide creating pockets of Appalachia where ever he hung his hat.

Agony of Defeat

I have read Full Cry Magazine for many years and hunted hounds for over 60 years. I have hunted for everything from possum to mountain lion in the United States and Canada. I have used every breed of hound that you can find.

Mr. Beckham's stories published in Full Cry Magazine are very good and I believe every word is true for example the story about the old gentleman hunting in the Ozark Mountains. Like he said, "They would never cut a den tree or say one bad word about their hunting partner or his dog." Very good.

I have been hunting bobcat in Washington State since 1961 and have had my trials and failures. Because we have plenty of rain and rough mountain country, we need good tough hounds that is wy I breed for performance only. I do not enter competition hunts or shows.

One of my favorite hounds is a Walker, but I like him much better if he is crossed with a Vaughn bred Bluetick or Wagoner bred Black & Tan. Some good Plott blood certainly does not hurt.

My belief is that pups inherit the desire to run the game their parents have been run on. For that reason, I breed to the best cat dogs available. I make sure they are not related in any way.

The dog that puts his head in the air runs by body scent, and keeps the cat moving is the dog that will pay for his feed. As long as he keeps his nose on the ground, he will never tree many cats.

Two of the best cat dogs I ever owned; one was half Black and Tan and half Plott, the other was Bluetick and Walker.

I heard it said by a wise old woman, "No one knows all about anything." In all the years I have hunted, I have never given the bobcat credit for being as smart as he really is. Now to my story.

Most people write stories of success. Few write stories of failure. This hunt took place in a strange land where everything went wrong. For that reason, I call it, "The Agony of Defeat."

In 1987, Champion Paper Company opened a large area for hunting in the foothills of Mt. Rainier in Washington State. The area comprises nearly one million acres, and had not been hunted with hounds for many years.

When the cat season opened, my son Tony and I loaded six hounds in my four-wheel drive truck, hooked on my camper and went through the gate. In two hours from my place, we drove seventeen miles and found a nice campground. We do not hunt cat at night. We took a drive to look over the country. Some fresh snow had fallen, ideal for hunting. We found plenty of cat tracks and mountain lion also.

No lion tag, so it would be bobcats only. We planned our strategy that night. Tony hunts Trigg Walkers and had three. I had three dogs, two veterans of many cats. I always thought that where cats had not been run, they would tree easy. I was bad wrong.

We knew we had the dog power. What we did not know was the kind of creatures we would be dealing with. We decided to split the pack, run two dogs on the first one, three on the second one and keep one dog in the box in case a cat crossed the road.

It looked like we would need a pack board for sure. Wrong again. We were high in the mountain at daybreak. We could look as far as we could see in every direction, not a sign of anyone anywhere. The scenery was the trip.

Below the road was small timber. Above, however, were high rocks and the lower edge of the old snow pack that never melts. I knew up in those rocks was where those cats were born and raised and would go there if they could possibly outrun the dogs and they did just that.

We found a good track going downhill and turned two dogs loose. They jumped the cat in an old cutover area grown up with briars and brush. Everything you touched seemed to have some kind of sticker.

The cat circled for awhile and turned downhill towards the timber. It will not be long now before he is looking for a tree to climb I thought. I walked back aways and three cats had come from below running for their lives. No dogs were after them.

I turned Jenny out and thought that she will never let them make it to those rocks. But they made it and we called her out. We found a road and drove close to the other race. I turned her in to help. She found a jumped cat before she got in the race. We turned every dog loose. They all went up on the old snow pack but Jenny – she was barking in a hole.

When they all came in, I looked them over, all bloody with thorns and scratches. Being a reader of the Bible, I thought of one verse that did apply, "You have been weighed in the balance and found wanting."

We did hunt more however, and caught nine cats in two weeks. We asked an old man why we run so many and caught so few, he said, "Dogs that have been run in a lower elevation would not perform up that high due to thin air."

Thin air or thick air, some excuse is better than none. I will go back.

Illustration by B. L. Dotson-Lewis

Bobcat Hunting

I hunted coon back east for many years and enjoyed it very much. In 1961, I moved to western Washington and hunted bear and mountain lion for a while. Then I got hooked on bobcat hunting.

I tried to break my dogs from everything except bobcats, as it takes a special kind of dog to make a good cat dog. I have done quite a bit of experimenting with different breeds. Coon hunting is so much different from hunting cats. We hunt coon at night when they are on the prowl; I hunt cats in the morning. They have fed all night and are sitting asleep and will not move, at least until a dog gets real close. So I need a good cold trailer that won't break off on trash. I use crossbred hounds as I mentioned in my story "Agony of Defeat" in Full Cry, February 1990.

I received twelve letters and phone calls asking me to write more on the subject of hunting bobcats. I am not a professional writer as I have indicated before, but it is easy to write a story if it is true and from your own experience.

A bobcat is a creature of habit. If you find a place where he crosses a forest road or a log across a creek, he will cross within ten steps of the same place three or four times a week. The cats here are small. We seldom ever catch one over thirty pounds. The female runs from fourteen to twenty pounds, the male eighteen to twenty-eight. I have only seen one which weighed thirty-four pounds.

I have nothing bad to say about any man's breed of dogs, but I will tell a story about the dogs I hunt.

One of my sons, Dennis, and I had found where a large tom was crossing a road, but he had already been gone too long. This was in February of this year, a little snow had fallen. When we got in the area, Sam, my other son, was in my truck with me and Dennis was behind with a box full of young dogs. He also had his old cat dog. The snow had melted in under the timber and there was some snow in the road. However, Sam saw the track and got out of the truck. He said, "It is the big tom but there is frost in it. It traveled early last night when the snow was soft."

They told me to put Ginger out, my red female I had raised from a pup. Her mother was a Wagoner Black & Tan. Her sire was Thunder, a Walker and Plott cross belonging to Dennis; never ran anything but cats. We could not find where the cat left the road. Ginger went up the hill, bawled twice, and crossed the ridge, but Sam had no dogs. Dennis opened his box. We had deer races all over, but we never heard Ginger.

After we got the deer dogs boxed up, we were delayed two more hours while the service crew unblocked the road. A mile on around the ridge we found Ginger. She had trailed the cat all morning behind a ridge out of our hearing. Where the cat came in the road, the snow was melting and left no scent. Most dogs would have quit there but she was still hunting for the track.

We tracked to where the cat had left the road. She opened up with that long bawl that she inherited from the old Black & Tan. This kind of trailing usually happens during the breeding season, when the old toms are looking for a mate.

I turned one other dog in. Sam and I followed. Two more miles and they jumped the cat. I told Sam the cat would be very thin at this time of year, and could outrun a greyhound and

drawing by B. L. Dotson-Lewis

not to get his hopes very high, plus I had one tired female.

The race was on. Ginger left the other dog when the cat crossed a lake. She ran for two more hours. Dennis came and turned in two fresh dogs. If Ginger was tired, she sure did not show it. She was right up front when the cat treed far off up a creek.

It did not take much arguing with the boys for me to agree to stay at the truck, as it was late and cold. It was so far away I never heard the shot. Ginger came out first with blood all over her head. She jumped all over me and looked up the creek as I petted her real good for a job well done.

They came in shortly with a twenty-nine and one/half pound tom. "What class have you got Ginger in now?" They asked.

"Well, according to the trophy she just brought in, I think she has qualified as the World's Champion Cat Dog. It only took her fifteen hours."

Ginger is still in my kennel, ready for the season to open and to help train up more crossbreed hounds. I guess she and I will both get old together.

Dennis Dotson, left, Sam Dotson, right. Ruby Young Dotson Collection

Illustration by B. L. Dotson-Lewis

Lost Bull on Strawberry Mountain

When elk season opened in 1972, I was 30 miles up in the Cascade Range in western Washington. I had spent one and one-half hours walking less than one-half mile. I was trying to slip up on two bull elk that bedded down close by. I had killed twelve bull elks in my time, but I had never killed one in its bed.

The sun was up and I knew the elk bedded down in the shade. I was walking an old elk trail. The Cherokee blood in my veins indicated I take one-step and stop. The white man's blood said, "Lay your rifle on your shoulder, light your smoke and try to kill one as they run." Timberline was to my right; the meadow was on my left. I crept like a cat, rifle up, safety off on my three hundred Magnum.

I had a swing scope. I moved it over so I could use the sights and bead. The smaller elk jumped up to my right, went over the hill like a bat out of hell. I knew the bull was watching me. I saw him get up but he was behind a fallen tree. I was ready. The first jump he made, I saw an opening and fired. He went over the hill like a big grey horse. I knew I hit him high in the back.

Strawberry Mountain was never a place for a lazy man to elk hunt, as the roads are few and far between. The entire top layer burned off long ago and grown up with grass. The grass dried out in late fall and the elk moved down, except the old bulls that stay until the snow drove them down. I had driven to the end of a road before daylight where I could look across a canyon and see part of the meadow. When the fog lifted, I could see two bull elk far out of rifle range, feeding. As the sun came up, they moved down towards the timber. It took me two hours to go to where I had last seen the elk. I could tell through my scope that one was a monster bull. That's where I started my stalk. We will now go back to where I fired my shot.

I sat down in the grass and had my first smoke since I left my truck that morning. I walked over and found no blood or hair. As I looked down the steep hill, it was evident that something had been dragging. Fifty yards down lay my winter's meat.

This should be the end of my story, but the elk hunt had just begun. I had all the tools and rope and butchered fast. I hung all the meat in scrub timber. It was dark when I found my truck. The next morning as I started to work, a large truck loaded with hay hit my truck and put me in the hospital. My boys came over that night. I drew a map the best I could. They hunted three days for the meat with no success. The fourth night they came in, it had come a snow in the mountains. They had found a bobcat's track and followed it to where it had been eating on the head. They, then, found the meat and brought it out. Ervin said the horns were the heaviest load they had.

As I lay in the hospital, all doped up and half asleep, I relived that hunt over again and again. I killed that elk over and over. I could hear the roar from my three hundred as it rocked against the canyon walls, vibrating from one to the other, finally fading out far below.

Then I thought about Strawberry Mountain the peace and quiet, the breath-taking scenery as far as the eye could see. All day long, I never saw another person or heard a shot fired except mine. I believe when God made that country, he had an elk hunter in mind.

My Father journeys to his last hunting ground:

Author's note: My Father left this hunting ground for a bigger, better hunting ground on March 24, 2004, at the age of 93 ½ years. Like the Sago miners, my father left a note for his family telling them how he felt about this life and the next. The letter was left in the care of the preacher.

Dear Preacher Paul & Violet,

We are pleased to hear from ya'll. Thanks for the nice card. We would be pleased if ya'll could visit us more.

Paul, I have been working on a song that much applies to the way I am thinking. I hope you will like it.

My Last Song – written by Earl Dotson 11-10-2002

"Years of time are swiftly passing
Bringing near my Heavenly goal
Soon I will be at Home with Jesus
While the ages roll
Oh, how precious is my promise
That with gladness fills my soul
Soon, I will be Home with Jesus
While internal ages roll.

Soon, I will meet my friends and love ones
That in time have gone before
We will live with God forever,
There will be no dying anymore"

Dear friend Paul,
I hope God will keep you long enough for you to come and preach at my funeral and read my Last Song to my family.

Earl.

My Father was well-prepared for this journey just as the many others he had traveled on - light in attire and well in heart and soul. Preacher Paul Justice held "Last Song" in secret as requested by my Father until his funeral in Rainey Valley.

Part 7 – A legacy for young mountaineers – genealogy

Coal Miner's family tree

Coal miner's family tree

What does my name mean?
What is a family tree?
Where is Appalachia?
Illustration by Phil Berry, Summersville, West Virginia

Illustration by Phil Berry

Coal Miner's Family Tree
page 1

Do you know you may be part Indian or a member of royalty? Think about that. If your great, great grandfather had stayed in England instead of coming to America, he may have inherited a king's throne. Have you thought about how different your life would be if your ancestors had stayed in Scotland, Ireland, Italy or Africa instead of coming to America? Do you know how or why he came to America?

Well, there are lots and lots of unsolved mysteries about you and your family that you can solve by studying a tree – a family tree.

Genealogy, that is another word they use when talking about a family tree or ancestors. Have you heard this word before?

Genealogy is a big word. But, I know what it means and I can explain it to you.

I will tell you my story of how I learned about my family tree - my genealogy - my ancestors.

Coal Miner's Family Tree
page 2

I first heard the word genealogy when I went on a trip to our family reunion with my parents. Aunt Nora, Daddy's sister, rode with us.

Daddy said, "I have been studying our family tree for a year now-ever since Dad died."

I remember when Grandpa died last year. That was scary and sad. I saw my dad cry for the first time.

Aunt Nora said, "I'm studying our genealogy too."

That was the first time I heard that word. Genealogy.

Illustration by Phil Berry

Try to say it, ge-ne-al-o-gy
Good Job! My aunt, my mom and dad
all said that word on the trip.

Illustration by Phil Berry

Coal Miner's Family Tree
page 3

Dad, Mom and Aunt Nora all talked about family trees, genealogy and Grandpa dying. I started thinking, "What does genealogy or a family tree have to do with my grandpa dying?" Daddy said that Grandpa had black lungs. He worked in a coal mine and got black lungs. Grandpa was sick for a long time. It was hard for him to breathe.

But now, they were talking about Grandpa dying and genealogy, I wondered if genealogy was a dangerous disease or contagious like the measles or chicken pox. If I caught it, could I stay home from school. I figured out family tree and genealogy were connected somehow but I didn't know how or what the words meant.

Coal Miner's Family Tree
page 4

Was this why momma had dressed me up in a white shirt, bowtie and navy blue shorts? Were they going to study my genealogy?

At Grandma's house everyone started hugging me and kissing me and calling me their relative. They asked my dad if I had been added to the family tree. They thought this would be a good time to add me.

I was a little scared of being added to the family tree. Would this be painful? Could I just sit on a limb? Would I be allowed to come down when I got hungry?

Illustration by Phil Berry

Coal Miner's Family Tree
page 5

After eating the fried chicken and chocolate cake, Aunt Nora said, "Time to take a look at the family tree. Time to study our genealogy."

Was that what Dad was looking for when he went in the yard in the evenings and stared at the trees? Was he trying to find our family tree?

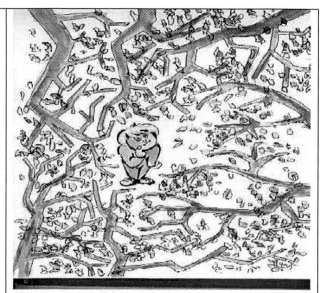

Illustration by Phil Berry

Coal Miner's Family Tree
page 6

Dad was talking to Aunt Nora about Grandpa passing away and how his death would affect the family tree. Then, a woman everyone called Aunt Lydia arrived. I had not met her before. She brought out a scroll, and two cousins rolled it down, all the way. They asked me to help hold it at the bottom while they added new branches for more names.

You could see on the scroll someone had used a crayon to draw a big tree with lots of branches. The tree did not have leaves but it had lots of names of people in my daddy's family written on the branches. All the people at the family reunion called this our "family tree." They said it was the study of our genealogy– our ancestors. They told me Aunt Nora was going to add me to the family tree.

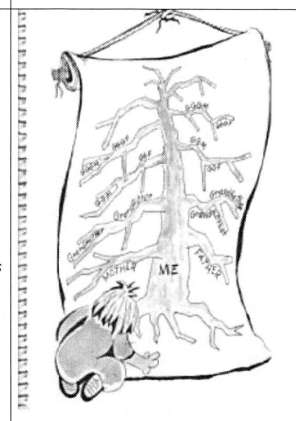

Aunt Nora got a crayon, and she wrote my name very carefully right beside Momma and Daddy's name, "James Madison Zachary Giuliano." I was their son. They said I could start tracing my genealogy.

Coal Miner's Family Tree
page 7

I finally understood what "family tree" and genealogy meant. They tell a story about you and your family, who you are, and where you came from.

You can make your own family tree. You can draw a tree like the one in this story or make one of your own.

Ask your parents to help you start tracing your genealogy on the family tree. Write the name of your momma's family on one side of the tree and the names of your dad's family on the other side of the tree. Keep them separate.

By making a family tree you can find out if you are Irish, English, American Indian, African-American, Italian, Spanish or Japanese. You will learn why you have blonde hair and blue eyes or dark hair and brown eyes, red hair and freckles.

Coal Miner's Family Tree
page 8

You may even find out one of your relatives was a pirate or came over on the Mayflower Ship and landed on Ellis Island in New York. You can find this out by tracing your last name, called surname, on your family tree.

First names tell who you are. Last names (surname) tell about your family. Last names were invented a long time ago to tell which family you belonged to. There were too many Roberts, too many Elizabeths and too many Johns, so they added a last name. They had a hard time finding ways to give people last names (surnames). The type of work a person did was one interesting way to give a family a surname, for example, your relative in Europe named Charlie was a baker, so he became Charlie Baker. Everyone in his family took the last name (surname) Baker. Mark, the son of Peter, became Mark Peterson.

Sarah, who lived near the woods became Sarah Woods. A surname was added so you didn't get mixed up with other families.

People often changed their first names or surnames when they came to America. If the name was long and sounded strange in the new world or people could not pronounce it correctly, the name was shortened or the spelling was changed.

Some famous people have changed their names. Did you know Pocahontas, who was an American Indian, changed her name? When she was young she was taken prisoner by white men. A man named John Rolfe was there being held prisoner also. They fell in love and married. Pocahontas changed her name from Pocahontas to Rebecca Rolfe.

You will like studying your family tree. You will learn about your genealogy. The next time Dad calls your sister, "his little princess", he may be talking about his relationship to Queen Elizabeth or some other member of royalty.

Illustration by B. L. Dotson-Lewis

When someone asks you where you got your red hair and freckles, you can tell them, they came from your "family tree".

The end.

Acknowledgments

It is impossible to me to thank all those who have helped me with this book. I know if I try to list each person or organization that gave me support or documentation, I will surely leave someone out. I thank them all.

To those I have called on mercilessly, without ceasing, I thank many times over. I have written to you or called you in the early morning or late, late at night without much consideration for you because of this mission I cannot cast off. I offer my apologies for that. This book would not have happened without you. This may not seem like such a big project to those who are experienced, but for me, a novice at this entire business, it has been a huge undertaking:

Jim Branscome – a constant source of inspiration, support and advisor

Jeannie Bischoff – assisting me with getting this information in a logical order and constant support

Sammie Wade – editing the entire document

Nelson and Delores Tinnel – assisting me with the technical aspect of this project. Nelson responded with a concise written report on Sago. They also provided me with details of what a miner's family life is like which was easy for them, since Delores had 4 sons and a husband working in the mines.

Arnold And Sandra Nicholas – assisting me with information about Sago Mine

Homer Hickam – giving me permission to reprint his tribute to the Sago miners made at the Sago Memorial Service

Angela (Angel) Errett – giving me permission to use the Logo from the Sago Memorial Service

Angela Gay Kincaid – giving me permission to copy the inside pages of the Sago Memorial Service bulletin

The Charleston Gazette, The Herald-Dispatch, The Register Herald, Todd Maisel – New York Daily News, The Nicholas Chronicle, The Logan Banner, West Virginia Department of Health & Safety Training, MSHA

Eula Hall, Dr. Donald Rasmussen, Ralph and Mary Baber, Larry Gibson, John Cline, Ralph and Charlie Roberts, Robert and Boots Sattler

Builder Levy – giving me permission to use his photos of the Appalachian coalfields

Nancy Taylor & The Gauley Bridge Historical Society – information on Hawks Nest Tunnel

Charlotte Yeager Nielsen, Helen Fogleman, H. C. White, Kathy Eakle, Owen Symes, Ida Belmont, Phyllis Armes, Phil Berry, Charlie and Patty Duffield, Mr. and Mrs. Cecil Butcher

Photograph Credits

Baber, Ralph and Mary - p. 30, 31, 207, 209

Berry, Phil (Illustrations) – p. 279, 280, 281, 282, 283

Errett, Angela, www.angelicdesigns.com – p. 15

Charleston Gazette Newspaper – p. 1, 21, 36, 182

Dotson-Lewis, B. L. – p. 4 (top and bottom), 5 (top and bottom), 6 (top and bottom), 8 (bottom), 9 (top and bottom), 10, 12 (bottom), 20, 29 (top and bottom), 32, 44, 163 (top), 184, 185, 222 (top), 223 (top and bottom), 224, 245 (bottom), 254, 257, 273, 274, 276, 284 (family photos, 260, 267, 268, 269, 270, 275)

Gauley Bridge Historical Society – p. 24 (top), 25 (top and bottom), 163 (bottom), 169

Gee, Gene, Appalachian Voices – p. 230

Given, Paul – Self-portrait of a West Virginia Coal Miner, front of book after Letter to Readers

Herald-Dispatch Newspaper – p. 7 (top and bottom), 13 Randy Snyder (top), 23 Randy Snyder, p 46

Inter-Mountain Newspaper – p. 3, 11, 19 (top)

Kincaid, Angela Gay – p. 16, 17, 18

Levy, Builder – "Prepare to Meet God" photo in front of book, p. 26, 27, 28, 35, 37, 229, 233, 251

Logan Banner Newspaper – p. 22, 154

Maisel, Todd, New York Daily News – p. 2 (bottom), 8 (top), 13 (bottom), 14 (top)

Pride, Keith, West Virginia Pictures – p. 19 (bottom)

Sattler, Robert – p. 252 (photo courtesy of Robert Sattler)

Toler, Karen and Tom – Note written by Martin Toler (Sago Mine Disaster) front of book

U.S. Department of Labor, Mine Safety and Health Administration – p. 2 (top), 12 (top), 14 (bottom)

WV Geological and Economic Survey – p. 222

Glossary of Coal Mining Terms

Abutment - The base structure of an arch of rock spanning a passageway and supporting the weight of the rocks above passageway; and the solid rock ahead of the face and the settled packs behind the face, supporting the weight of the rocks over a longwall face.

Acid mine water - Mine water that contains free sulfuric acid, mainly due to the weathering of iron pyrites.

Active workings - Any place in a mine where miners are normally required to work or travel and which are ventilated and inspected regularly.

Adit - A nearly horizontal passage from the surface by which a mine is entered and dewatered. A blind horizontal opening into a mountain, with only one entrance.

Advance - Mining in the same direction, or order of sequence; first mining as distinguished from retreat.

Air split - The division of a current of air into two or more parts.

Airway - Any passage through which air is carried. Also known as an air course. Anemometer - Instrument for measuring air velocity.

Arching - Fracture processes around a mine opening, leading to stabilization by an arching effect.

Area (of an airway) - Average width multiplied by average height of airway, expressed in square feet.

Auger - A rotary drill that uses a screw device to penetrate, break, and then transport the drilled material (coal).

Auxiliary operations - All activities supportive of but not contributing directly to mining.

Auxiliary ventilation - Portion of main ventilating current directed to face of dead end entry by means of an auxiliary fan and tubing.

Back - The roof or upper part in any underground mining cavity.

Backfill – Mine waste or rock used to support the roof after coal removal.

Barricading - Enclosing part of a mine to prevent inflow of noxious gasses from a mine fire or an explosion.

Barrier - Something that bars or keeps out. Barrier pillars are solid blocks of coal left between two mines or sections of a mine to prevent accidents due to inrushes of water, gas, or from explosions or a mine fire.

Beam - A bar or straight girder used to support a span of roof between two support props or walls.

Beam building - The creation of a strong, inflexible beam by bolting or otherwise fastening together several weaker layers. In coal mining this is the intended basis for roof bolting.

Bearing – A surveying term used to designate direction. The bearing of a line is the acute horizontal angle between the meridian and the line. The meridian is an established line of reference.

Bearing plate - A plate used to distribute a given load. In roof bolting, the plate used between the bolt head and the roof.

Bed - A stratum of coal or other sedimentary deposit.

Belt conveyor -	A looped belt on which coal or other materials can be carried and which is generally constructed of flame-resistant material or of reinforced rubber or rubber-like substance.
Belt idler -	A roller, usually of cylindrical shape, which is supported on a frame and which, in turn, supports or guides a conveyor belt. Idlers are not powered but turn by contact with the moving belt.
Belt take-up -	A belt pulley, generally under a conveyor belt and inby the drive pulley, kept under strong tension parallel to the belt line. Its purpose is to automatically compensate for any slack in the belting created by start-up, etc.
Bench -	One of two or more divisions of a coal seam separated by slate or formed by the process of cutting the coal.
Binder -	A streak of impurity in a coal seam.
Bit -	The hardened and strengthened device at the end of a drill rod that transmits the energy of breakage to the rock. The size of the bit determines the size of the hole. A bit may be either detachable from or integral with its supporting drill rod.
Bituminous coal –	A middle rank coal (between subbituminous and anthracite) formed by additional pressure and heat on lignite. Usually has a high Btu value and may be referred to as "soft coal."
Black damp -	A term generally applied to carbon dioxide. Strictly speaking, it is a mixture of carbon dioxide and nitrogen. It is also applied to an atmosphere depleted of oxygen, rather than having an excess of carbon dioxide.
Blasting agent -	Any material consisting of a mixture of a fuel and an oxidizer.
Blasting cap -	A detonator containing a charge of detonating compound, which is ignited by electric current or the spark of a fuse. Used for detonating explosives.
Blasting circuit -	Electric circuits used to fire electric detonators or to ignite an igniter cord by means of an electric starter.
Bleeder or bleeder entries -	Special air courses developed and maintained as part of the mine ventilation system and designed to continuously move air-methane mixtures emitted by the gob or at the active face away from the active workings and into mine-return air courses.
Borehole -	Any deep or long drill-hole, usually associated with a diamond drill.
Boss -	Any member of the managerial ranks who is directly in charge of miners (e.g., "shift-boss," "face-boss," "fire-boss," etc.).
Brattice or brattice cloth -	Fire-resistant fabric or plastic partition used in a mine passage to confine the air and force it into the working place. Also termed "line brattice," "line canvas," or "line curtain."
Break line -	The line that roughly follows the rear edges of coal pillars that are being mined. The line along which the roof of a coal mine is expected to break.
Breakthrough -	A passage for ventilation that is cut through the pillars between rooms.
Bridge carrier -	A rubber-tire-mounted mobile conveyor, about 10 meters long, used as an intermediate unit to create a system of articulated conveyors between a mining machine and a room or entry conveyor.
Bridge conveyor -	A short conveyor hung from the boom of mining or lading machine or haulage system with the other end attached to a receiving bin that dollies along a frame supported by the room or entry conveyor, tailpiece.

Brow -	A low place in the roof of a mine, giving insufficient headroom.
Btu –	British thermal unit. A measure of the energy required to raise the temperature of one pound of water one degree Fahrenheit.
Bug dust -	The fine particles of coal or other material resulting form the boring or cutting of the coal face by drill or machine.
Bump (or burst) -	A violent dislocation of the mine workings which is attributed to severe stresses in the rock surrounding the workings.
Butt cleat -	A short, poorly defined vertical cleavage plane in a coal seam, usually at right angles to the long face cleat.
Butt entry -	A coal mining term that has different meanings in different locations. It can be synonymous with panel entry, submain entry, or in its older sense it refers to an entry that is "butt" onto the coal cleavage (that is, at right angles to the face).
Cage -	In a mine shaft, the device, similar to an elevator car, that is used for hoisting personnel and materials.
Calorific value -	The quantity of heat that can be liberated from one pound of coal or oil measured in BTU's.
Canopy -	A protective covering of a cab on a mining machine.
Cap -	A miner's safety helmet. Also, a highly sensitive, encapsulated explosive that is used to detonate larger but less sensitive explosives.
Cap block -	A flat piece of wood inserted between the top of the prop and the roof to provide bearing support.
Car -	A railway wagon, especially any of the wagons adapted to carrying coal, ore, and waste underground.
Car-dump -	The mechanism for unloading a loaded car.
Carbide bit -	More correctly, cemented tungsten carbide. A cutting or drilling bit for rock or coal, made by fusing an insert of molded tungsten carbide to the cutting edge of a steel bit shank.
Cast -	A directed throw; in strip-mining, the overburden is cast from the coal to the previously mined area.
Certified -	Describes a person who has passed an examination to do a required job.
Chain conveyor -	A conveyor on which the material is moved along solid pans (troughs) by the action of scraper crossbars attached to powered chains.
Chain pillar -	The pillar of coal left to protect the gangway or entry and the parallel airways.
Check curtain --	Sheet of brattice cloth hung across an airway to control the passage of the air current. Chock Large hydraulic jacks used to support roof in longwall and shortwall mining systems.
Cleat -	The vertical cleavage of coal seams. The main set of joints along which coal breaks when mined.
Clean Air Act – Amendments of 1990	A comprehensive set of amendments to the federal law governing the nation's air quality. The Clean Air Act was originally passed in 1970 to address significant air pollution problems in our cities. The 1990 amendments broadened and strengthened the original law to address specific problems such as acid deposition, urban smog, hazardous air pollutants and stratospheric ozone depletion.

Coal -	A solid, brittle, more or less distinctly stratified combustible carbonaceous rock, formed by partial to complete decomposition of vegetation; varies in color from dark brown to black; not fusible without decomposition and very insoluble.
Coal dust -	Particles of coal that can pass a No. 20 sieve.
Coal Gasification –	The conversion of coal into a gaseous fuel.
Coal mine -	An area of land and all structures, facilities, machinery, tools, equipment, shafts, slopes, tunnels, excavations, and other property, real or personal, placed upon, under, or above the surface of such land by any person, used in extracting coal from its natural deposits in the earth by any means or method, and the work of preparing the coal so extracted, including coal preparation facilities. British term is "colliery."
Coal reserves -	Measured tonnages of coal that have been calculated to occur in a coal seam within a particular property.
Coal washing –	The process of separating undesirable materials from coal based on differences in densities.
Coke –	A hard, dry carbon substance produced by heating coal to a very high temperature in the absence of air.
Continuous miner -	A machine that constantly extracts coal while it loads it. This is to be distinguished from a conventional, or cyclic, unit which must stop the extraction process in order for loading to commence.
Conventional mining –	The first fully-mechanized underground mining method involving the insertion of explosives in a coal seam, the blasting of the seam, and the removal of the coal onto a conveyor or shuttle car by a loading machine.
Conveyor -	An apparatus for moving material from one point to another in a continuous fashion.
Core sample –	A cylinder sample generally 1-5" in diameter drilled out of an area to determine the geologic and chemical analysis of the overburden and coal.
Cover -	The overburden of any deposit.
Creep -	The forcing of pillars into soft bottom by the weight of a strong roof. In surface mining, a very slow movement of slopes downhill.
Crib -	A roof support of prop timbers or ties, laid in alternate cross-layers, log-cabin style. It may or may not be filled with debris. Also may be called a chock or cog.
Cribbing -	The construction of cribs or timbers laid at right angles to each other, sometimes filled with earth, as a roof support or as a support for machinery.
Crop coal -	Coal at the outcrop of the seam.
Crossbar -	The horizontal member of a roof timber set supported by props located either on roadways or at the face.
Crosscut -	A passageway driven between the entry and its parallel air course or air courses for ventilation purposes. Also, a tunnel driven from one seam to another through or across the intervening measures; sometimes called "crosscut tunnel", or "breakthrough."
Cross entry -	An entry running at an angle with the main entry.
Cutter; Cutting machine -	A machine, usually used in coal, that will cut a 10- to 15-cm slot. The slot allows room for expansion of the broken coal. Also applies to the man who operates the machine and to workers engaged in the cutting of coal by pick or drill.

Cycle mining -	A system of mining in more than one working place at a time, that is, a miner takes a lift from the face and moves to another face while permanent roof support is established in the previous working face.
Detectors -	Specialized chemical or electronic instruments used to detect mine gases.
Detonator -	A device containing a small detonating charge that is used for detonating an explosive, including, but not limited to, blasting caps, exploders, electric detonators, and delay electric blasting caps.
Diffusion -	Blending of a gas and air, resulting in a homogeneous mixture. Blending of two or more gases.
Diffuser fan -	A fan mounted on a continuous miner to assist and direct air delivery from the machine to the face.
Dilute -	To lower the concentration of a mixture; in this case the concentration of any hazardous gas in mine air by addition of fresh intake air.
Dragline –	A large excavation machine used in surface mining to remove overburden (layers of rock and soil) covering a coal seam. The dragline casts a wire rope-hung bucket a considerable distance, collects the dug material by pulling the bucket toward itself on the ground with a second wire rope (or chain), elevates the bucket, and dumps the material on a spoil bank, in a hopper, or on a pile.
Draw slate -	A soft slate, shale, or rock from approximately 1 cm to 10 cm thick and located immediately above certain coal seams, which falls quite easily when the coal support is withdrawn.
Drift -	A horizontal passage underground. A drift follows the vein, as distinguished from a crosscut that intersects it, or a level or gallery, which may do either.
Drift mine –	An underground coal mine in which the entry or access is above water level and generally on the slope of a hill, driven horizontally into a coal seam.
Drill -	A machine utilizing rotation, percussion (hammering), or a combination of both to make holes. If the hole is much over 0.4m in diameter, the machine is called a borer.
Drilling -	The use of such a machine to create holes for exploration or for loading with explosives.
Dummy -	A bag filled with sand, clay, etc., used for stemming a charged hole.
Dump -	To unload; specifically, a load of coal or waste; the mechanism for unloading, e.g. a car dump (sometimes called tipple); or, the pile created by such unloading, e.g. a waste dump (also called heap, pile, tip, spoil pike, etc.).
Electrical grounding -	To connect with the ground to make the earth part of the circuit.
Entry -	An underground horizontal or near-horizontal passage used for haulage, ventilation, or as a mainway; a coal heading; a working place where the coal is extracted from the seam in the initial mining; same as "gate" and "roadway," both British terms.
Explosive -	Any rapidly combustive or expanding substance. The energy released during this rapid combustion or expansion can be used to break rock.
Extraction -	The process of mining and removal of coal or ore from a mine.
Face –	The exposed area of a coal bed from which coal is being extracted.
Face conveyor -	Any conveyor used parallel to a working face which delivers coal into another conveyor or into a car.

Fall -	A mass of roof rock or coal which has fallen in any part of a mine.
Fan, auxiliary -	A small, portable fan used to supplement the ventilation of an individual working place.
Fan, booster -	A large fan installed in the main air current, and thus in tandem with the main fan.
Fan signal -	Automation device designed to give alarm if the main fan slows down or stops.
Feeder -	A machine that feeds coal onto a conveyor belt evenly.
Fill -	Any material that is put back in place of the extracted ore to provide ground support.
Fire damp -	The combustible gas, methane, CH_4. Also, the explosive methane-air mixtures with between 5% and 15% methane. A combustible gas formed in mines by decomposition of coal or other carbonaceous matter, and that consists chiefly of methane.
Fixed carbon –	The part of the carbon that remains behind when coal is heated in a closed vessel until all of the volatile matter is driven off.
Float dust -	Fine coal-dust particles carried in suspension by air currents and eventually deposited in return entries. Dust consisting of particles of coal that can pass through a No. 200 sieve.
Fly ash –	The finely divided particles of ash suspended in gases resulting from the combustion of fuel. Fuse -A cord-like substance used in the ignition of explosives. Black powder is entrained in the cord and, when lit, burns along the cord at a set rate.
Gallery -	A horizontal or a nearly horizontal underground passage, either natural or artificial.
Gasification –	Any of various processes by which coal is turned into low, medium, or high Btu gases.
Gathering conveyor; - gathering belt	Any conveyor which is used to gather coal from other conveyors and deliver it either into mine cars or onto another conveyor. The term is frequently used with belt conveyors placed in entries where a number of room conveyors deliver coal onto the belt.
Gob -	The term applied to that part of the mine from which the coal has been removed and the space more or less filled up with waste. Also, the loose waste in a mine.
Ground control -	The regulation and final arresting of the closure of the walls of a mined area. The term generally refers to measures taken to prevent roof falls or coal bursts.
Gunite -	A cement applied by spraying to the roof and sides of a mine passage.
Haulage -	The horizontal transport of ore, coal, supplies, and waste. The vertical transport of the same is called hoisting.
Haulageway -	Any underground entry or passageway that is designed for transport of mined material, personnel, or equipment, usually by the installation of track or belt conveyor.
Heading -	A vein above a drift. An interior level or airway driven in a mine. In longwall workings, a narrow passage driven upward from a gangway in starting a working in order to give a loose end.
Head section -	A term used in both belt and chain conveyor work to designate that portion of the conveyor used for discharging material.
Heaving -	Applied to the rising of the bottom after removal of the coal; a sharp rise in the floor is called a "hogsback."
Highwall –	The unexcavated face of exposed overburden and coal in a surface mine or in a face or bank on the uphill side of a contour mine excavation.

Highwall miner –	A highwall mining system consists of a remotely controlled continuous miner which extracts coal and conveys it via augers, belt or chain conveyors to the outside. The cut is typically a rectangular, horizontal cut from a highwall bench, reaching depths of several hundred feet or deeper.
Hoisting -	The vertical transport coal or material.
Horseback -	A mass of material with a slippery surface in the roof; shaped like a horse's back.
Inby -	In the direction of the working face.
Incline -	Any entry to a mine that is not vertical (shaft) or horizontal (adit). Often incline is reserved for those entries that are too steep for a belt conveyor (+17 degrees -18 degrees), in which case a hoist and guide rails are employed. A belt conveyor incline is termed a slope.
Intake -	The passage through which fresh air is drawn or forced into a mine or to a section of a mine.
Intermediate section -	A term used in belt and chain conveyor network to designate a section of the conveyor frame occupying a position between the head and foot sections.
Kettle bottom -	A smooth, rounded piece of rock, cylindrical in shape, which may drop out of the roof of a mine without warning.
Kerf -	The undercut of a coal face.
Lamp -	The electric cap lamp worn for visibility. Also, the flame safety lamp used in coal mines to detect methane gas concentrations and oxygen deficiency.
Layout -	The design or pattern of the main roadways and workings. The proper layout of mine workings is the responsibility of the manager aided by the planning department.
Lift -	The amount of coal obtained from a continuous miner in one mining cycle.
Load -	To place explosives in a drill hole. Also, to transfer broken material into a haulage device.
Loading machine -	Any device for transferring excavated coal into the haulage equipment.
Loading pocket -	Transfer point at a shaft where bulk material is loaded by bin, hopper, and chute into a skip.
Longwall Mining –	One of three major underground coal mining methods currently in use. Employs a steal plow, or rotation drum, which is pulled mechanically back and forth across a face of coal that is usually several hundred feet long. The loosened coal falls onto a conveyor for removal from the mine.
Loose coal -	Coal fragments larger in size than coal dust.
Main entry -	A main haulage road. Where the coal has cleats, main entries are driven at right angles to the face cleats.
Main fan -	A mechanical ventilator installed at the surface; operates by either exhausting or blowing to induce airflow through the mine roadways and workings.
Manhole -	A safety hole constructed in the side of a gangway, tunnel, or slope in which miner can be safe from passing locomotives and car. Also called a refuge hole.
Man trip -	A carrier of mine personnel, by rail or rubber tire, to and from the work area.
Manway -	An entry used exclusively for personnel to travel form the shaft bottom or drift mouth to the working section; it is always on the intake air side in gassy mines. Also, a small passage at one side or both sides of a breast, used as a traveling way for the miner, and sometimes, as an airway, or chute, or both.

Methane –   A potentially explosive gas formed naturally from the decay of vegetative matter, similar to that which formed coal. Methane, which is the principal component of natural gas, is frequently encountered in underground coal mining operations and is kept within safe limits through the use of extensive mine ventilation systems.

Methane monitor -   An electronic instrument often mounted on a piece of mining equipment, that detects and measures the methane content of mine air.

Mine mouth electric plant – A coal burning electric-generating plant built near a coal mine.

Miner -   One who is engaged in the business or occupation of extracting ore, coal, precious substances, or other natural materials from the earth's crust.

Mining Engineer -   A person qualified by education, training, and experience in mining engineering. A trained engineer with knowledge of the science, economics, and arts of mineral location, extraction, concentration and sale, and the administrative and financial problems of practical importance in connection with the profitable conduct of mining.

MSHA -   Mine Safety and Health Administration; the federal agency which regulates coal mine health and safety.

Mud cap -   A charge of high explosive fired in contact with the surface of a rock after being covered with a quantity of wet mud, wet earth, or sand, without any borehole being used. Also termed adobe, dobie, and sandblast (illegal in coal mining).

Natural ventilation - Ventilation of a mine without the aid of fans or furnaces.

Nip -   Device at the end of the trailing cable of a mining machine used for connecting the trailing cable to the trolley wire and ground.

Open end pillaring - A method of mining pillars in which no stump is left; the pockets driven are open on the gob side and the roof is supported by timber.

Outby; outbye -   Nearer to the shaft, and hence farther from the working face. Toward the mine entrance. The opposite of inby.

Outcrop –   Coal that appears at or near the surface.

Overburden –   Layers of soil and rock covering a coal seam. Overburden is removed prior to surface mining and replaced after the coal is taken from the seam.

Overcast (undercast) Enclosed airway which permits one air current to pass over (under) another without interruption.

Panel -   A coal mining block that generally comprises one operating unit.

Peat –   The partially decayed plant matter found in swamps and bogs, one of the earliest stages of coal formation.

Percentage extraction - The proportion of a coal seam which is removed from the mine. The remainder may represent coal in pillars or coal which is too thin or inferior to mine or lost in mining. Shallow coal mines working under townships, reservoirs, etc., may extract 50%, or less, of the entire seam, the remainder being left as pillars to protect the surface. Under favorable conditions, longwall mining may extract from 80 to 95% of the entire seam. With pillar methods of working, the extraction ranges from 50 to 90% depending on local conditions.

Percussion drill -   A drill, usually air powered, that delivers its energy through a pounding or hammering action.

Permissible -	That which is allowable or permitted. It is most widely applied to mine equipment and explosives of all kinds which are similar in all respects to samples that have passed certain tests of the MSHA and can be used with safety in accordance with specified conditions where hazards from explosive gas or coal dust exist.
Permit –	As it pertains to mining, a document issued by a regulatory agency that gives approval for mining operations to take place.
Piggy-back -	A bridge conveyor.
Pillar -	An area of coal left to support the overlying strata in a mine; sometimes left permanently to support surface structures.
Pillar robbing -	The systematic removal of the coal pillars between rooms or chambers to regulate the subsidence of the roof. Also termed "bridging back" the pillar, "drawing" the pillar, or "pulling" the pillar.
Pinch -	A compression of the walls of a vein or the roof and floor of a coal seam so as to "squeeze" out the coal.
Pinch –	A compression of the roof and floor of a coal seam so as to "squeeze" out the coal.
Pinning -	Roof bolting.
Plan -	A map showing features such as mine workings or geological structures on a horizontal plane.
Pneumoconiosis -	A chronic disease of the lung arising from breathing coal dust.
Portal -	The structure surrounding the immediate entrance to a mine; the mouth of an adit or tunnel.
Portal bus -	Track-mounted, self-propelled personnel carrier that holds 8 to 12 people.
Post -	The vertical member of a timber set.
Preparation plant -	A place where coal is cleaned, sized, and prepared for market.
Primary roof -	The main roof above the immediate top. Its thickness may vary from a few to several thousand feet.
Prop -	Coal mining term for any single post used as roof support. Props may be timber or steel; if steel--screwed, yieldable, or hydraulic.
Ranks of coal –	The classification of coal by degree of hardness, moisture and heat content. "Anthracite" is hard coal, almost pure carbon, used mainly for heating homes. "Bituminous" is soft coal. It is the most common coal found in the United States and is used to generate electricity and to make coke for the steel industry. "Subbituminous" is a coal with a heating value between bituminous and lignite. It has low fixed carbon and high percentages of volatile matter and moisture. "Lignite" is the softest coal and has the highest moisture content. It is used for generating electricity and for conversion into synthetic gas. In terms of Btu or "heating" content, anthracite has the highest value, followed by bituminous, subbituminous and lignite.
Reclamation –	The restoration of land and environmental values to a surface mine site after the coal is extracted. Reclamation operations are usually underway as soon as the coal has been removed from a mine site. The process includes restoring the land to its approximate original appearance by restoring topsoil and planting native grasses and ground covers.
Recovery -	The proportion or percentage of coal or ore mined from the original seam or deposit.

Red dog -	A nonvolatile combustion product of the oxidation of coal or coal refuse. Most commonly applied to material resulting from in situ, uncontrolled burning of coal or coal refuse piles. It is similar to coal ash.
Regulator -	Device (wall, door) used to control the volume of air in an air split.
Reserve -	That portion of the identified coal resource that can be economically mined at the time of determination. The reserve is derived by applying a recovery factor to that component of the identified coal resource designated as the reserve base.
Resin bolting -	A method of permanent roof support in which steel rods are grouted with resin.
Resources -	Concentrations of coal in such forms that economic extraction is currently or may become feasible. Coal resources broken down by identified and undiscovered resources. Identified coal resources are classified as demonstrated and inferred. Demonstrated resources are further broken down as measured and indicated. Undiscovered resources are broken down as hypothetical and speculative.
Respirable dust -	Dust particles 5 microns or less in size.
Respirable dust sample -	A sample collected with an approved coal mine dust sampler unit attached to a miner, or so positioned as to measure the concentration of respirable dust to which the miner is exposed, and operated continuously over an entire work shift of such miner.
Retreat mining -	A system of robbing pillars in which the robbing line, or line through the faces of the pillars being extracted, retreats from the boundary toward the shaft or mine mouth.
Return -	The air or ventilation that has passed through all the working faces of a split.
Return idler -	The idler or roller underneath the cover or cover plates on which the conveyor belt rides after the load which it was carrying has been dumped at the head section and starts the return trip toward the foot section.
Rib -	The side of a pillar or the wall of an entry. The solid coal on the side of any underground passage. Same as rib pillar.
Rider -	A thin seam of coal overlying a thicker one.
Ripper -	A coal extraction machine that works by tearing the coal from the face.
Rob -	To extract pillars of coal previously left for support.
Robbed out area -	Describes that part of a mine from which the pillars have been removed.
Roll -	(1) A high place in the bottom or a low place in the top of a mine passage, (2) a local thickening of roof or floor strata, causing thinning of a coal seam.
Roof -	The stratum of rock or other material above a coal seam; the overhead surface of a coal working place. Same as "back" or "top."
Roof bolt -	A long steel bolt driven into the roof of underground excavations to support the roof, preventing and limiting the extent of roof falls. The unit consists of the bolt (up to 4 feet long), steel plate, expansion shell, and pal nut. The use of roof bolts eliminates the need for timbering by fastening together, or "laminating," several weaker layers of roof strata to build a "beam."
Roof fall -	A coal mine cave-in especially in permanent areas such as entries.
Roof jack -	A screw- or pump-type hydraulic extension post made of steel and used as temporary roof support.

Roof sag -	The sinking, bending, or curving of the roof, especially in the middle, from weight or pressure.
Roof stress -	Unbalanced internal forces in the roof or sides, created when coal is extracted.
Roof support –	Posts, jacks, roof bolts and beams used to support the rock overlying a coal seam in an underground mine. A good roof support plan is part of mine safety and coal extraction.
Roof trusses -	A combination of steel rods anchored into the roof to create zones of compression and tension forces and provide better support for weak roof and roof over wide areas.
Room and pillar mining –	A method of underground mining in which approximately half of the coal is left in place to support the roof of the active mining area. Large "pillars" are left while "rooms" of coal are extracted.
Room neck -	The short passage from the entry into a room.
Royalty -	The payment of a certain stipulated sum on the mineral produced.
Rubbing surface -	The total area (top, bottom, and sides) of an airway.
Safety lamp -	A lamp with steel wire gauze covering every opening from the inside to the outside so as to prevent the passage of flame should explosive gas be encountered.
Scaling -	Removal of loose rock from the roof or walls. This work is dangerous and a long bar (called a scaling bar) is often used.
Scoop -	A rubber tired-, battery- or diesel-powered piece of equipment designed for cleaning runways and hauling supplies.
Scrubber –	Any of several forms of chemical/physical devices that remove sulfur compounds formed during coal combustion. These devices, technically know as flue gas desulfurization systems, combine the sulfur in gaseous emissions with another chemical medium to form inert "sludge," which must then be removed for disposal.
Seam -	A stratum or bed of coal.
Secondary roof -	The roof strata immediately above the coalbed, requiring support during the excavating of coal.
Section -	A portion of the working area of a mine.
Self-contained breathing apparatus	A self-contained supply of oxygen used during rescue work from coal mine fires and explosions; same as SCSR (self-contained self rescuer).
Self-rescuer –	A small filtering device carried by a coal miner underground, either on his belt or in his pocket, to provide him with immediate protection against carbon monoxide and smoke in case of a mine fire or explosion. It is a small canister with a mouthpiece directly attached to it. The wearer breathes through the mouth, the nose being closed by a clip. The canister contains a layer of fused calcium chloride that absorbs water vapor from the mine air. The device is used for escape purposes only because it does not sustain life in atmospheres containing deficient oxygen. The length of time a self-rescuer can be used is governed mainly by the humidity in the mine air, usually between 30 minutes and one hour.
Shaft -	A primary vertical or non-vertical opening through mine strata used for ventilation or drainage and/or for hoisting of personnel or materials; connects the surface with underground workings.

Shaft mine –	An underground mine in which the main entry or access is by means of a vertical shaft.
Shearer -	A mining machine for longwall faces that uses a rotating action to "shear" the material from the face as it progresses along the face.
Shift -	The number of hours or the part of any day worked.
Shortwall –	An underground mining method in which small areas are worked (15 to 150 feet) by a continuous miner in conjunction with the use of hydraulic roof supports.
Shuttle car –	A self-discharging truck, generally with rubber tires or caterpillar-type treads, used for receiving coal from the loading or mining machine and transferring it to an underground loading point, mine railway or belt conveyor system.
Sinking -	The process by which a shaft is driven.
Skid -	A track-mounted vehicle used to hold trips or cars from running out of control. Also it is a flat-bottom personnel or equipment carrier used in low coal.
Slack -	Small coal; the finest-sized soft coal, usually less than one inch in diameter.
Slag -	The waste product of the process of smelting.
Slate -	A miner's term for any shale or slate accompanying coal. Geologically, it is a dense, fine-textured, metamorphic rock, which has excellent parallel cleavage so that it breaks into thin plates or pencil-like shapes.
Slate bar -	The proper long-handled tool used to pry down loose and hazardous material from roof, face, and ribs.
Slip -	A fault. A smooth joint or crack where the strata have moved on each other.
Slope -	Primary inclined opening, connection the surface with the underground workings.
Slope mine –	An underground mine with an opening that slopes upward or downward to the coal seam.
Sloughing -	The slow crumbling and falling away of material from roof, rib, and face.
Sounding -	Knocking on a roof to see whether it is sound and safe to work under.
Spad –	A spad is a flat spike hammered into a wooden plug anchored in a hole drilled into the mine ceiling from which is threaded a plumbline. The spad is an underground survey station similar to the use of stakes in marking survey points on the surface. A pointer spad, or sight spad, is a station that allows a mine foreman to visually align entries or breaks from the main spad.
Split -	Any division or branch of the ventilating current. Also, the workings ventilated by one branch. Also, to divide a pillar by driving one or more roads through it.
Squeeze -	The settling, without breaking, of the roof and the gradual upheaval of the floor of a mine due to the weight of the overlying strata.
Stripping ratio –	The unit amount of overburden that must be removed to gain access to a similar unit amount of coal or mineral material.
Stump -	Any small pillar.
Subsidence –	The gradual sinking, or sometimes abrupt collapse, of the rock and soil layers into an underground mine. Structures and surface features above the subsidence area can be affected.

Sump -	The bottom of a shaft, or any other place in a mine, that is used as a collecting point for drainage water.
Sumping -	To force the cutter bar of a machine into or under the coal.
Support -	The all-important function of keeping the mine workings open. As a verb, it refers to this function; as a noun it refers to all the equipment and materials--timber, roof bolts, concrete, steel, etc.--that are used to carry out this function.
Surface mine –	A mine in which the coal lies near the surface and can be extracted by removing the covering layers of rock and soil.
Suspension -	Weaker strata hanging from stronger, overlying strata by means of roof bolts.
Tailgate -	A subsidiary gate road to a conveyor face as opposed to a main gate. The tailgate commonly acts as the return airway and supplies road to the face.
Tailpiece -	Also known as foot section pulley. The pulley or roller in the tail or foot section of a belt conveyor around which the belt runs.
Timber -	A collective term for underground wooden supports.
Timbering -	The setting of timber supports in mine workings or shafts for protection against falls from roof, face, or rib.
Timber set -	A timber frame to support the roof, sides, and sometimes the floor of mine roadways or shafts.
Tipple -	Originally the place where the mine cars were tipped and emptied of their coal, and still used in that same sense, although now more generally applied to the surface structures of a mine, including the preparation plant and loading tracks.
Ton –	A short or net ton is equal to 2,000 pounds.
Top -	A mine roof; same as "back."
Torque wrench -	A wrench that indicates, as on a dial, the amount of torque (in units of foot-pounds) exerted in tightening a roof bolt.
Tram -	Used in connection with moving self-propelled mining equipment. A tramming motor may refer to an electric locomotive used for hauling loaded trips or it may refer to the motor in a cutting machine that supplies the power for moving or tramming the machine.
Trip -	A train of mine cars.
Undercut -	To cut below or undermine the coal face by chipping away the coal by pick or mining machine. In some localities the terms "undermine" or "underhole" are used.
Underground mine -	Also known as a "deep" mine. Usually located several hundred feet below the earth's surface, an underground mine's coal is removed mechanically and transferred by shuttle car or conveyor to the surface.
Underground station -	An enlargement of an entry, drift, or level at a shaft at which cages stop to receive and discharge cars, personnel, and material. An underground station is any location where stationary electrical equipment is installed. This includes pump rooms, compressor rooms, hoist rooms, battery-charging rooms, etc.
Unit train –	A long train of between 60 and 150 or more hopper cars, carrying only coal between a single mine and destination.

Universal coal cutter -	A type of coal cutting machine which is designed to make horizontal cuts in a coal face at any point between he bottom and top or to make shearing cuts at any point between the two ribs of the place. The cutter bar can be twisted to make cuts at any angle to the horizontal or vertical.
Upcast shaft -	A shaft through which air leaves the mine.
Ventilation -	The provision of a directed flow of fresh and return air along all underground roadways, traveling roads, workings, and service parts.
Violation -	The breaking of any state or federal mining law.
Virgin -	Unworked; untouched; often said of areas where there has been no coal mining.
Void -	A general term for pore space or other reopenings in rock.
Volatile matter -	The gaseous part, mostly hydrocarbons, of coal.
Waste -	That rock or mineral which must be removed from a mine to keep the mining scheme practical, but which has no value.
Wedge -	A piece of wood tapering to a thin edge and used for tightening in conventional timbering.
Weight -	Fracturing and lowering of the roof strata at the face as a result of mining operations, as in "taking weight."
White damp -	Carbon monoxide, CO. A gas that may be present in the afterdamp of a gas- or coal-dust explosion, or in the gases given off by a mine fire; also one of the constituents of the gases produced by blasting. Rarely found in mines under other circumstances. It is absorbed by the hemoglobin of the blood to the exclusion of oxygen. One-tenth of 1% (.001) may be fatal in 10 minutes.
Working -	When a coal seam is being squeezed by pressure from roof and floor, it emits creaking noises and is said to be "working." This often serves as a warning to the miners that additional support is neede
Working face -	Any place in a mine where material is extracted during a mining cycle.
Working place -	From the outby side of the last open crosscut to the face.
Workings -	The entire system of openings in a mine for the purpose of exploitation.
Working section -	From the faces to the point where coal is loaded onto belts or rail cars to begin its trip to the outside.

Resource: University of Pennsylvania and local coal miners.

Additional terms associated with coal mining:

Black Lung -	Black lung is a legal term describing man-made, occupational lung diseases that are contracted by prolonged breathing of coal mine dust.
Coal Impoundments -	Coal impoundments hold a thick, sludge-like mixture of water, coal waste particles, and rock and clay from the process of cleaning coal.
Dogholes-	Mines employing less that 50 workers.
Mine Disaster -	The term "mine disaster" historically applies to mine accidents claiming five or more lives

Mountaintop removal -   Mountaintop removal (MTR) is a relatively new form of coal mining that involves the mass restructuring of earth in order to reach sediment as deep as 1,000 feet below the surface. MTR requires that the targeted land be first clear-cut and then leveled by use of explosives. The debris_created is typically scraped into a valley fill.

UMWA -   The United Mine Workers of America (UMW or UMWA) is a United States labor union that represents workers in mining.